Asia-Pacific Diplomacy

The emergence of Asia-Pacific regionalism represents one of the major trends in late twentieth-century geopolitics and international relations. What are the origins of this regional impetus? Who has led the way? How have they operated? How successful have they been? In *Asia-Pacific Diplomacy*, Lawrence Woods traces the evolution of the Pacific economic cooperation movement by examining the diplomatic contributions of a trio of international nongovernmental organizations (INGOs): the scholarly Pacific Trade and Development Conference (PAFTAD, 1968-); the business-oriented Pacific Basin Economic Council (PBEC, 1968-); and the multipartite (predominantly academic, business, and government) Pacific Economic Cooperation Council (PECC, 1980-). In addition, he provides an innovative historical perspective of an earlier INGO, the Institute of Pacific Relations (IPR, 1925-61), the often overlooked forerunner of the three INGOs which are the focus of this study.

Asia-Pacific Diplomacy provides the first in-depth examination of the origins, structure, and activities of these crucial nongovernmental networks. Meticulously researched and derived from personal interviews and organizational documents, this book also makes an important contribution to the study of international political and economic institutions. When assessing the future diplomatic relevance of INGOs in light of the recently established intergovernmental organization, Asia Pacific Economic Cooperation, the author argues that as the regional cooperation movement expands at the governmental level, an understanding of the nongovernmental roots of that movement is required if the diplomatic contributions of INGOs are to be retained.

Lawrence T. Woods is an associate professor of international studies and Asia-Pacific politics at the University of Northern British Columbia, Prince George.

Canada and International Relations

Lawrence T. Woods

Asia-Pacific Diplomacy:
Nongovernmental Organizations
and International Relations

UBCPress / Vancouver

ISBN 0-7748-0440-8
ISSN 0847-0510 (Canada and International Relations series)

Canadian Cataloguing in Publication Data

Woods, Lawrence Timothy, 1960-
  Asia-Pacific diplomacy

(Canada and international relations, ISSN 0847-0510; v. 7)
  Includes bibliographical references and index.
  ISBN 0-7748-0440-8

  1. Pacific Area cooperation. 2. Pacific Area – Foreign economic
relations. 3. East Asia – Foreign economic relations. 4. Nongovernmental organizations – Pacific Area. 5. Non-governmental
organizations – East Asia. I. Title. II. Series.

HF1642.55.W65 1993   337.11'823   C93-091415-5

UBC Press gratefully acknowledges the ongoing support to its publishing program
from the Canada Council, the Province of British Columbia Cultural Services
Branch, and the Department of Communications of the Government of Canada.

UBC Press
University of British Columbia
6344 Memorial Road
Vancouver, BC V6T 1Z2
(604) 822-3589
Fax: (604) 822-6083

To my parents

Contents

Tables and Figures

Preface and Acknowledgments

The establishment of the intergovernmental Asia Pacific Economic Cooperation (APEC) forum in November 1989 marked the beginning of a new phase in pan-Pacific regionalism. Previously, three international nongovernmental organizations (INGOs) – the Pacific Trade and Development Conference (PAFTAD), the Pacific Basin Economic Council (PBEC), and what is now known as the Pacific Economic Cooperation Council (PECC, formerly Conference) – had been leading the way, the presence of less substantial intergovernmental initiatives notwithstanding. This book is about this trio of INGOs and is intended as a study of the nongovernmental diplomacy underpinning the regional economic cooperation movement. It also casts an earlier INGO, the Institute of Pacific Relations (IPR), as an often overlooked precursor. In his volume, *The New Regionalism in Asia and the Pacific* (1991), Norman D. Palmer observes that the experiences of PAFTAD, PBEC, and PECC 'merit careful examination' (p. 154). My work is, in part, a response to this call.

Many references to private papers and correspondence utilized during the research stage – including those held by the Australia-Japan Research Centre (AJRC, Canberra), the Canadian Chamber of Commerce (CCC, Ottawa), and SRI International (formerly Stanford Research Institute; Menlo Park, California) – have been omitted here. I also wish to acknowledge that earlier versions of elements of this book have been published in academic journals: Chapter 3 has been published as 'Regional Diplomacy and the Institute of Pacific Relations' in the *Journal of Developing Societies* 8 (July-October 1992):212-22; Chapter 5 was published as 'A House Divided: The Pacific Basin Economic Council and Regional Diplomacy' in the *Australian Journal of International Affairs* 45 (1991):264-79; and parts of Chapter 7 have appeared in 'Delicate Diplomatic Debuts: Chinese and Soviet Participation in the

Pacific Economic Cooperation Conference' in *Pacific Affairs* 63 (1990):210-27. Permission to use these components here is appreciated.

I am grateful for funding received during the preparation of this book from the Commonwealth Scholarship and Fellowship Plan, the Department of International Relations in the Research School of Pacific Studies at the Australian National University, the Senate Research and Publication Committees of Bishop's University, and the Asia Pacific Foundation of Canada. During my fieldwork, fine treatment was forthcoming from my many individual hosts and the following institutions: the Centre for Strategic and International Studies (Jakarta); the Japan National Committee for Pacific Economic Cooperation (Tokyo); the Canadian Chamber of Commerce; SRI International; and the Australia-Japan Research Centre, National Library of Australia, and Archives of Business and Labour (Canberra). Permission to observe the proceedings of the Fifth Pacific Economic Cooperation Conference (Vancouver, November 1986) and the Sixteenth Pacific Trade and Development Conference (Wellington, January 1987) must also be acknowledged, as must the time, patience, and help offered by the almost ninety academics, businesspeople, organizational officials, and public servants in Canberra, Jakarta, Tokyo, Vancouver, Ottawa, Toronto, Menlo Park, and Wellington, who granted confidential personal interviews. The assistance and hospitality of the Institute of International Relations at the University of British Columbia was similarly appreciated during the final stages of editing.

Many people have offered invaluable constructive criticism, advice, and encouragement during the production of this book. I thank, in particular, the staff and reviewers at UBC Press, my students at Bishop's University, and the following colleagues: J.D.B. Miller, Peter Drysdale, John Girling, Richard Higgott, Hugh Collins, James Richardson, William O'Malley, Peter Rimmer, Michael Roschlau, Paul Kattenburg, Christopher Thorne, Nancy Viviani, Michael Donnelly, Ted English, Frank Langdon, Mark Zacher, Brian Job, Charles Burton, Andrew Fenton Cooper, Gerald Segal, James Cotton, Kim Richard Nossal, Tim Shaw, Anton de Man, Michael Bourke, Ernest Yee, Robert Glasser, and Robert Ham. Coping with manuscript changes along the way was the talented team of Diane Mills, Lynda Raymond, Mary Ann Bell, Jean Bourke, and Lynne Payne.

Finally, I thank my wife Joan, my daughter Elizabeth, and my extended family for their unfailing support, understanding, prayers, and love.

Abbreviations

ACMA	Associated Chambers of Manufacturers of Australia
ADB	Asian Development Bank
AJBCC	Australia-Japan Business Cooperation Committee
AJRC	Australia-Japan Research Centre
ANU	Australian National University
APD	ASEAN-Pacific Dialogue (also ASEAN Post-Ministerial Conferences)
APEC	Asia Pacific Economic Cooperation
APFC	Asia Pacific Foundation of Canada
ASEAN	Association of Southeast Asian Nations
CCC	Canadian Chamber of Commerce
CCI	Chamber of Commerce and Industry
CSIS	Centre for Strategic and International Studies (Jakarta)
EAEC	East Asian Economic Caucus (formerly Grouping)
EC	European Community
EEC	European Economic Community
EPA	Economic Planning Agency (Japan)
ESCAP	United Nations Economic and Social Commission for Asia and the Pacific
FAO	Food and Agriculture Organization of the United Nations
FEER	*Far Eastern Economic Review*
GATT	General Agreement on Tariffs and Trade
HOC	Host Organizing Committee
IGO	international governmental organization
ILO	International Labor Office/Organization
INGO	international nongovernmental organization

IPR	Institute of Pacific Relations
ISC	International Steering/Standing Committee
ISEAS	Institute of Southeast Asian Studies (Singapore)
JERC	Japan Economic Research Centre
MTN	multilateral trade negotiations
NATO	North Atlantic Treaty Organization
NIRA	National Institute for Research Advancement (Japan)
NLA	National Library of Australia
NPCCA	National Pacific Cooperation Committee of Australia
OECD	Organization for Economic Cooperation and Development
OPTAD	Organization for Pacific Trade (Aid) and Development
PAFTA	Pacific Free Trade Area
PAFTAD	Pacific Trade and Development Conference
PBCSG	Pacific Basin Co-operation Study Group (Japan)
PBEC	Pacific Basin Economic Council
PBO	Pacific Basin Organisation for Economic Cooperation and Development
PCN	Pacific Cooperation Newsletter (Japan)
PEC	Pacific Economic Community
PECC	Pacific Economic Cooperation Council (formerly Conference)
PRC	People's Republic of China
RMC	Regional Member Committee
SRI	SRI International (formerly Stanford Research Institute)
UN	United Nations
UNCTAD	UN Conference on Trade and Development
YMCA	Young Men's Christian Association

Asia-Pacific Diplomacy

1
Introduction: The Pacific Economic Cooperation Movement

The discussion of 'things Asia-Pacific' is prominent in the contemporary parlance of international relations. The world's economic centre of gravity, it is routinely asserted, has moved from the mid-Atlantic to the mid-Pacific in recent decades. Glowing assessments of post-Second World War development abound, as do forecasts of a forthcoming 'Pacific century' and claims that a 'Pacific community' is emerging amidst the cultural, linguistic, economic, and political diversity of the region.[1]

Descriptions of the Asia-Pacific as a region of growing economic, political, and military/strategic significance, in which multilateral or collective action among states provides the best chance of securing continued prosperity and stability, commonly focus on at least six factors believed to promote regional cooperation. These are: (1) unmatched economic growth rates since 1960 and a concomitant increase in intraregional trade (now accounting for over or near 60 per cent of all trade flows for many Asia-Pacific countries); (2) the threat to the regional and global trading systems posed by rising protectionism and the use of subsidies; (3) Japan's emergence as a regional and global economic power; (4) a decline in American economic and political influence and military presence; (5) the growing diplomatic and economic importance of the Association of Southeast Asian Nations (ASEAN – Brunei, Indonesia, Malaysia, the Philippines, Singapore, and Thailand) and the newly industrialized countries/economies of East Asia (Hong Kong, Taiwan, and South Korea); and (6) economic reforms undertaken by the leadership of the People's Republic of China and its efforts to expand regional ties. The theme of economic *interdependence* is conspicuous in many analyses, the implication being that improved mechanisms for the multilateral management of the regional economy are needed if the economic, political, and social well-being of the people of the Asia-Pacific is to be preserved and strengthened.[2] Above all, it is suggested, efforts must be made to avoid the negative and sometimes unintended consequences of unilateral or bilateral policy implementation and to counter the dangers posed by an increasingly hostile global economic environment. The pursuit of *Pacific economic cooperation* (i.e., 'improved forms of cooperation, communication, and consultation' on economic policy issues)[3] represents one such effort to cope with the region's economic and political dynamism and vulnerability.

An active interest in the positive effects of cooperation among nations might seem to fall primarily within the domain of legislators and bureaucrats directly involved in the formulation and administration of public policy. Yet, until the intergovernmental Asia Pacific Economic Cooperation (APEC) forum was initiated in November 1989,[4] the promotion of Pacific regionalism had largely been undertaken by *international nongovernmental organizations* (INGOs) – international institutions neither created nor maintained by an intergovernmental agreement.[5] According to one participant, 'these networks of private communication have ... been imbued with a public purpose.'[6] This often observed but rarely examined feature of the pursuit of Pacific economic cooperation (i.e., the utility of a nongovernmental approach) is the subject of the present study. The concomitant need to adapt conventional conceptions of diplomacy in order to account for the contemporary use of official *and* unofficial diplomatic agents will also be explored.

The notion of Pacific economic cooperation has been widely scrutinized in certain academic, business, and government circles since the mid-1960s. Two INGOs, the Pacific Trade and Development Conference (PAFTAD) and the Pacific Basin Economic Council (PBEC), are commonly associated with this concept. A third INGO, the Pacific Economic Cooperation Council (PECC, formerly Conference), is generally considered to have arisen as a direct result of PAFTAD and PBEC efforts.[7] These organizations may be conceived as the main nongovernmental elements of a Pacific economic cooperation movement,[8] the activities of which demonstrate the virtues and shortcomings of a nongovernmental approach to regional diplomacy. The study of these organizations is even more relevant in the wake of the symbiotic relationship agreed upon between APEC and PECC[9] and in light of the ongoing debate over regional institutionalization.[10]

This book seeks to answer the following question: How have the INGOs promoting the idea of Pacific economic cooperation contributed to the regional diplomatic framework? While articles and volumes on the Pacific community and Pacific economic cooperation concepts are legion, detailed comparative analyses of the nongovernmental organizations examining and promoting the cooperation theme are not.[11] Yet, as is frequently the case when trying to comprehend or explain an idea, a more complete understanding may be acquired by studying the persons or groups voicing support. Similarly, if the promotion of a concept is successful, it may be possible to glean valuable lessons from the methods used. Unsuccessful efforts may also be instructive.

The analytical perspective adopted here regards PAFTAD, PBEC, and PECC as INGOs with the potential to contribute to regional diplomacy. This approach is based on two premises. The first holds that these nongovernmental entities qualify as relevant units of analysis in a study of international relations focusing on the issue of Pacific economic cooperation. The second maintains that nongovernmental entities can be assessed as diplomatic actors or agents. Some participants in, and observers of, the movement invoke the term *international regime* (i.e., a set 'of implicit or explicit principles, norms, rules and decision-making procedures around which actors' expectations converge in a given [issue] area of international relations')[12] when describing the object of their pursuit or analysis.[13] However, the present study seeks to examine the roles of nongovernmental organizations participating in the promotion of regional cooperation as opposed to the notion of cooperation itself. Thus, while it may be possible to conclude that PAFTAD, PBEC, and PECC are engaged in the process of regime development or transformation, the conceptual approach utilized here takes the view that this recent terminology is merely providing new labels for elements of a much older concept in the language of international relations – diplomacy.[14]

An analytical framework for the study of diplomacy and INGOs is presented in Chapter 2. In Chapter 3, this perspective is applied to the Institute of Pacific Relations (IPR), a now defunct organization which may be seen as the oft-forgotten precursor of the nongovernmental components within today's regional cooperation movement. The main objective of this study is to examine the diplomatic roles of PAFTAD, PBEC, and PECC. The origins and structure of each organization are explored in chapters 4, 5, and 6, respectively, along with a review of their diplomatic utility and involvement in the regional economic cooperation movement. Chapter 7 presents four case studies drawn from the activities of PECC.

States and governments are commonly recognized as the most significant actors in international relations. As a result, a great deal of attention is paid to official bilateral and multilateral diplomacy in which only these actors are involved. Yet, few would dispute that, today, INGOs are also important international actors in many issue areas. As shall be discussed in Chapter 2, an international nongovernmental organization may only be considered an international actor if that organization has an impact on international relations. For observers such as Wolfers, this means that the activities of an INGO must be 'able on occasion to affect the course of international events' and/or to provoke responses from other international actors, particularly states: 'When this happens, these entities become actors in the international arena and competitors of the nation-state. Their ability to operate as international or transnational actors may be traced to the fact that men identify themselves and their interests with corporate bodies other than the nation-state.'[15]

Thus, a nongovernmental body seeking to influence international affairs cannot be totally devoid of interaction with states or governments. Often, the objectives pursued by an INGO and its membership cannot be achieved without such interaction. Similarly, it is at their peril that governments ignore the presence and activities of INGOs. To do so would be to ignore the constraints and the opportunities which INGOs present in interstate relations. Although groups like Greenpeace and Amnesty International may be thorns in the sides of many governments, they and other INGOs, such as the International Red Cross and Oxfam, often carry out functions that governments are unable to perform or unable to agree on how to perform. While environmental, human rights, relief, and development assistance organizations join multinational corporations among those bodies commonly referred to as politically significant INGOs, the central hypothesis to be tested in this study holds that nongovernmental groups such as PAFTAD, PBEC, and PECC qualify as international actors by contributing in different ways, and to varying degrees, to Asia-Pacific diplomacy.[16]

But if diplomacy is commonly regarded as 'the dialogue between independent states'[17] and an activity involving only official state representatives, how can diplomatic qualities be ascribed to INGOs? I argue that the traditional conception of diplomacy as an activity involving only official state agents is too narrow, given the complexities and necessities of international relations in the closing decades of the twentieth century.

An answer to the conceptual problem faced by an attempt to include INGOs in a discussion of diplomacy may be found by examining the functions of diplomats: *representation, information, communication,* and *negotiation.* Representation refers to the act of representing or symbolizing one's country in relations with other countries. Normally, this means acting as the representative of the state or government, but the interests of the private citizen or other members and sectors of the diplomat's society may also be represented. The information function involves the generation, collection, analysis, and dissemination of information about the countries to which the diplomat is accredited or the issue areas which he/she is expected to monitor. Another important aspect of this function is the act of reporting information to the persons or groups the diplomat represents. Communication refers to the act of facilitating the exchange of views, positions, and/or policies between states, and the negotiation function suggests a role in resolving any differences which arise during these exchanges. Whether or not an international actor contributes to the diplomatic framework within which interstate relations are conducted will thus be dependent upon that actor's performance and/or facilitation of one or more diplomatic tasks.

An analytical perspective able to account for nongovernmental entities is also strengthened by a review of the rationale which has perpetuated an exclusive view of diplomatic agents, the impact of commercial and academic interests upon diplomatic practices, the adaptive qualities of diplomacy, and the implications of the traditional conception's European origins.

When assessing the claim that the pursuit of Pacific economic cooperation is well served by the diplomatic contributions made by PAFTAD, PBEC, and PECC, it should be noted that nongovernmental promotion of this concept has a history dating back to the formation of the Pan-Pacific Union in 1907. The union's activities led directly to the creation of several other INGOs. One of these offspring was the Institute of Pacific Relations (IPR).[18] Founded in 1925, the IPR operated as a private forum in which national delegations of leading academics, businesspeople, labour leaders, and journalists, together with politicians, bureaucrats, and statespeople, undertook to discuss and research domestic and regional issues. It rose to prominence as a respected international forum prior to, during, and immediately following the

Second World War but was disbanded in 1960-1 after falling victim to the prevailing Cold War mentality in the United States.

Given the desirability of a private regional forum in which mutual understanding and reconciliation could be fostered, it is not surprising to find two new organizations, PAFTAD and PBEC, arriving on the scene shortly after the IPR's demise. Today, these groups remain major components of the regional economic cooperation movement, having been joined, in 1980, by PECC.

Launched in 1968, the Pacific Trade and Development Conference has been the intellectual driving force of the cooperation movement.[19] The first gathering was sponsored by the Japanese Ministry of Foreign Affairs and was held to discuss Kiyoshi Kojima's proposal for a Pacific Free Trade Area (PAFTA). While this proposal was deemed premature, several participants acknowledged that the practice of bringing together professional and academic economists from around the region was valuable and should be continued. As a result, the study of problems encountered within the regional economy has formed the basis for an ongoing conference series. The invited delegates initially came from Japan, Australia, New Zealand, Canada, and the United States (the countries envisaged as members of Kojima's PAFTA), but efforts were soon undertaken to ensure regular participation from as many nations as could be considered feasible, including China and the former Soviet Union.

Another organization filling the void created by the demise of the IPR is the Pacific Basin Economic Council. Whereas PAFTAD adopts a policy-oriented, scholarly approach to regional economic questions, PBEC's business is business.[20] Its members are concerned with the creation and maintenance of a climate of opinion and public policy favourable to the orderly conduct of commercial transactions. Established in 1967-8 by business leaders from Japan, Australia, New Zealand, Canada, and the United States, the council now operates as a network of some 850 fee-paying firms and business executives. The five founding national committees were joined by member committees from South Korea and Chinese Taipei in 1984, Mexico and Chile in 1989, Hong Kong and Peru in 1990, Malaysia in 1991, and Fiji and the Philippines in 1992. Annual conferences are held each May to examine regional economic and commercial conditions, the attendance of the senior corporate officers being a major feature of PBEC activities.

In 1980, academics, business leaders, and state officials attended a Pacific Community Seminar held in Canberra under the sponsorship of the prime ministers of Japan and Australia. The participants, present as private individuals, were organized on the basis of tripartite national delegations in a bid to ensure balanced sectoral input. Representatives of PAFTAD and PBEC were also in attendance. The tripartite format of this gathering has become a prominent feature of what became known as the Pacific Economic Cooperation Conference. The name of the organization was changed to the Pacific Economic Cooperation Council in January 1992 to acknowledge an ongoing process of institutional development.[21] The Canberra Seminar (PECC I) has been followed by a series of similar conferences, each organized in accordance with the principle of nonexclusiveness – that is, the desire to allow representatives from any country, region, or organization to participate as long as they demonstrate a genuine commitment to the theme of cooperation.[22] Delegations from Australia, Brunei Darussalam, Canada, Chile, China, Chinese Taipei, Hong Kong, Indonesia, Japan, Malaysia, Mexico, New Zealand, the Pacific Island nations (via the South Pacific Forum), Peru, the Philippines, Russia, Singapore, South Korea, Thailand, and the United States hold full membership in PECC as of 1992. PAFTAD and PBEC are non-voting institutional members. An international standing committee including many long-time leaders of PAFTAD and PBEC is charged with the task of overseeing conference preparations, coordinating communications between national PECC committees, and authorizing the research programs of PECC task forces.

Similarities and differences between the primary nongovernmental components of today's Pacific economic cooperation movement are evident in these introductory sketches. Each organization holds regular conferences, each is directed by an international standing/steering committee, and each is centrally concerned with foreign and domestic economic policy issues. At the same time, each of these INGOs has a distinct character: economists are the chief participants in PAFTAD meetings; PBEC has a fee-paying corporate membership; and tripartite sectoral participation is unique to PECC. In addition, although each organization has followed the example set by the IPR and is engaged in the facilitation of the diplomatic functions of representation, information, and communication, the nature and impact of their respective contributions varies greatly. Indeed, while PAFTAD appears to have consolidated its place within the regional cooperation movement in recent years, the inadequacies of PBEC and the successes of PECC, including the latter's ability to facilitate diplomatic negotiations, have threatened the future of their roles as unofficial diplomatic actors.

The need to appreciate differences is applicable not only to a comparative study of PAFTAD, PBEC, and PECC but also to the study of these respective organizations as individual entities. None of these groups is homogeneous or single-minded. Although each is concerned with regional trade and economic development, participants become engaged for a variety of reasons (i.e. personal, altruistic, philanthropic, political, commercial, academic, or symbolic).[23] As a result, interests and objectives vis-à-vis the concept of, and movement promoting, Pacific economic cooperation will often vary not only between organizations but among individuals, across countries, and within national delegations. Like other INGOs, each is dependent on the will of the membership or a committee of senior members. Consensus decision-making[24] is the norm at the regional level, and the same is often true at national and subnational levels of operation. Therefore, when considering the activities and contributions of the INGOs discussed here, their underlying heterogeneity must be recognized. An understanding of the diplomatic utility of a nongovernmental approach to accommodating and reconciling these national, sectoral, personal, and cultural differences is a main objective of this study.

2
INGOs, International Relations, and Diplomacy

The suggestion that international nongovernmental organizations contribute to diplomacy is immediately confronted by traditional conceptions of this activity which exclude nongovernmental actors. In this chapter, it will be argued that the depiction of diplomacy as a dialogue involving only official state representatives unwisely and errantly overlooks the possibility of diplomatic functions being performed or facilitated by and within INGOs. In making this argument, it will be necessary to examine definitions of diplomacy and to consider these in terms of classifications of diplomatic functions and agents, the dynamism of diplomatic practices, and the implications of the cultural setting in which the traditional conception of diplomacy has been shaped.

INGOs as International Actors

An *international nongovernmental organization* may be defined as an international institution which is not created by an agreement among governments.[1] Institutions which owe their establishment and continuing existence to an 'agreement among two or more sovereign states for the conduct of regular political interactions' may be referred to as *international governmental organizations* (IGOs) and can be distinguished by the tendency of their members to be states or for participants to be official state representatives under the direction or control of governments.[2] As a result, it is often argued that a true INGO should refuse all forms of state support, exclude government officials from being participants or members, and, thereby, maintain an autonomous decision-making process. Some analysts add the proviso that INGOs should be operated on a nonprofit basis – a stipulation which poses a difficulty for anyone wishing to classify a multinational corporation as an INGO.[3]

INGOs appear in many forms and typologies are plentiful. For example, Feld's categories (business enterprises and collaborative efforts, labour organizations, development assistance and relief organizations, and miscellaneous political groups)[4] highlight the nature of the activities being undertaken, as do those proposed by Huntington (bureaucratic, association, and transaction).[5] Similarly, Taylor emphasizes the type of issue area (economic, security, political, and cultural/ ideological)[6] in which the INGO is active. The criterion of geographical scope of membership (regional and supraregional) is also invoked by Taylor, as it is by Jacobson (limited and universal), who, in turn, adds range of organizational pursuits (general or specific) to the methods of classification.[7]

None of these typologies necessitates the consideration of INGOs as important units of analysis in the study of international relations. Instead, one is left to consider White's observation that 'the importance of an INGO is to be measured not so much by the importance which its national members may have in their own countries as by the importance of the work they do together on the international level'[8] and Feld's belief that such associations should only be 'recognized as acquiring international actor status when they engage in behaviour that transcends national boundaries and play purposeful roles affecting the international arena.'[9]

Classifications based on function include Cox and Jacobson's distinction between *service* and *forum* organizations. A service organization conducts activities such as the collection, analysis, and dissemination of information or the representation of viewpoints and interests as a service to its members. A forum organization provides a framework within which members undertake activities ranging from the exchange of views to the negotiation of binding agreements, and it may be used by state and nonstate entities for the 'collective legitimization' of one's policies, existence, or role as an international actor.[10] Mansbach et al. cite the tasks of physical protection, economic development and regulation, residual public interest, and group status,[11] while White suggests that INGOs 'usually function as agents of international understanding, as molders of public opinion, and as pressure groups, both on the national and international level.'[12]

Willetts chooses to classify some INGOs as sectoral or promotional pressure groups – groups which 'seek to protect the interests of a particular section of society' or which 'seek to promote causes arising from a given set of attitudes.' He reminds us that 'it is the act of applying pressure that brings them into politics'[13] and argues that, although the conception of interest groups having a political role is derived from studies of domestic politics, the concept is equally applicable to international politics – particularly when considering the origins and movement of issues on the international political agenda.[14] Building upon the pressure group perspective, Lador-Lederer classifies INGOs by the social functions they perform and their relationships with states and IGOs:

(1) those which are delegated by states and IGOs the authority to perform certain tasks or acts of administration (i.e., the International Red Cross).

(2) those which collaborate with states and IGOs in the performance of consultative, judicial, technical, or informational tasks (i.e., scientific societies, the International Chamber of Commerce, Amnesty International, development assistance organizations, and Rotary International).

(3) autonomous organizations undertaking international activities, be these religious, ideological, regulatory, humanitarian, or recreational.[15]

Not all attempts to categorize functions are helpful. For example, one must be wary of typologies which distinguish between *official* and *unofficial* functions or between *political* and *nonpolitical* international interactions.[16] These theoretical distinctions become problematic in practice because of their separation of politics from economics and other social issues. Moreover, allegedly unofficial or nonpolitical activities of private individuals frequently involve the interests of states as political units and affect power relationships.[17] One might also reflect on attitudes of unofficial actors, such as nongovernmental pressure groups, and the reasons why both official and unofficial actors might seek to uphold the political/nonpolitical and official/unofficial dichotomies.[18]

These points reinforce Nye and Keohane's characterization of *world politics* as 'all political interactions between significant actors,' a significant actor being 'any somewhat autonomous individual or organization that controls substantial resources and participates in political relationships with other actors across state lines ... At any point where [an actor] employs techniques ... to achieve the modification of other actors' behavior, it is acting politically.'[19] The question which must be asked when assessing the role of INGOs in the study and practice of international relations thus revolves around whether or not their actions are politically significant. Do their activities influence international events?[20] The answer must not be prejudged by the application of misleading labels. For example, it may be possible to construct a continuum displaying the relative significance of INGOs in international relations – a continuum which may situate service organizations at the least significant extreme and move through autonomous forum organizations and pressure groups to those working with, or delegated authority by, states and IGOs. The task of placing groups on the continuum would be complicated by the fact that these categories would not be mutually exclusive and that the significance of few groups could be assessed by attention to only one activity or function. Similarly, groups in each category may fall under Lador-Lederer's heading of autonomous organizations and would be scattered across the continuum in accordance with the consequences their activities might have for states and the state responses these consequences may evoke.

Key factors in determining an entity's status as an international actor thus include the nature of an INGO's relationships (i.e., autonomous, symbiotic, dependent) with other actors and the impact of nongovernmental activities upon those actors. A typology based upon function or action (as opposed to issue area, scope and nature of membership, or range of organizational pursuits) is, subsequently, better suited for the determination of international actor status. The same might be said of the utility of a function-based typology versus the utility of a typology based upon organizational structure, given the notion that function often dictates form.

The degree of control leaders of, or participants in, an INGO have over their organization's activities is another analytical consideration. An organization controlled by a state or states and primarily serving state interests would not be recognized as an international actor, whereas an organization controlled by private individuals but utilized by a state to pursue state interests would qualify.[21] A more complex analytical problem arises when an otherwise private organization accepts state support (i.e., material, human, and/or financial assistance). The organization's decision-making process may continue to be controlled from within, but one must consider the extent to which action would be limited in the absence of such support.

In addition, having gained state assistance, tension may arise between the state and an INGO if the state attempts to assert control over an organization which it finds useful. State officials and nongovernmental leaders will attempt to protect their own interests. The former will seek to ensure that INGO activities complement state activities, while the latter will endeavour to preserve their organization's nongovernmental status and flexibility. The limits to which a state will attempt to assert control are restricted only by whether or not it is willing to risk explicit politicization or collapse of the organization in which it has invested. Thus, an INGO's survival may depend upon the degree to which it is recognized as valuable by a state and by that state's willingness to support the organization's existence or status.

As highlighted by Reynolds, *action* includes both 'process and output.'[22] Hence, the stress placed upon autonomous decision-making should not overshadow the need for outputs to have relevance for international politics. To be classified as an international actor, an entity's actions must have a political purpose. Usually this means that actions must have consequences for other international actors. Given that states are commonly recognized to be among the most significant international actors, the significance of other actors may be gleaned by attention to the impact their actions have upon states as well as the interaction between the latter. Observers who believe that private international organizations do not engage in, or have an impact upon, international relations ignore the possibility that INGOs may at times be as adept or better at performing tasks of interest to states than are states themselves or IGOs.[23] Similarly, they are ignoring the possibility that nongovernmental activities may have important consequences for state action and interstate interaction – consequences to which a state may feel obliged to respond. These consequences may include

(1) attitude changes or the creation of new myths, symbols, and norms which gain legitimacy and thus become politically significant.

(2) the promotion of international pluralism through the linking of national elites or interest groups and the increased capability these links might give such elites or groups in their attempts to influence state policies.

(3) the rise of further constraints on state activity, as perceived by statesmen and bureaucrats, due to the heightened significance of international pluralism, increasing international interdependence, or the need for joint decision-making among states in the face of costly unilateral state actions, all of which may affect a state's ability to achieve its objectives.

(4) an increase in the ability of certain states to influence others by using the nongovernmental interactions at hand as 'new instruments of influence' or 'governmental foreign policy.'

(5) the emergence of autonomous or quasi-autonomous nonstate actors possessing private foreign policies in the company of significant political resources, which they use to reinforce their legitimacy and potential to influence state policy and interstate relations.[24]

Nye and Keohane have derived these consequences from studies of what they term *transnational relations* – 'contacts, coalitions, and interactions across state boundaries that are not controlled by the central foreign policy organs of governments.'[25] Given this definition, their use of the term *instrument* (a term which normally connotes control on the part of the user) with regard to the fourth consequence requires clarification. The authors are not utilizing the word instrument in this narrow sense but, rather, as a synonym for means or techniques.[26] They are also allowing for consent, commenting that 'transnational organizations are particularly serviceable as instruments of governmental foreign policy whether through control or willing alliance.'[27]

These nuances aside, when confronted by such consequences, states may choose to respond passively. However, in situations in which this is not judged to be the prudent course, response options include

(1) the unilateral implementation of defensive policies to thwart the domestic nongovernmental activities.
(2) extending the impact of state laws beyond state boundaries through controls on mobile factors.
(3) the pursuit of defensive policy coordination with other states, possibly involving (the creation of) an IGO.
(4) an effort to coopt the nongovernmental activities or actor in the pursuit of state objectives alone.
(5) the pursuit of a symbiotic relationship with a nongovernmental actor.[28]

The first and second options carry potential social and political costs for the state in question as a result of the retaliatory measures taken by the nongovernmental actors or other states which might be affected by such unilateral action. The third option may lead to cooperation among states and the pursuit of optimal solutions, but it may also increase the danger of a continued loss of domestic state control or, at least, a situation in which legislators and elected officials lose control to bureaucrats and technocrats. A decision to respond defensively to transnational relations through interstate policy coordination may also lead to the acceptance of a joint policy which restricts, rather than seeks benefit from, nongovernmental activities.[29]

For a vast range of transnational activities confronting policy-makers in democratic settings, options 1-3 may not be viable options. Policy-makers in authoritarian states may be able to respond without fear of public or electoral reprisals, but, in democratic polities, responses which seek to accommodate, rather than to directly curb, the activities of INGOs may be more desirable from the state's perspective. The fourth and fifth options provide scope for INGOs to be seen as the potential allies of states in the formulation and implementation of state policy and in the achievement of interstate policy coordination. Opening channels for societal participation in the development of public policy (i.e., the creation of advisory committees involving nongovernmental actors) can provide the state with an additional source of ideas, information, legitimacy, and control, whether these benefits are pursued solely in the self-interest of the state or with a recognized element of cooperation for mutual benefit underlying the interaction between governmental and nongovernmental interests.[30] Accordingly, 'fitting private persons or groups into the policy process may be inspired by variable doses of principle, astute politics, and practicality in the shaping and application of policy.'[31] More to the point, in studies of transnational politics and the resultant interdependence, 'policy is portrayed as set, not so much by states as unitary actors, or by markets, but by transnational networks of government and private actors, acting to coordinate policies by combinations of formal and informal collaboration, through and around institutional settings.'[32]

Interdependence in this context approximates Keohane and Nye's *complex interdependence*, a contemporary condition characterized by multiple channels of communication between societies, the absence of a hierarchy among issues, and a minor role for the use of military force.[33] The first element is of greatest interest here, for it suggests that the channels of interstate relations routinely ascribed significance by works on diplomatic history (i.e., formal foreign office arrangements) have today been joined by a host of other channels. Additions include informal ties between governmental elites and between nongovernmental elites and organizations. These multiple channels of communication help to blur even more the distinction between domestic and international politics. The opportunities and constraints presented by nongovernmental activities therefore portend the greater sensitivity and vulnerability of all actors to changes elsewhere in the system. Patterns of political action will be affected in a variety of ways by a greater degree, or more complex form, of interdependence.

Complex interdependence increases the potential for international institutions, such as INGOs, to have an impact upon interstate bargaining as they assume roles in which they help to set the international agenda, act as catalysts for coalition-formation, or serve as arenas for political initiatives and linkages. As in IGOs, these roles will tend to be particularly useful for weaker states (especially where the principle of equality among participants or national delegations prevails) in the sense that their appeals to institutional norms may make opposition by stronger states to majority or consensual decisions and attempts at unilateral domination appear 'harshly self-interested and less defensible.'[34] In essence, Keohane and Nye are observing that INGOs can play roles as international actors in diplomatic relations between states – that they are, like states, 'personifications of social functions.'[35]

But how do INGOs become involved in diplomacy? If traditional conceptions of international relations are adhered to, nongovernmental channels could be utilized by states as a means of achieving foreign policy objectives. For example, a 'bottom-up' approach may be attractive to states wary of becoming closely associated with a vague concept or deeply involved in an issue area over which an air of uneasiness and unfamiliarity might linger.[36] Uncertainty plays an important role in each instance, necessitating a period in which states and governments can familiarize themselves with ideas or with one another.[37] The bottom-up diplomatic strategy therefore becomes a way of reducing risks, of lowering potential costs, and of ensuring that other state interests are not impinged upon.

The notion of a state-initiated, bottom-up approach, which relies upon other societal sectors to take the lead, does not necessarily mean that the nongovernmental entities in question are, or can be, controlled by states. A distinction between utilization and control must be drawn. It may be the leaders or members of an INGO who are pursuing a nongovernmental approach to diplomacy. One must be willing to explore the possibility that academics, businesspeople, and other nongovernmental actors perceive themselves and/or the associations in which they participate as being able, and/or as having a need, to contribute to the diplomatic framework. INGOs might then be characterized as *interest groups* or collections of *political entrepreneurs* which have succeeded in placing and maintaining an issue on the diplomatic agenda.[38]

Lying between the *foreign policy means* and *self-perception/self-interest* propositions is the possibility that, although state input and support are helpful, the nongovernmental players and state officials involved have realized that the primacy of the state in a variety of issue areas should not be overstated. Indeed, the presence of an effective business or research network may mean that state leadership is not required in order to achieve cooperation or the attendant objectives of nongovernmental interests. Under such conditions, it may be that states are accommodating the desires of nongovernmental actors and vice-versa as part of a symbiotic arrangement which serves the diplomatic interests of state and nongovernmental actors alike.[39]

Diplomacy and Diplomatic Functions

This said, diplomacy is still commonly considered to be one means of achieving the policy objectives of states through the exercise of 'national power.'[40] Satow's oft-cited definition refers to the practice of diplomacy as 'the application of intelligence and tact to the conduct of official relations between the governments of independent states, extending sometimes also to their relations with vassal states; or more briefly still, the conduct of business between states by peaceful means ... skill or address in the conduct of international intercourse and negotiations.'[41]

At a more elementary level, diplomacy is what Nicolson calls 'an essential element in any reasonable relation between man and man and between nation and nation.'[42] Implicit in Nicolson's conception is the notion of interdependence and an acknowledgment that there are links between domestic politics and the external environment.[43] This view also offers an opening for the possible inclusion of nongovernmental actors. Accordingly, a more concise way of defining diplomacy may be by reference to the functions or tasks involved. Watson proposes that the tasks of the diplomatic agent are fourfold: (1) *'finding out or guessing intelligently* what one power needs to know about another,' (2) *'sifting and collating* the information received,' (3) *'determining the options* available to a government and submitting them for decision,' and (4) *'communicating and explaining* a government's decisions to another government.'[44] The stress in this conception is on *information*, and thus it coincides with Wight's suggestion of three functions – 'communication, negotiation and information.'[45] Though negotiation is a major element, Satow draws attention to the complementary roles of communication and information, stating that 'the duty of the diplomatic agent is to watch over the maintenance of good relations, to protect the interests of his countrymen, and to report to his government on all matters of importance, without being always charged with the conduct of a specific negotiation.'[46]

The diplomatic tasks of representation, information, communication, and negotiation are similar to those derived by Plischke. Accepting the proposition that 'functionally [diplomacy] embraces both the making and implementation of foreign policy at all levels, centrally and in the field,' he suggests that this 'involves essentially, but is not restricted to, the functions of representation, reporting, communicating, negotiating, and maneuvering, as well as caring for the interests of nationals abroad.'[47] Equating the 'caring' function with representation and 'maneuvering' with negotiating, we arrive at a fourfold classification of diplomatic functions. Whether or not an international actor engages in or contributes to diplomacy is therefore dependent upon whether or not that actor performs and/or facilitates one or more diplomatic tasks.

Plischke concludes that, in addition to the element of function, a definition of diplomacy must consider the nature of the participants and the process in which they are engaged:

> Diplomacy is the political process by which political entities (generally states) establish and maintain official relations, direct and indirect, with one another, in pursuing their respective goals, objectives, interests, and substantive and procedural policies in the international environment; as a political process it is dynamic, adaptive, and changing, and it constitutes a continuum.[48]

Plischke supports those who argue that the study of diplomacy should be limited to the study of official states and government agents. In his view, 'there is merit ... in such precision which, while acknowledging similarities, recognizes dissimilarity ... Failure to recognize these distinctions tends to confuse rather than to clarify.'[49] Yet, one senses that if Plischke had reflected upon the remaining elements of his own definition before formulating his position on the involvement of actors other than states, a serious conceptual problem posed by attempts to restrict the study of diplomacy to the study of states would have been exposed. For if we accept that diplomacy is 'dynamic, adaptive and changing,' an examination of actors based upon their performance of diplomatic functions may provide us with a clue as to the nature of the flexibility inherent in the practices which characterize the diplomatic continuum he acknowledges.

Diplomacy and Diplomatic Agents

Like Plischke, many people perceive diplomacy as an activity undertaken by the official representatives of states alone; in other words, as those interactions conforming to what Wight terms 'traditional diplomatic standards.'[50] *Diplomats* are usually considered to be persons charged by a state with the responsibility and task of representing that state in its relations with other states.[51] This restriction is sometimes expressed in classifications of *diplomatic agents* – classifications routinely based upon regulations governing the conduct of international relations adopted at the Congress of Vienna in 1815, amended at the Congress of Aix-la-Chapelle in 1818, and reconfirmed by the adoption of the Vienna Conventions on Diplomatic Relations in 1961.[52]

How has the practice of diplomacy come to be viewed in this way? Nicolson observes that it was realized even in primitive societies that, though all foreigners were to be regarded as potentially dangerous and impure, a dialogue between groups was not possible unless messengers from one group were allowed to be heard (rather than killed) by another group and to return home with a response. But it was not until the period spanning the thirteenth to the fifteenth centuries that the now traditional standards of diplomacy began to emerge in the Italian state system.[53]

That there is general agreement on the links between diplomatic practice and the development of the European state system from the fifteenth century onward reflects, in part, the scholarly and political emphasis placed upon order and institutionalization as well as upon the development of diplomacy as an organized activity. The evolution of traditional diplomatic practices is considered to have been synonymous with the emergence of powerful, centralized, and territorial states impinging on one another but aware of the advantages for all in the establishment of 'procedures for constant communication, discussion of disputed issues and the making of agreements.'[54] Procedures for the management of international relations were formally established in 1815 and remained the bases for conduct until the First World War. The perceived need for formal standards of diplomatic conduct (as distinct from efforts at the Congress of Vienna to institutionalize a European balance of power) arose from difficulties encountered in the sixteenth and seventeenth centuries with the management and maintenance of the representative qualities of ambassadors.[55]

The belief that diplomacy involves only official state representatives has also been perpetuated by theories governing the extension of diplomatic immunities and privileges and the dominance of the *warrior* conception of diplomacy over the *shopkeeper* school. As Wilson notes, theories of personal representation, extraterritoriality, and functional necessity have promoted the belief that 'the diplomatic agent is the personification of his ruler or of a sovereign state whose independence must be respected.'[56] Given the increasingly complex nature of international relations, official diplomats are less able to claim that they are the only legitimate or functionally necessary diplomatic agents.[57] It is unlikely that the pressures of economic growth and environmental stress, the expansion of international trade and investment flows, and the mounting limitations on the use of force will allow a narrow definition of diplomacy to be sustained as we approach the twenty-first century.

The warrior school of diplomacy corresponds with the realist suggestion that the state must be primarily concerned with matters of war, peace, and security.[58] Negotiation is equated with 'a military campaign, or, at best, autumn manoeuvres,' and negotiators' means are considered 'more akin to military tactics than to the give and take of civilian intercourse ... the purpose of negotiation is victory, and ... the denial of complete victory means defeat.' Diplomacy is thus a zero-sum game in which conciliation, confidence-building, and fair play are not apparent. Involvement in diplomatic affairs is properly left to the state, the guardian of force and the protector of the people. Any actors not officially fulfilling offensive or defensive roles on behalf of the state are not to be considered diplomats.[59]

In contrast, the *shopkeeper* school of diplomacy has its roots in an activity which provided much of the impetus for the establishment of the modern diplomatic corps: trade. Reflecting what might be termed the 'civilian theory of negotiation,' the commercial conception is 'based upon the assumption that compromise between rivalries is generally more profitable than the complete destruction of the rival.' It is thus the source of the distinction between diplomacy and other means of attaining policy objectives. Mutual concessions are seen as leading to mutual understanding among nations and 'questions of prestige should not be allowed to interfere with a sound business deal.' Reconciliation is possible, given frank discussion, honesty, and human rationality.[60]

The view that diplomacy should not involve questions of commerce thus ignores one of the original motivations for the creation of diplomatic practice. Nicolson contends that diplomacy as an organized profession owes as much to commerce as to politics, and that the main impulse transforming previously ad hoc or amateur diplomacy into a specialized service was trade. For example, the Venetian diplomatic service originated from commercial machinery, and early British representation in the Near and Far East was often maintained by trading companies, with the state lending moral support. Envoys exhibited dual allegiance to a board of directors and to a government. This semi-official, semi-mercantile status was abolished in 1815, when the envoy formally became the personal representative of his/her sovereign. Thereafter, diplomats sought to dissociate themselves from the stereotype of the company agent because they felt it lowered their status to that of commercial travellers. It was not until the late nineteenth century that German and American statesmen sought to combine political and commercial influence in the practice of diplomacy.[61]

By 1900, economic goals and war had led business groups in many states to demand state support and a place in the making and implementation of foreign policy. As these demands were acknowledged, there followed a large-scale reassertion of commerce in the diplomatic intercourse between states. Industrial syndicates, exporters, and chambers of commerce gained prominent roles as foreign policy advisors and decision-makers. Business leaders also influenced the selection of diplomats, and commercial competency became a prerequisite for entrance into the diplomatic service.[62]

Today, one finds domestic and external forces similar to those present at the close of the last century, again emphasizing the link between 'the pouch and the pocketbook.'[63] The number of international economic organizations in existence is further evidence of this linkage. The reorganization of state bureaucracies (as in the recent restructuring of the foreign ministries of Canada and Australia in 1982 and 1987, respectively) as a reflection of this renewed economic focus is thus to be expected.[64] As Nicolson reminds us, 'the main formative influence in diplomatic theory ... is common sense. And it was through trade and commerce that people first learnt to apply common sense in their dealings with each other.'[65]

Just as diplomacy has once again become enmeshed in economic matters, many of the increasingly technical social and environmental concerns of foreign policy and diplomatic practice now require the advice of scholars and private individuals, further altering the shape of diplomacy as experts on specific subjects operate beside experts in dealing with foreign governments. Like businesspeople, scholars and interest group members have become necessary participants in the policy formulation process. They are also functional parts of many negotiating teams and conference delegations, encouraging multisectoral societal participation in diplomatic contexts.[66]

Nonetheless, there is much debate over the utility and actual importance of technical experts. While noting that the theory of functionalism suggests it is possible for 'the increasingly tight and continuous network of contacts between experts to be not merely an expansion of the diplomatic dialogue ... but the embryo of a new collective administration of the world's affairs,' Watson sees such predictions as 'in part wishful thinking given restraints presented by state concerns, especially on more controversial issues.' Recognizing appointed or independent technical experts to be engaged in diplomacy, he does not foresee loyalties being easily shifted away from the state and does not expect that the logic of functionalism will eventually result in states being replaced as the primary units of analysis in international relations.[67] Yet, these observations indicate that we must be willing to accept actors other than official state agents as potentially significant contributors to, or components of, the dialogue between states.

Diplomacy as a Dynamic Activity

Many scholars cite 1914 as a turning point in the evolution of diplomatic theory and practice. This is because the trauma of the First World War ushered in a variety of changes and/or accelerated existing trends: the increased use of conference diplomacy involving senior state officials; the demands for democratic control of diplomatic interaction in countries with representative political institutions; the rise of the moral factor in international relations in response to the destruction wrought during the war; the increased use of the media and propaganda; the growing support for, and participation in, multilateral intergovernmental organizations; and the rising importance of commerce as a concern of diplomacy. Change was precipitated, in part, by technological improvements to communications, transportation, and weaponry, which combined to provide the spectre of greater risks when engaging in, and fewer prospects for success through, the use of force.[68]

Diplomacy is not a static phenomenon. As Watson observes, the acceptance and vitality of traditional diplomatic channels[69] does not preclude new forms of interaction or types of actors from playing roles in peaceful relations between states: 'On the contrary there is a great need for adaptability in the dialogue between states. Most of the valuable innovations in diplomatic practice began as ad hoc arrangements and evolved experimentally, and were formalized only when their utility in practice had been demonstrated.'[70]

The need to adapt to the changing circumstances accompanying the emergence of the European state system was a primary reason for the development of formal diplomatic practices during the fifteenth and sixteenth centuries.[71] The use of nonprofessional diplomats and nongovernmental organizations in the latter half of the twentieth century reflects yet another phase in the ongoing process of diplomatic adaptation.

The tasks of diplomacy (i.e., representation, information, communication, and negotiation) can be and are being pursued through official *and* unofficial channels. Accordingly, an analytical perspective based upon a narrow definition of diplomacy and choosing to distinguish between diplomatic actors and semi-diplomatic, quasi-diplomatic, extra-diplomatic, and/or non-diplomatic agents runs the risk of understating or overlooking the functions of those placed in the latter categories. It also obscures the flexibility of diplomatic practices and techniques.

This observation is consonant with Scott's suggestion that nongovernmental entities may serve diplomatic as well as subversive forms of informal penetration[72] and Cottam's inclusion of the activities of 'nonofficials' in his typology of *competitive interference* in twentieth century diplomacy.[73] Similarly, Bryant invokes the concept of 'private economic diplomacy,'[74] Watson cites the diplomatic utility of 'unofficial proxenoi,'[75] Kertesz lists the 'activities of private groups and individuals' as a distinct category of diplomacy,[76] and Kriesberg notes 'the growth of Track 2 diplomacy (non-official)' involving 'quasi-mediators.'[77]

Perhaps the most concise assessment of 'unofficial diplomats' (i.e., 'private citizens acting alone or attached to nongovernmental organizations [who] become involved in the conduct of interstate relations [by having] contact with private citizens or government officials from other countries as well as with their own government')[78] is provided by Berman and Johnson. They suggest that nongovernmental actors may contribute to the practice of diplomacy by

(1) serving as intermediaries and performing third-party functions related to negotiation and mediation.

(2) providing alternate settings in which government officials may meet.

(3) providing alternate channels of communication when official channels are blocked or unfeasible.

(4) serving as sounding boards and thereby lessening the risks faced by governments when putting forward or testing new policy ideas or positions, given that the activities of nongovernmental actors can be disavowed at anytime.

(5) performing tasks related to research, analysis, and observation.

(6) formulating alternative courses of action and improved decision-making procedures.

(7) increasing the salience of many economic and social issues on the international agenda by demonstrating to authorities public support for long-term, global approaches to policymaking.[79]

Furthermore, case studies lead Berman and Johnson to conclude that the success of unofficial diplomacy in democratic societies (i.e., the ability of unofficial diplomats to reach key decision-makers and to demonstrate to them compelling reasons for utilizing unofficial channels) is dependent upon at least eight factors:

(1) a recognized competence in an area of specialization.

(2) the prominence of the private individuals involved.

(3) contacts private citizens have gained from previous government service and personal associations.

(4) a clear statement of intent.

(5) the maintenance of a private and confidential setting.

(6) the building and delivery of a constituency and the ability to demonstrate the support of that constituency and the public at large for alternative approaches to policy matters.

(7) the ability to create an 'environment of accommodation' in which perceptions become malleable, contacts are made between nations at many levels, and participants become aware of inherited premises and cultural differences.

(8) 'dedication, sophistication and perseverance.'[80]

Once again, prominent throughout this assessment is an emphasis on the ability of private citizens and organizations to perform or to facilitate the diplomatic tasks of information, representation, communication, and negotiation.

Diplomacy as a Dialogue between Cultures

The final point to be made regarding the need to be wary of a state-centric conception of diplomacy is derived from the observation that, because the so-called traditional diplomatic practices developed alongside the European state system during the fifteenth to the nineteenth centuries, they are imbued with European and Christian values. Several non-Western societies had developed their own diplomatic practices much earlier.[81] Watson suggests that European traditions became predominant because only in Europe were diplomatic practices not consumed by one empire; diplomacy is necessary and functions best under conditions similar to that of the multiple balance of power which developed around 1500 in Europe. Only in the twentieth century 'has a states system become for the first time truly global, encompassing a variety of civilizations and beliefs.' He also stresses that recognition of the European roots of contemporary diplomacy is necessary 'if we are to see where it has become inadequate and how it can successfully be adapted and in some respects wholly transformed to meet the requirements of its global expansion and of radical change.'[82]

The post-Second World War era has demonstrated the functional necessity of adapting diplomatic practices to decolonization and the attendant creation of new and less developed independent states, most of which lack a European cultural heritage from which traditional diplomatic standards have evolved. Strategic, economic, social, and environmental interdependence has presented a similar need. Studies of contemporary international relations would be wise to heed such observations, for they highlight yet again the advantages of conceiving diplomacy as a dynamic activity, the shape of which can be adjusted to accommodate the many contending cultures and aspirations.

Conclusion

Provided they maintain autonomous decision-making processes, international nongovernmental organizations may be usefully categorized by reference to the functions they perform. It is as a result of their actions having an impact upon other political entities that INGOs obtain international actor status. Many activities of INGOs have political consequences necessitating state responses. Cases in which states seek to utilize or cooperate with INGOs are of particular interest, as it is in such contexts that the diplomatic roles played by INGOs may be better understood.

Diplomacy is commonly characterized as an activity in which only states or their official representatives are involved. This conception has been perpetuated despite the role which commerce and commercial interests have played in shaping the practice of diplomacy and the rise to prominence of technical and academic experts. The necessity of adapting practices to a changing diplomatic environment and cultural differences has also been noted. Thus, restrictive notions of diplomacy must be questioned. A more useful way of examining the practice of diplomacy may be to assess international actors with regard to their performance or facilitation of the diplomatic functions of representation, information, communication, and negotiation. Recent examinations of environmental politics,[83] the 1992 Earth Summit,[84] global social change,[85] international organizations,[86] foreign policy,[87] global public policy,[88] epistemic communities,[89] international regimes,[90] and state-business relations[91] reinforce the utility of moving in this direction and suggest fruitful areas for further research. Using INGOs prominent in the Pacific economic cooperation movement as subjects, the chapters which follow seek to pursue this line of inquiry.

3
The Institute of
Pacific Relations

Proponents and observers of the recently created intergovernmental body, Asia Pacific Economic Cooperation, are reminded that the promotion of the regional cooperation by international nongovernmental organizations has a history spanning more than eight decades. Although the time may be right to advance beyond the level of unofficial diplomacy, one should be cognizant of the utility of the path travelled prior to APEC's appearance in 1989. This chapter considers an INGO prominent during the early part of this journey, the Institute of Pacific Relations (IPR), and argues that the diplomatic contributions made by this organization set an example which was followed by the nongovernmental components of the present regional cooperation movement.

Origins and Structure
The impetus for Pacific regionalism can be traced to the years immediately before and after the First World War, when increasing international economic growth, expansionism, competition, and disorder sparked the search for ways to ensure the peaceful settlement of disputes. This was true not only in Western Europe, the major battleground of the First World War, but also in East Asia and the Pacific, where Sino-Japanese and Russo-Japanese conflicts had already signalled regional unease and imminent danger.[1] Organized nongovernmental action in response to regional concerns was first taken in 1907 with the founding, in Honolulu, of the Pan-Pacific Union, which sought to bring 'greater unity to the region through the development of communities in microcosm.'[2] Among the several similarly functional but nonofficial fora which emerged in the 1920s as a result of the union's activities was the IPR. The discussion of postwar problems in the Pacific by members

of the Young Men's Christian Association (YMCA) also played a role in the Institute's creation. These discussions began in 1919, when the idea of 'a self-governing and self-directing body concerned with promoting the best relations between Pacific peoples to avoid misunderstandings and conflicts and to promote friendship and cooperation' was canvassed. The proposed organization was to be guided by a 'Christian spirit of cooperation and fellowship,' an overt reference quickly jettisoned as a non-starter. By 1923, plans for an inaugural conference on this theme were well advanced, the stated objective having been reformulated as 'the promotion ... of a community of interest among the peoples of the Pacific basin.'[3]

The IPR was founded in 1925 at a Honolulu gathering, which included private individuals and delegations from Australia, Canada, China, Great Britain, Hawaii, Japan, Korea, New Zealand, the Philippines, and the mainland United States. The organization's stated purpose was 'to study the conditions of the Pacific peoples with a view to the improvement of their mutual relations,'[4] and discussions of the regional cooperation idea can be found in the proceedings of the first IPR conference.[5] A 1943 IPR publication portrays the Institute as

> an unofficial and non-political organization ... composed of autonomous National Councils in the principal countries having important interests in the Pacific area, together with an International Secretariat. It is privately funded by contributions from National Councils, corporations and institutions. The Institute, as such, does not advocate policies or doctrines and is precluded from expressing opinions on national or international affairs. It is governed by a Pacific Council composed of members appointed by each of the National Councils.[6]

Outlining a format which remained intact for most of the Institute's existence, this description also reflects a staunch defence of the organization's nongovernmental status.

Diplomatic Contributions

Although some founding members might have perceived the IPR 'primarily as a means of crosscultural contact and exchange of individual views in a private framework,' scholars such as Thomas, Thorne, and Johnson have noted that not all participants shared this 'restricted view.'[7] Likewise, the following denial of a diplomatic role (coming, as it does, at the opening of a summary of a 1929 IPR conference roundtable discussion of diplomatic relations in the Pacific) suggests that, early in the Institute's life, the public perception of the organization acknowledged that it did play such a role and hints that IPR participants themselves were conscious of their contributions to official relations:

The [IPR] is not a diplomatic body. It has no official connection in any way with governmental policy. Its genius is educational rather than political. None of its officers or members hold positions of official responsibility; but on the contrary, when official positions are accepted, that fact has been taken as necessitating the resignation from the Institute of the individual concerned ...

The fact must also be re-stated emphatically that the Institute, as such, does not engage in the search for solutions of pressing political problems. Still less does it endeavor to formulate policies and press them upon the governmental officials whose business it is to conduct international negotiations. Some confusion of understanding inevitably arises from the fact that some members may use the new light gained from their fellow-members in the round-tables to bring whatever influence they have in their private capacities to bear on their home governments ... For such by-products, however, the Institute takes no responsibility and can claim no credit. It merely provides a forum for the exchange of ideas and opinions. What happens as a result of the mutual education which comes of this exchange is a matter of individual not collective responsibility.

Necessarily the round-table discussions are concerned with the backgrounds of diplomatic questions ... Beyond endeavoring to illuminate these backgrounds, the Institute has not gone, and does not intend to go, further. The utilization of its discussions is a matter for the proper governmental officials, influenced as may be by individual members of the conference either by direct representation or by their efforts in awakening public opinion.[8]

Several features of the IPR's operations reinforce the perception of the organization as a diplomatic forum performing the functions of representation, information, communication, and, perhaps, even negotiation. Although individual members did not hold public office, the level of past or present national public status among IPR leaders and conference delegates was (in current comparison with PAFTAD, PBEC, and PECC) relatively high. Participants included former prime ministers, foreign ministers, ambassadors, and senior bureaucrats together with corporate executives, industry association personnel, academics, labour leaders, philanthropists, and newspaper editors.[9] They attended as private individuals but, as a result of their affiliations with national delegations, were routinely considered to be representatives of their respective societies and/or governments.

Over time, circumstances dictated an attempt to engage persons actively involved in policy-making and implementation, thereby further enhancing the Institute's representative qualities. When the possibilities for wartime and postwar cooperation in the region were scheduled to be discussed during the IPR's December 1942 conference at Mont Tremblant,

> an important departure from previous [IPR] practice was authorized in inviting persons holding government positions to participate in discussions, though only in their personal capacities. This step was considered necessary because so many of the competent authorities in the field of Far Eastern and Pacific problems had gone into government service and because without the presence of some officials the discussions on such a topic as cooperation of the United Nations in the Pacific would inevitably be unrealistic if not actually misleading.[10]

In another departure, this conference 'was completely private and its discussions were not reported by the press,' again indicating the sensitive diplomatic nature of the Institute's activities.[11]

Similarly, the IPR itself drew attention to the significance of the attendance of Soviet and French 'full member' delegations in 1936, which brought the number of national groups represented at the organization's pre-Second World War peak to eleven: Australia, Canada, China, France, Japan, the Netherlands-Netherlands Indies, New Zealand, the Philippines, the Soviet Union, the United Kingdom, and the United States.[12]

The diplomatic nature of participation in Institute activities was complemented by the organization's informational pursuits, which included 'studies of economic, social and political problems, particularly those which seem chiefly to endanger the friendly relations of governments and peoples.'[13] The centre-piece of these efforts was an international research program, which culminated in the holding of a conference every two to three years. A journal, *Pacific Affairs*, was published by the International Secretariat, and each national council maintained a research committee. Those studies exceeding the capabilities and resources of individual national councils were submitted to the International Research Committee (composed of National Research Committee chairpeople) and subject to the approval of the Pacific Council. Once authorized, these projects and study groups were delegated by the International Secretariat to a coordinating institution or national council. The research program was financed by local contributions and matching grants administered by the International Secretariat, whose main sources of funds were, for many years, the Rockefeller and Carnegie foundations.[14]

Contemporary assessments of the IPR also highlight its role in the facilitation of diplomatic communication. An Australian state official and participant in the Mont Tremblant conference recounts that

> it became apparent that governments themselves saw the conference as a very useful sounding board and as an opportunity for exploring further some of the problems of post-war settlement. Consequently the membership of the ... conference included persons who were able to make a highly useful contribution to discussion because of their closeness to official thinking and, perhaps even more importantly, who were part of a small corps of officials who would continue to work in postwar planning in future years ...
>
> Part of the value of international conferences of this kind is that in out-of-session discussions a number of persons from various countries who are working in the same field get to know each other, learn from each other and hence are better equipped to work with each other in the future.[15]

In his study of Ozaki Hotsumi's participation in the Sorge spy ring, Johnson's comments about pre-Second World War Japanese involvement in the Institute tend to support the communication theme:

> During the period when Sino-Japanese and Japanese-American relations were deteriorating, IPR conferences naturally became forums for expressing differences of national policy. The 1936 conference, held in Yosemite National Park in California, was the last one in which the Japanese genuinely tried to influence world public opinion through the IPR.
>
> ... Ozaki's paper ... entitled 'Recent Developments in Sino-Japanese Relations,' was as forceful and cogent a presentation of the Japanese case for its continental policies as could have been made at the time ...

Attendance at the IPR conference signified Ozaki's acceptance into the ranks of the civilian political elite of Japan, and his selection as a member of the delegation marked him as a recognized spokesman for Japan's China policy.[16]

Thorne's observations about British participation in the IPR are similarly instructive. Commenting on the links between the 1942 and 1945 British delegations (coordinated by the Royal Institute of International Affairs at Chatham House) and the British Foreign Office (Whitehall), Thorne notes that 'foreign assumptions about the limited extent of the Royal Institute's independence for once had some validity.' He, too, emphasizes the IPR's communication function, especially with respect to 'the climate of opinion and specific attitudes to be found in those areas in both Britain and the United States where officialdom overlapped with prominent outsiders who had an interest in international affairs.' Accordingly, these 'IPR conferences did help to bring home to officials and influential members of the public on both sides of the Atlantic the extent of the mistrust and, in some degree, misunderstandings that surrounded such Far Eastern issues as the future of South-east Asian colonial territories and the postwar international role of China'.[17]

However, Thorne discounts the suggestion that the IPR's role in moulding opinion was at any time translated into direct influence upon foreign policy formulation in many of the countries represented. Nor does he have sympathy for the claim that some IPR leaders actively sought such influence – a claim levied against members of the Institute's International Secretariat and American Council during a 1951-2 investigation conducted by the Subcommittee on Internal Security of the United States Senate's Committee on the Judiciary. The Senate investigators alleged that the IPR had been infiltrated and/or used by communist elements to manipulate, to mislead, and to misinform U.S. foreign policy and policy-makers in relation to America's diplomacy in the Asia-Pacific region over the preceding two decades. It is now commonly accepted that, while testimony did reveal channels of communication between IPR leaders and the U.S. Department of State, the high degree of influence ascribed to the International Secretariat and American Council of the IPR was exaggerated amidst the McCarthyism and anti-communist hysteria which pervaded the Senate inquiry, and that, given the evidence presented, the conclusions drawn are not sustainable.[18]

The communication function can also be seen within IPR publications, with the reader's attention frequently being drawn to the Institute's cordial and cooperative relations with organizations which sent observers to IPR conferences. These interested parties included the International Labor Office (ILO, later Organization), the League of Nations, the United Nations (UN), the International Institute of Intellectual Cooperation, the Rockefeller Foundation, and the Carnegie Corporation.[19]

However, it should be noted that, although the participation of active government officials at the 1942 and 1945 conferences of the IPR did present the possibility of these gatherings serving as fora for negotiation, none of the participants was at liberty to enter into formal agreements. Even so, the proceedings of these meetings did go somewhat beyond a simple exchange of views, as participants and national delegations attempted to define, to redefine, to expose, and to alter the policies being intimated by the representatives of other countries (even if they were allies), while defending those of their own government. As Thorne concludes:

> In essence what occurred was that the international conferences convened by the IPR became a forum for the debating of Allied war aims in Asia, with representatives of several of the constituent national bodies showing themselves eager to attack the colonial record and policies of Britain in particular (France and the Netherlands were sometimes placed in the dock as well). And in doing so they had behind them a substantial body of public opinion in the United States, as well as in Asian countries.[20]

The IPR and Regional Cooperation

Further evidence of the IPR's contributions to diplomacy is found in Institute studies of, and debates about, the regional diplomatic framework. At the 1936 conference, Quincy Wright, professor of international law at the University of Chicago, presented a paper entitled 'Diplomatic Machinery in the Pacific Area.'[21] Wright concluded that there was 'less than a comprehensive network of bilateral treaties among Pacific powers for arbitration and conciliation of disputes.' He also found that, due to the nature of membership inclusions and exclusions, the existing multilateral agreements (the Washington treaties and the supplementary London treaties together covering insular possessions, naval limitations, and relations with China) could 'hardly be said to constitute a regional Pacific grouping,' and that the general machinery – provided under the Hague Conventions (1899 and 1907), the League of Nations Covenant (1919), the Kellogg-Briand Pact (1928), and the Argentine Anti-War Treaty (1933) – had failed to deter or quell aggression.[22]

It is important to note the breadth of Wright's study when assessing his comments on the regional diplomatic framework of the day. Reflecting the traditional conception of diplomacy and abiding by the preferences of the IPR leadership, Wright limits his exploration of 'possible new instruments or modifications' by defining *diplomatic machinery* as 'procedures and institutions for dealing with problems in the relations of independent states ... Such problems may, of course, be taken up by states officially in which case their handling is by diplomatic machinery.' Though willing to consider the option, given that the Pacific had 'become such a focus of world interest that there is at present no possibility of an official organization of the powers with interests only or mainly in that area,' he was not optimistic about the chances of establishing a new intergovernmental organization with a strictly regional approach.[23]

The traditional and narrow scope of Wright's assessment discounts the possibility of regional diplomatic machinery being nongovernmental in nature. He ultimately sides with those IPR participants who, in 1929, had 'urged that the existing diplomatic machinery in the Pacific – the official channels of diplomacy ... were adequate if they were fully and properly used. The need, it was argued, was to make existing machinery effective rather than to create more.' Dissent was, nonetheless, forcefully expressed. The proceedings of the 1929 IPR conference make a point of recording that, despite observations of significant growth in the pan-Pacific economy and the nascent 'Pacific consciousness' which was accompanying this increased interaction,

> there remain difficulties of international intercourse. In part these arise from factors of distance and isolation ...
>
>   This is all the more important because the social structure of the chief Asiatic countries differs so radically from the social structure familiar to western peoples. Not only spatial but 'social distance' enters into the problems ...
>
>   One important result of this situation is a distinct distrust of European and, to a somewhat less extent, American diplomacy and diplomatic machinery, on the part of many leaders of Oriental thought ...

... Any consideration of the need for further international machinery of a regional character in the Pacific must bear these attitudes in mind.[24]

Thus, while the IPR leadership would have been pleased with Wright's 1936 perspective because it precludes the suggestion that the Institute itself had a role to play in regional diplomatic affairs, by 1929 there already seemed to be a number of participants who felt 'that the very existence of the [IPR] was proof of a widely-felt need for more adequate means of international cooperation ... [because] of inadequate diplomatic understandings and contacts,' and that the Institute itself 'should sponsor the creation of such machinery, or should use its research program to gather useful material for diplomatic negotiation.'[25] This said, the prevailing wisdom within the IPR (i.e., that effective regional cooperation could only be achieved by governmental action) was understandably strengthened by the outbreak of the Second World War and dominated the proceedings of the 1942 Mont Tremblant conference.[26]

The governmental approach also dominated regional cooperation proposals made outside the IPR. One of the earliest of such conceptions was put forward by John Crawford (later Sir) in 1938. Expressing a cooperative theme which was to form the foundation for much of his later involvement in international relations as an Australian academic, bureaucrat, and university administrator, Crawford sought to ensure his country's economic and political integrity and to deal with Japan's rise as an economic and military power. He advocated that the Australian government pursue 'the path of appeasement or alleviation of international economic grievances, accompanied by measures which directly link such appeasement to collective agreements in the interests of political security.' Leaving open the option of creating a permanent regional organization, he emphasized the need for an official regional accord: 'For their part the Powers making concessions could expect from Japan a more reasonable attitude towards the problems of security in the Pacific. The only alternative to mutual agreement is international anarchy, and in this game of power politics we may not always be the winners.' Crawford's version of economic appeasement may have succumbed to the 'storm over the Pacific,' which he sought to avoid, but the concept of regional cooperation was to remain a cornerstone of his economic and political thought.[27]

At about the same time, a somewhat different form of regionalism was being conceived in Japan – a Greater East Asian Co-Prosperity Sphere. The roots of this idea have been traced to the notions of an East Asian Cooperative Body and a New Order in Eastern Asia, which were deliberated by the Showa Kenkyukai (Showa Research Society) led by Prince Fumimaro Konoe (prime minister three times between 1937-41). Immediately prior to and during the Second World War, this study group discussed ways of implementing peace policies in Asia. Its activities are notable in the context of today's Pacific economic cooperation movement because of the participation of Saburo Okita in the Showa-juku (Showa Institute), a private school established by the Showa Kenkyukai.[28] They are less notable as a result of another major feature of twentieth century history: the adoption and alteration of these East Asian cooperation ideas by the Japanese military and their subsequent promotion as the Co-Prosperity Sphere.[29] While 'there always is the danger of reading too much out of a person's history of involvement in the development of a concept,'[30] it is evident from Okita's memoirs that his exposure to the regional cooperation idea at this time (and to its corruption at the hands of the Japanese military) ingrained in him an understanding of the virtues and pitfalls of promoting such a framework.[31]

Okita initially rose to prominence in this issue area when, as a director of Japan's Economic Planning Agency (EPA), he co-authored a 1961 UN Economic Commission for Asia and the Far East study of regional economic cooperation.[32] In 1963, Okita left the bureaucracy to head the newly formed Japan Economic Research Centre (JERC), an organization funded by four major business groups. The centre's first published report, 'Economic Cooperation in the Pacific Area,' proposed annual meetings of representatives from Japan, Australia, New Zealand, Canada, and the United States. Exhibiting a reluctance to support only a governmental approach, the report did not specify the preferred status of these representatives.[33]

In 1960-1, the IPR was disbanded as a result of the vicissitudes wrought by the U.S. Senate investigation, which, ten years earlier, had irreparably damaged the Institute's status as an impartial and respected international nongovernmental organization.[34] Thus, the JERC report remains important because it marks the earliest rekindling of interest in the nongovernmental approach to regional cooperation evident in the IPR's activities. Its release in 1963, just two years after the death of the IPR, coincided with the first discussions amongst Japanese and Australian businesspeople of what was to become PBEC, and at least one observer has suggested a causal link.[35] Okita's association with Kiyoshi Kojima, whose 1965 proposal of a Pacific Free Trade Area eventually led to the birth of PAFTAD, is also significant. Perhaps even more notable is Okita's subsequent relationship with Crawford – a relationship which began via PAFTAD and was to play a crucial role in the launching of the PECC process. Okita and Crawford had first-hand experience with frustrated intergovernmental proposals, and both went on to become leading proponents of a nongovernmental approach.[36]

Intergovernmental action may be desirable, given the primary significance accorded to states in the international system today, but one must question whether promoting cooperation with a governmental solution held high as the ultimate objective is prudent. Not only does such an approach risk running afoul of those suspicious of the promoters' motives and intentions, it also allows the possibility that the utility of pursuing nongovernmental courses of action will be overlooked. Despite their reluctance to characterize their organization's efforts as diplomatic, participants in the IPR appear to have understood the diplomatic value of multipartite nongovernmental activities, the virtues of which have been rediscovered within the PECC process.

Conclusion

The diplomatic tasks of representation, information, and communication were facilitated by the IPR. Prior to, during, and immediately after the Second World War, the need for a private forum to assist in the promotion of mutual understanding was evident, and the IPR became a respected international organization. However, the opportunities presented by this status also proved to be liabilities, and the Institute fell victim to the prevailing Cold War mentality of the 1950s. Yet, given that it was followed soon after by the founding of PAFTAD and PBEC, the demise of the Institute in 1961 appears to have extinguished neither the spirit nor the utility of nongovernmental diplomacy – characteristics even more evident in PECC. Its form, functions, and impetus thus suggest that the IPR represents the institutional precursor of the INGOs today involved in the Pacific economic cooperation movement.[37]

There has been a tendency, during most of the past three decades, for the examination and promotion of the concept of economic cooperation in the Asia-Pacific region to be led by INGOs rather than by states or governments.[38] This aspect of the Pacific economic cooperation movement reflects an easing of the tension seen earlier in IPR debates on regional diplomatic machinery. It also reflects an acknowledgment of the role and value of nongovernmental networking in a region in which Western diplomatic values and customs must be reconciled with those of non-Western cultures if cooperation among people and nations is to be achieved.

Factors such as Japan's economic ascendancy, the rise of other newly industrialized economies in East Asia, the conflict in Indochina, the emergence of ASEAN and the reemergence of China, an ongoing superpower rivalry, and an underlying perception of economic interdependence have dramatically altered the circumstances in which Pacific diplomacy has been conducted in the post-Second World War period. The problem of ensuring peace and cooperation remains, but the necessity of broadening diplomatic practices to include a nongovernmental approach and of following the lead set by the IPR would appear to have been widely accepted, the contentious circumstances surrounding the Institute's demise notwithstanding. The proponents of APEC may wish to take note, as they seek to extend the path of the cooperation movement beyond the nongovernmental boundary.

4

The Pacific Trade and Development Conference

Without the work of a host of ... scholars from a variety of countries within the region, consciousness of Pacific economic and governmental cooperation could not have reached its current level.[1]

Filling part of the vacuum left by the disbanding of the IPR, the Pacific Trade and Development Conference has led the scholarly promotion of the Pacific 'consciousness' referred to above.[2] At first glance, PAFTAD is a regular gathering of policy-oriented academic and professional economists interested in Pacific affairs, but a closer look reveals it to be 'the key regional forum for exchanges on foreign economic policy research [and] among the most effective instruments for promoting Pacific economic cooperation.'[3] One key participant has remarked that the organization's history 'is an interesting story in the practice of Pacific cooperation at the research level. It is an important story as well, because of the policy influence that has emanated from these conferences.'[4] In this chapter, a short review of the PAFTAD 'story' will precede an examination of its performance of three diplomatic functions: representation, information, and communication. This assessment will then be extended to consider PAFTAD's role in the regional cooperation movement.

Origins and Structure

As noted in Chapter 3, the research efforts of Okita and JERC in the early 1960s were complemented by those of Kiyoshi Kojima, an economist at Tokyo's Hitotsubashi University and the founding father of PAFTAD. Kojima's attendance at a 1964 East-West Center conference in Honolulu on 'Economic Cooperation for Development and Trade in the Pacific' sparked within him a conception of Pacific economic cooperation that had been nurtured during his work with one of the foremost experts on regional economic integration, Bela Balassa.[5] In 1965, Kojima unveiled his proposal for a Pacific Free Trade Area (PAFTA) in the form of an intergovernmental agreement on trade liberalization and production specialization between Japan, Australia, New Zealand, Canada, and the United States.[6] This proposal has served as a reference point for much of the subsequent academic, business, and governmental consideration of the Pacific economic cooperation concept.

Within Japan, consideration had earlier been given to the idea of reviving the IPR (to whose publications Okita had contributed), but, given the Institute's tainted reputation, it was conceded that such a move would not be looked upon with favour in the Tokyo, Canberra, Wellington, Ottawa, and Washington of the day.[7] The Japanese Ministry of Finance was actively examining the prospect of regional economic development schemes in East Asia and the Pacific at the time and

in March and April 1967 Professor Kojima, at the request of the Japanese Ministry of Foreign Affairs [Gaimusho], undertook a study tour of industrialised nations in the region to look at trade policies. The aim was ... also to gauge the amount of interest amongst academics in establishing an international conference to explore the question of a Pacific free-trade area. This tour provided the opportunity for setting up the PAFTAD Conference series.[8]

This Gaimusho-financed tour took Kojima first to Canberra, for discussions with Peter Drysdale of the Australian National University (ANU), who had previously studied and worked with Kojima in Japan, and John Crawford, director of the ANU's Research School of Pacific Studies. Kojima subsequently travelled to New Zealand for talks with Frank Holmes of the Institute of Policy Studies at Victoria University of Wellington; to the United States for meetings with Howard P. Jones of the East-West Center in Honolulu, Harry G. Johnson of the University of Chicago and head of the London-based Trade Policy Research Centre, and Hugh T. Patrick of Yale University; and to Canada for discussions with H. Edward English of Carleton University in Ottawa.[9]

Foreign Minister Takeo Miki's May 1967 announcement of an Asian Pacific policy clearly demonstrated the regional thrust of Japanese foreign relations.[10] His support for Kojima's academic initiative, coupled with that lent by the Rockefeller Foundation (which had also been involved with the IPR) via the International House of Japan,[11] led directly to the Gaimusho's sponsorship of the first PAFTAD conference of 11-13 January 1968. Held under the auspices of JERC and chaired by its president, Okita, the meeting now known as PAFTAD 1 allowed delegates to discuss the viability of a PAFTA involving industrialized nations as well as the potential for cooperation between the developed and developing countries of the region.[12] As a result of problems with the free trade area concept pointed out during his tour, Kojima recast his idea in the form of an Organization for Pacific Trade and Development (OPTAD). To be patterned after the Organization for Economic Cooperation and Development (OECD), the proposed organization would seek to establish regional codes for the conduct of trade policy and overseas investment and to facilitate the coordination of aid and trade policies towards developing countries. Drysdale also introduced his version of an OPTAD at this conference.[13]

While the PAFTA and OPTAD proposals did not provoke overwhelmingly positive responses, they were perceived by some participants as concepts around which an ongoing scholarly forum designed to study regional and global trade and development issues might arise. As Drysdale recalls, the 'impetus' for Kojima's PAFTA idea and for the PAFTAD series 'emanated from a regional concern at the time that the European Economic Community (EEC) might develop into an exclusive trading bloc for Europe and Africa, with detrimental consequences for developed and developing nations.'[14] This said, the organizational efforts which have since led to the convening of regular PAFTAD conferences (usually every eighteen months) were noticeably ad hoc in the early years. Indeed, without the assistance of the Asia Foundation, PAFTAD 2 might never have been held, and only in the late 1980s was a broad and relatively stable funding arrangement secured.[15] Table 4.1 outlines the subsequent breadth of PAFTAD conference themes and participation.

A discernible organizational structure (Figure 4.1) began to emerge in 1973-4, when the previously informal organizing committee was transformed into an International Steering Committee (PAFTAD-ISC), initially composed of Kojima, Okita, Johnson, Patrick, Jones, English, Crawford, and Drysdale. In recent years, the fifteen- to seventeen-member PAFTAD-ISC (Figure 4.2) has consisted of one to three representatives from most participating countries and has met at each PAFTAD conference. Two decades after the founding of the conference series several original members (Kojima, Okita, Patrick, Drysdale, and English) remained on the PAFTAD-ISC. This continuity is a prominent

Table 4.1

Pacific Trade and Development Conference series

No.	Year	Place	Economies represented for first time	Theme
1	1968	Tokyo	Japan, Australia, New Zealand, Canada, U.S.	Alternative trade arrangements
2	1969	Honolulu	Indonesia, South Korea, Philippines, Chinese Taipei	Role of developing countries
3	1970	Sydney	Thailand	Direct foreign investment
4	1971	Ottawa	Hong Kong, Singapore	Obstacles to trade
5	1973	Tokyo	Mexico	Structural adjustment
6	1974	Mexico City	Peru, Venezuela, USSR, Brazil, India	Technology transfer
7	1975	Auckland	Papua New Guinea, Fiji	Relations between large & small countries
8	1976	Pattaya	Malaysia	Trade & employment
9	1977	San Francisco	Chile	Mineral resources
10	1979	Canberra	China	ASEAN
11	1980	Seoul		Trade & growth of advanced developing countries
12	1981	Vancouver		Renewable resources
13	1983	Manila		Energy & structural change
14	1984	Singapore		Growth & financial interdependence
15	1985	Tokyo	Colombia	Industrial policies
16	1987	Wellington	Western Samoa, Tonga	Trade & investment in services
17	1988	Bali		Technological change
18	1989	Kuala Lumpur		Macroeconomic management
19	1991	Beijing		Economic reform & internationalization
20	1992	Washington		Pacific dynamism & the international system
21	1994	Hong Kong		Economic transformation & subregional cooperation

Note: International and regional organizations represented at various sessions: World Bank, Food and Agriculture Organization (FAO), Asian Development Bank (ADB), United Nations Economic and Social Commission for Asia and the Pacific (ESCAP), Andean Group (Bolivia, Chile, Colombia, Ecuador, Peru, and Venezuela), Organization for Economic Cooperation and Development (OECD), Association of Southeast Asian Nations (ASEAN), International Labor Organization (ILO), United Nations Conference on Trade and Development, and South Pacific Bureau for Economic Cooperation

Sources: H.E. English, 'The Emerging Pacific Community,' Carleton University, Ottawa, 1982, mimeo, 12; various PAFTAD proceedings and issues of *PAFTAD Newsletter*; *Pacific Trade and Development Conference: The First Twenty Years* (Canberra: PAFTAD Secretariat, April 1989)

feature of PAFTAD's history and an important reason for the organization's success.[16]

Figure 4.1

Pacific Trade and Development Conference: organizational structure

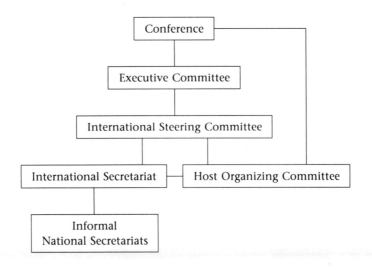

The PAFTAD-ISC chooses conference themes and locations and arranges institutional support and funding. When the conference location is agreed upon (decision-making is by consensus), a Host Organizing Committee (HOC) is formed by the PAFTAD-ISC member(s) from the next host country. Working in consultation with the PAFTAD-ISC, the HOC is responsible for drawing up a conference program and issuing invitations to prospective participants. The HOC also contributes 2-3 members of the PAFTAD-ISC's Executive Committee, a body which was formed in 1975 'for reasons of administrative convenience,' and which included Okita, Kojima, Patrick, and Drysdale amongst its membership through the late 1980s.[17] The organizational guidelines adhered to in the planning of each conference are set out in Appendix A.

Consolidation of PAFTAD's Role
Until 1983, PAFTAD was funded in what is usually described as an ad hoc manner. Financial support from the Japanese Ministry of Foreign Affairs (which has for some time had a member of its Information

Figure 4.2

PAFTAD International Steering Committee, 1992

Australia
Ross Garnaut
Department of Economics
Research School of Pacific Studies
Australian National University

Canada
H.E. English
Department of Economics
Carleton University

Indonesia
M. Hadi Soesastro
Director of Studies
Centre for Strategic and
    International Studies

Japan
Hiromuchi Mutoh
Senior Economist
Japan Economic Research Centre

Ippei Yamazawa
Faculty of Economics
Hitotsubashi University

Malaysia
Mohammed Ariff
Faculty of Economics and
    Administration
University of Malaya

Noordin Sopiee
Director
Institute of Strategic and
    International Studies

New Zealand
Allan Bollard
New Zealand Institute of Economic
    Research

Philippines
Filologo Pante, Jr.
President
Philippine Institute for
    Development Studies

Singapore
Lim Chong-Yah
Department of Economics and
    Statistics
National University of Singapore

South Korea
Wontack Hong
Department of International
    Economics
College of Social Sciences
Seoul University

Taiwan
Tai-ying Liu
Taiwan Institute of Economic
    Research

Thailand
Narongchai Akrasanee
Managing Director
Industrial Management Co. Ltd.

United States
Hugh Patrick (Chairman, 1985-)
Graduate School of Business
Columbia University

Lawrence B. Krause
Graduate School of International
    Relations and Pacific Studies
University of California, San Diego

ADB
Seiji Naya
Economic Office
Asian Development Bank, Manila

Secetariat Director
Peter Drysdale
Executive Director
Australia-Japan Research Centre
Research School of Pacific Studies

Senior Advisors
Kiyoshi Kojima (Chairman,
    1968-83)
International Christian University,
    Tokyo

Saburo Okita (Chairman, 1983-5)
Chairman
Institute for Domestic and
    International Policy Studies,
    Tokyo

Sir Frank Holmes
Institute of Policy Studies
Victoria University of Wellington

Sources: PAFTAD Secretariat and *PAFTAD Newsletter*, no. 6 (March 1991):4, and no. 7 (July 1992):6

Analysis, Research and Planning Division assigned to monitor PAFTAD activities and handle requests for funding) and related agencies has aided Japanese participation throughout.[18] There has also been a long history of support from the Asia Foundation, the Ford Foundation, and the Asian Development Bank (ADB).[19] However, in most cases such funds have not covered the total cost of a single conference and the related research program. The PAFTAD-ISC and respective HOCs have thus been forced to seek help from governments and government agencies, corporations, and academic institutions in host countries for the provision of financial assistance, personnel, and facilities.[20]

The uncertainty of government funding, in particular, has often been crucial to the siting of PAFTAD conferences. For example, the 1984 conference was originally scheduled for New Zealand, but the HOC withdrew because 'for domestic political reasons [a change in government in 1982 and an economic recession] it had been decided to postpone bringing the matter to the highest level of government until the new fiscal year approached.' Singapore (with the sponsorship of the Economic Society of Singapore and the National University of Singapore having been secured) assumed the role of host country, although consideration was given to Thailand and Japan, the latter being described as the 'ultimate fall-back host' or 'backstop.'[21]

Similarly, Canada was suggested as a possible host of the 1986 PAFTAD meeting, with the hope that the conference would be held in conjunction with the World Exposition in Vancouver. However, the PAFTAD leadership was subsequently advised that the prospect of attracting sufficient government funding for a PAFTAD conference was poor because of an impending federal election in 1984, the primacy of PECC V (scheduled for Vancouver in 1986) in the eyes of the federal government, and earlier efforts to secure funding for PECC from the government-sponsored Asia Pacific Foundation of Canada (APFC).[22] As a result, the New Zealand HOC, buoyed by the support of a new national government seeking to utilize organizations such as PAFTAD as diplomatic conduits, was asked to reassume the role of host, and PAFTAD 16 was held in Wellington in January 1987.[23]

Intent on consolidating their organization's role within the cooperation movement in the early 1980s, the PAFTAD leadership sought to address the previously acknowledged need for long-term planning and stable financing with the formation of a central secretariat and consortium funding arrangement. The matter of establishing a secretariat had been on the PAFTAD agenda for some years, but fears of institutionalizing costs and bureaucratic inertia had prevented moves in this direction. It was not until the Seoul meeting in 1980 and the imminent appearance of PECC that the idea began to take root. Informal national secretariats (at JERC, at the ANU's Australia-Japan Research Centre [AJRC], and at the Economic Growth Centre within Yale University's Graduate School of Business) had already assisted PAFTAD. Kojima was among those who expressed the view that it was time for PAFTAD to 'be remodelled into a research institution ... with a permanent office and research facilities in say, Canberra.'[24] Conscious that the growing need to strengthen PAFTAD's research role would necessitate changes in the organization of the conference series, the PAFTAD-ISC made special reference in September 1980 to the desirability of a central secretariat, observing that heightened interest in Pacific economic cooperation 'in policy circles ... and the proliferation of centres for research on Pacific affairs, pointed to the urgent need for a contact point and a centre for communication about Conference activity.'[25]

The commitment to establish a secretariat was reaffirmed in Vancouver in September 1981, and AJRC was invited to take on the task and to seek financial support. The intention was to ensure the continuity of networking activities, to improve the distribution of conference publications, to establish a five-year or five-conference forward planning program, and to secure a consortium funding scheme.[26] The following month, Kojima, in his capacity as PAFTAD chairperson, wrote to Crawford, the chancellor of ANU, to seek his assistance, noting that the Vancouver PAFTAD-ISC meeting had unanimously agreed that ANU was the best location for an 'effective liaisonpoint,' and adding: 'We hoped that the Australian Government may see a clear interest in funding the initiative.'[27]

Canberra was probably suggested as the best site for a secretariat for two reasons. The first pertains to the long-standing desire that PAFTAD (and, indeed, the entire cooperation movement) not be seen as dominated or controlled by Japanese or American interests. Second, the existence of a national secretariat at AJRC, the long history of support from Drysdale and Crawford, and the established Japanese-Australian research effort (which, with Japanese and Australian government funding, had led to the establishment of AJRC in 1980) would naturally have drawn attention to the Australian option.[28] Likewise, the Australian government's co-sponsorship of the Canberra Seminar (PECC I) in 1980 signalled its interest in exploring regional economic issues through informal channels.

The process of establishing the PAFTAD Secretariat took over three years (September 1980 to October 1983), largely due to the time-consuming process of applying to philanthropic foundations for contributions to a consortium funding arrangement.[29] Applications portrayed PAFTAD as an organization which could provide funding bodies 'with an effective channel through which to respond to key issues and to identify the right people and institutions in Pacific countries to engage in research on them.'[30]

Plans for a consortium funding scheme to support a permanent secretariat and a three- to five-year research program were well under way by the 1983 Manila meeting. The PAFTAD-ISC noted that it had received a 'commitment of support in effect by the Australian government' for general financial support to be provided through the 'Drysdale-[Ross] Garnaut activities at the ANU' as well as expressions of interest and support in principle from the Ford Foundation, the Asia Foundation, the Rockefeller Brothers Fund, and Japan's National Institute for Research Advancement (NIRA).[31]

Financial support was sufficiently in place for the opening of the PAFTAD Secretariat at AJRC in October 1983, just prior to PAFTAD 14 in Singapore, the proposed budget being U.S.$180,000 per year for five years.[32] Perhaps the most significant advance to date in the institutionalization of PAFTAD, the secretariat was initially comprised of a director (Drysdale), executive officer, and secretary. The latter two positions were shared with the National Pacific Cooperation Committee of Australia (NPCCA). The growing sense of maturity, stability, and forward planning in PAFTAD activities which accompanied the creation of the secretariat was enhanced by the publication of the *PAFTAD Newsletter*, which was distributed to interested persons and organizations as a means of publicizing and monitoring PAFTAD work, and by the establishment of a PAFTAD Research Fellowship to assist young scholars studying matters related to each conference theme.[33]

Efforts to secure a consortium funding scheme for a second three-year conference program began in August 1985 but ran into difficulty with the withdrawal of the Asia Foundation and NIRA. The Foundation for Advanced Information and Research stepped in to provide sustained Japanese funding, while the inclusion of the Henry Luce Foundation and Rockefeller Foundation bolstered American involvement in the consortium. The Taiwan Institute of Economic Research also joined. A third three-year funding arrangement began in December 1989, with the addition of the Korea Development Institute, the Tokyo Chamber of

Commerce and Industry, and the Kansai Federation of Economic Organizations in Japan.[34]

The financing of activities points to an operational feature which leaves PAFTAD's independent and nongovernmental character vulnerable: its dependence upon external funding derived from sources other than membership dues or subscriptions. Whereas PBEC, like many other private groups, covers its costs by levying membership and conference fees, PAFTAD is reliant upon governments and foundations to pay most of its bills. Therefore, if PAFTAD is to retain the ability to contribute to the diplomacy and the regional cooperation movement, it must continue to demonstrate to these donors the diplomatic utility of supporting a nongovernmental research network.

Representation

The forty to fifty delegates at each PAFTAD conference (usually two to three per country), whether academics or professional economists from businesses, state agencies, and international organizations, participate as private individuals. Attendance is by invitation, with the number, quality, and selection of participants monitored by the PAFTAD-ISC. Observers may also be permitted. Paper-writers are commissioned to do their research, and invited participants have their expenses paid. Thus, there is no financial constraint for persons invited to become members of the PAFTAD network, whereas financial cost is often a major consideration for persons considering membership in many other voluntary nongovernmental organizations.

The economists participating in PAFTAD 1 came from Japan, Australia, New Zealand, Canada, and the United States (the five countries envisaged as members of the PAFTA proposed by Kojima), but attendance of presenters and discussants from developing countries has been a salient feature of PAFTAD deliberations since 1969, when the Asia Foundation made its funding for PAFTAD 2 conditional upon there being an attempt to broaden the geographic scope of participation.[35] While many of the long-standing PAFTAD enthusiasts might be classified as liberal economic thinkers espousing the virtues of an outward-looking, export-oriented national economic strategy and seeking to accommodate the political realities which confront trade and development in the Asia-Pacific region, the wide range of political and economic systems from which conference participants are now drawn would tend to indicate that adherence to a particular brand of economic thought is not a prerequisite.

Strong support has been received from the countries of ASEAN since PAFTAD 2, whereas Latin American scholars only began participating in 1973. Despite the Ford Foundation's keen interest in seeing their participation increase, they have appeared only sporadically. The reasons usually given involve technical or logistical difficulties rather than philosophical differences. The PAFTAD-ISC has also had trouble finding Latin American economists with a sustained interest in the Pacific Basin.[36]

Soviet academics first accepted invitations to participate in 1974, and their participation, like that of Latin American academics, has also been sporadic. Still, given that foreign business and state attitudes towards Soviet involvement were less accommodating at the time of the first Soviet entry than they are towards Russian involvement in the 1990s, the earlier willingness of PAFTAD leaders to welcome Soviet participation is indicative of an important difference in the academic approach to Pacific affairs and cooperation efforts. It also reflected the PAFTAD leadership's desire to set a precedent for participation from other than market economies.[37]

The PAFTAD-ISC finally succeeded in attracting participants from China in 1979. In 1982, Kojima, as chairperson, wrote to the vice-president of the Chinese Academy of Social Sciences formally requesting 'that the Chinese Academy of Social Sciences appoint a scholar who can serve as liaison within the International Steering Committee on a continuing basis.' The purpose of this request was to consolidate and strengthen the relationship with China and to ensure appropriate participation in the future.[38] Chinese economists have since become regular participants. A Chinese scholar was awarded a PAFTAD Research Fellowship in 1987,[39] and the Institute of Industrial Economics acted as host of PAFTAD 19 in 1991. The Tiananmen Square massacre of June 1989 did cast a cloud over the conference, but the nongovernmental nature of PAFTAD allowed the organization to proceed once satisfactory assurances about the situation in China and the integrity of the conference program were provided by Chinese officials. Chinese involvement in PAFTAD is particularly significant in light of China's entry into PECC in 1986 and the presence of delegates from Taiwan in PAFTAD and PECC. The Taiwanese first appeared in PAFTAD in 1969. This involvement may have initially impeded Chinese participation. The Chinese willingness to contribute to PAFTAD since 1979 alongside Taiwanese delegates seems to be linked to China's 'coming out' and to the renewed Chinese desire to participate in intergovernmental and nongovernmental international organizations.[40]

Economists from South Korea, Hong Kong, and the Pacific Island nations have been participating in PAFTAD since 1969, 1971, and 1975, respectively. More recently, expressions of interest have been received from Vietnamese researchers, and the extension of invitations, 'when that becomes appropriate,' has been encouraged by donors such as the Ford Foundation and the Rockefeller Brothers Fund.[41]

PAFTAD participant lists are also dotted with the names of economists in the employ of global and regional governmental and non-governmental institutions. These organizations include the Asia Foundation, the World Bank, the Food and Agriculture Organization (FAO) of the UN, the UN Economic and Social Commission for Asia and the Pacific (ESCAP), the UN Conference on Trade and Development (UNCTAD), the UN Asian Development Institute, OECD, ASEAN, ADB, ILO, the International Chamber of Commerce, the South Pacific Bureau for Economic Cooperation, and the Andean Group. Similarly, government ministries and agencies from Japan, Australia, New Zealand, the Philippines, the United States, and Papua New Guinea have contributed participants and observers.[42]

Information and Communication
Inherent in the planning of each PAFTAD conference is the desire to define a research program on a particular theme one to two years in advance, to allow for a discussion of research results and their implications for policy, and to ensure publication of research findings.[43]

The dissemination of PAFTAD research findings has been problematic due to a limited publication and distribution scheme. This ad hoc system changed in 1983, when a commercial arrangement was struck with the publishing house Allen and Unwin (Australia), and a more rigorous editing and distribution process was undertaken.[44] Yet, while the conference organizers are interested in communicating the main themes and findings of the proceedings to a wider audience, PAFTAD conferences are normally closed to journalists in order to ensure the frank discussion of research and ideas.

The organization's success as a regional forum has largely been due to the control exercised by the PAFTAD-ISC. Several participants have suggested that a major attraction of this forum is the usually high quality of the research presented and the ensuing discussions. The majority of participants have been specialists, who are invited to prepare and to present the papers to be considered – an arrangement which has been instrumental in maintaining the organization's academic and policy-oriented credentials. The presence of government officials and bureaucrats from international economic organizations is also attractive to academic participants because the conferences then serve as useful settings for the exchange of views between academic and non-academic economists and provide important opportunities to influence the policy-making process. For some attendees, the synergy between the poles of government and academe has been the most enlightening aspect of their PAFTAD experience.[45]

While most participants are academics, many have considerable experience within state apparatuses. Other PAFTAD participants have proceeded to make notable contributions in the field of public administration following their initial contact with PAFTAD.[46] The potential for influence increases when PAFTAD conferences become the scene for an appraisal of economic policies. High stakes are often placed on the outcomes of such discussions, especially by participants in the employ of government agencies or with direct access to policy-makers. Such was the case in 1980, when the question of when to switch from an import substitution to an export promotion strategy became a central issue. In 1971, senior bureaucrats from foreign investment review and promotion agencies in the Philippines, Indonesia, South Korea, and Thailand were present, and the conference sessions spilled over into four to five days of post-conference meetings.[47]

PAFTAD's influence upon scholarly relations in the Pacific and the study of regional economic issues is even more evident to observers and participants with the development and refinement of common concepts or definitions, such as industrial policy (1985) or services trade (1987), repeatedly cited.[48] As an attempt to harness academic research efforts pertaining to the regional economy and to provide a forum for economists from around the region, PAFTAD offers a focus that was lacking after the demise of the IPR. The conferences thus serve to promote a unified and common approach to the analysis of economic matters by demonstrating the different assumptions and perspectives being used by economists in different countries.

Of perhaps even greater importance than a unified approach is the continuity seen in the participation of key academic leaders and in the ongoing nature of the conference series itself. Both features have contributed to what PAFTAD leaders commonly refer to as the building of a research network of past participants (numbering over 450 by the early 1990s)[49] and institutions involved in generating and disseminating the basic research information needed in order to discuss regional economic issues.[50] At the very least, PAFTAD has exhibited a capacity to contribute to the diplomatic framework of the Asia-Pacific region by enhancing the quality and frequency of discussions on trade and development. While 'modes of communication, stages of thinking, and interest in problems that have been and are being addressed' vary across countries, institutional and state support (financial and organizational) for research is also on the rise around the Pacific Basin.[51] Given the range and stature of individual participants and supporting organizations, it is difficult to dispute the claim that the perceived significance of PAFTAD deliberations is increasing in policy-making circles.[52]

In their effort to foster the practice of networking, the PAFTAD-ISC members lead by example. Correspondence is routinely shared, in keeping with the desire that PAFTAD become a research network in which the circulation of information is crucial. The PAFTAD-ISC perceives PAFTAD's role in the movement as that of providing intellectual leadership, and the sharing of information ensures that the intellectual capital that has been accumulated in the PAFTAD network is well used.[53] Effective communication is vital to the relationship between PAFTAD and other nongovernmental components of the Pacific economic cooperation movement. Because several PAFTAD leaders are also leaders of, or participants in, other fora promoting the study of regional economic questions, an attempt is made to coordinate meeting schedules.[54] This effort provides further evidence that groups such as PAFTAD, PBEC, and PECC have a collective importance in the sense that attempts are made to ensure a continuous and regular circulation of elites who frequently participate in more than one of these organizations.

PAFTAD and the Cooperation Idea

According to Drysdale, PAFTAD

> conferences are designed primarily for the intelligent consideration of economic policy issues of importance to Pacific countries ... This intellectual contribution aims to assist and complement the contributions of practitioners, in government and in the business world, in dealing with the challenges of Pacific development.
>
> ... The extension of this network of communication about policy ideas forms an important underpinning to economic problem-solving in the Pacific and a major resource in building upon the practice of Pacific cooperation.[55]

This statement of purpose indicates that the fostering of regional cooperation was a major interest of the original PAFTAD leaders, who quickly 'recognised the dynamism and economic importance of the Pacific region, and anticipated the usefulness of a coherent research activity to the problems of policy making.'[56]

Even so, the concept of Pacific economic cooperation has not always appeared as a prominent topic of discussion at PAFTAD conferences. Consideration of the PAFTA and OPTAD proposals raised in 1968 continued at PAFTAD 2 in 1969, with the need to build upon existing institutional arrangements being stressed. The arrangements cited included the Japan-Australia and Japan-New Zealand trade agreements and a recently established regional business association, the Pacific Basin Economic Cooperation Committee (later renamed PBEC).[57] In 1970, the conference focused on direct foreign investment, marking the beginning of a shift away from the discussion of pan-Pacific organizational models or mechanisms and towards more specific policy concerns. A desire to consider issues in their global context was also evident.[58] The OPTAD option was revived at PAFTAD 4, but the search for policy solutions to obstacles to trade was overshadowed somewhat by a debate about the short- and long-term effects of the Nixon 'shocks' of 15 August 1971.[59] When the theme of structural adjustment was addressed in 1973, attention was again given to global rather than to regional policy alternatives, the latter continuing to be seen as 'second best' solutions.[60]

Foreign investment and technology transfer returned to the spotlight at the 1974 conference in Mexico City, the first to be held in a developing country. Soviet participants, attending for the first time, led the discussion of the regional cooperation idea. They were keen to attract support for Siberian development and spoke in favour of achieving 'collective security by promoting further development of friendly and neighbourly relations between countries of the Pacific area.'[61] The attitudes of the Latin American academics in attendance, with respect to technology transfer and the distribution of economic power, were more belligerent.[62] Their concerns about the need for a fair distribution of gains from trade, development assistance, and foreign investment were also stressed in 1975 in discussions of the relations between large and small countries. The OPTAD proposal was raised, but concern was again expressed about the economic disparities between potential participating nations and the second-best nature of a regional solution.[63] Subsequently, trade barriers and trade strategies became the major issues at

PAFTAD 8 in 1976, with little mention of possible institutional arrangements at the regional level being made.[64]

Regional cooperation regained prominence at the 1977 conference, when Drysdale reformulated and restated his conception of an Organization for Pacific Trade, Aid and Development. This body was conceived as 'a loose, unbureaucratized organization, including both developed and developing countries which could do much to reduce the uncertainties involved in resource security,' an idea described by Drysdale's PAFTAD colleague, Lawrence Krause of the Brookings Institution, as 'an important contribution to finding a pragmatic middle ground.'[65]

Drysdale's revised version of OPTAD encompassed four broad aims:

(1) to provide a safety valve for the discussion of trade and economic grievances in a rational and cooperative atmosphere, given the high levels of economic interdependence.

(2) to stimulate aid and investment flows to developing countries and to improve the quality and structure of these flows.

(3) to provide a forum for consultation and discussion about longer term developments.

(4) to provide a more secure framework of economic alliance in the development of closer economic integration free of the suspicions involved in the expansion of relations with China, the USSR, and Southeast Asia.[66]

Initially modelled after the OECD, this intergovernmental forum was to go beyond being simply an organization for the development of joint policy approaches. The participation of developed and developing countries was to give it a special quality – a quality which would allow it to serve the objectives of the General Agreement on Tariffs and Trade (GATT) and UNCTAD, while focusing upon practicalities rather than generalities. The OPTAD was therefore to be 'a reference point for thinking in *Pacific* terms and for building a practice of coordination and cooperation.' It was also to be an organization which would

> weld together the three major strands in the relationships among Asian Pacific countries: the crucial economic links with Japan and the United States; the political, diplomatic and economic involvements with the developing nations, both non-communist and communist, in the Western Pacific region; and the strategic interest in stable and constructive relationships among the superpowers in East Asia and the Pacific.[67]

In 1979 Kojima raised the prospect of an OPTAD-like policy and 'tension management' forum involving the governments of ASEAN and the five industrialized nations of the region. He noted that when he had suggested this option to the Seventh Williamsburg Conference in Canberra in 1977, Thanat Khoman, a former Thai foreign minister, and Soedjatmoko, former Indonesian ambassador to the United Nations, responded favourably to the idea of a body which 'might eventually become, together with other already existing institutions and networks, important building blocks for a structure for peace and equitable development in the Asia-Pacific region.'[68] The discussions at PAFTAD 10 also highlighted the increasing awareness of ASEAN's importance in international economic relations and the subsequent necessity of moving towards Pacific economic cooperation at a pace acceptable to the members of the association.

The views of these ASEAN statespeople are instructive, because they emphasize the need to build upon existing institutions and networks. Inherent in these responses is the idea that channels other than those which are formal and intergovernmental may be just as important in the promotion of Pacific economic cooperation, if not more so. Two American political scientists, David Yoffie and Robert Keohane, made a similar point in a submission to PAFTAD 11 in 1980. Observing that 'a new, highly salient, Pacific Basin trade organization,' such as that envisaged by some proponents of the OPTAD proposal, may tend to fuel rather than to quell political controversy, these authors noted that

rejecting formal institutionalized arrangements does not, however, imply that an informal, low-profile OPTAD would be undesirable. There is a good deal to be said for informal exchanges of information, both among private citizens and government officials. Multilateral contacts among bureaucrats on specific issues of mutual interest can be extremely valuable. Some of the most significant attempts to bring cohesion and good sense to international relations occur through relatively informal contacts, either loosely within the framework of an international organization or outside of one entirely. Thus the principal difficulty with plans for OPTAD is not the idea that multilateral discussions of common problems should be encouraged, but the implication in some formulations that these discussions should take place within a formally constituted organization.[69]

When presented with this argument, several PAFTAD leaders responded coolly, defending the OPTAD idea and criticizing Yoffie and Keohane for their negative attitude towards the utility, desirability, and feasibility of an intergovernmental organization.[70]

The criticisms levelled against these authors are interesting, because an organization in which several PAFTAD leaders are now engaged (PECC) resembles the informal forum Yoffie and Keohane had favoured. Indeed, much of the research and debate undertaken by PAFTAD since 1980 has inspired or been inspired by (if not directly aimed at assisting) the PECC process. For example, at PAFTAD 12 in 1981 a consensus was reached on the need for enhanced regional cooperation in fisheries, forests, and fuels. A provocative and somewhat pessimistic paper on fisheries development and management by Gordon Munro of the University of British Columbia eventually led to the establishment of a PECC Task Force on Fisheries Development and Cooperation, which was initially chaired by Munro.[71]

The examination of regional and global cooperation on energy matters in 1983 was timely, given the recent establishment of a PECC Task Force on Minerals and Energy.[72] Likewise, discussions of financial interdependence in 1984 complemented the PECC Task Force on Foreign Investment and Technology Transfer, while the subsequent studies of industrial policies (1985), trade in services (1987), macroeconomic management (1989), economic reform in China (1991), and regional versus global trade liberalization (1992) have been designed as contributions to the PECC Trade Policy Forum, the Uruguay Round of GATT negotiations initiated in 1986, and/or the nascent APEC.[73]

Possible negotiating strategies for Pacific nations in bilateral, regional, and global settings were also reviewed at PAFTAD 16, 18, 19, and 20. Moreover, an organizational meeting of the PECC Trade Policy Forum held at PAFTAD 16 sought to clarify the interconnections between the various trade policy fora. Negotiations within GATT were seen as being complemented by PECC, with the PAFTAD leadership perceiving their organization as 'a pillar of the PECC process'[74] – a position the creation of APEC has since caused them to reaffirm.[75]

PAFTAD and the Cooperation Movement
PAFTAD's role as a prime element of the Pacific economic cooperation movement was evident to observers and participants alike by the late 1970s. Despite its still ad hoc coordination, the organization had become known as the leading academic forum for the discussion and

study of Pacific trade issues and theorizing about the feasibility of a regional economic arrangement.

In response to discussions at PAFTAD 7 in 1975 and PAFTAD 9 in 1977, Drysdale and Patrick were asked by Senator John Glenn, chairperson of the Subcommittee on East Asian and Pacific Affairs of the U.S. Senate's Committee on Foreign Relations, to provide a report on the feasibility of a pan-Pacific intergovernmental economic organization. Their report was issued in July 1979 and advocated the establishment of an OECD-style OPTAD. Recognized as one of the most authoritative conceptions of a regional intergovernmental institution, this submission revitalized the idea of Pacific economic cooperation, and its very commissioning signalled that (at least in the eyes of the U.S. legislators) the concept was still worth examining.[76] The legitimacy of scholarly efforts was further enhanced by the participation of several Japanese academics and PAFTAD contributors in the Pacific Basin Co-operation Study Group (PBCSG) established by Prime Minister Ohira in 1978 and chaired by Okita before he accepted the post of foreign minister.[77]

Neither the Drysdale/Patrick proposal nor the PBCSG report received widespread support. Each was looked upon suspiciously by those who perceived that a regional economic organization would serve the national interests of the countries and governments which commissioned the reports.[78] Nevertheless, these submissions did succeed in instilling renewed vigour in the study of the regional cooperation idea. The PBCSG recommendation that any ongoing discussions should include academics, business leaders, and state officials also confirmed a format which has become the hallmark of the PECC process. By placing these three sectors on the same level, the stage was set for PAFTAD to consolidate its position within the regional cooperation movement.

In September 1980, almost two decades of ground preparation by the PAFTAD research network culminated in the holding of the Pacific Community Seminar in Canberra. This gathering, now referred to as PECC I, was initiated by Crawford and Okita, the former having responded in his capacity as chancellor of ANU to a query from the latter, then foreign minister of Japan, with the observation that Prime Minister Fraser of Australia might be amenable to a proposal from Prime Minister Ohira that the two leaders co-sponsor a seminar on regional cooperation to be chaired by Crawford.[79] Thus, two key players in the launching of PAFTAD set the stage for the beginning of the PECC process. In a written submission to the seminar on 16 September 1980, Kojima, as chairperson of PAFTAD, noted that it had, over the years,

'given birth to a Pacific Economists Community.'[80] With the beginning
of the PECC process, the PAFTAD leadership had now parented an even
broader community than had hitherto been the case.

Not surprisingly, PAFTAD was one of two regional INGOs invited to
participate in the Canberra Seminar (the other INGO being PBEC). The
formal PAFTAD submission to the conference proceedings read as
follows:

> At its meeting on September 3, 1980 the International Steering Com-
> mittee of the Pacific Trade and Development Conference (PAFTAD)
> series:
> (1) Expressed gratification that the Canberra Seminar will be held later
>   this month. We regard it in some respects as an outgrowth of the
>   research and Conference activities of PAFTAD and its individual
>   participants over the past thirteen years ...
> (2) Indicated a strong willingness to cooperate with the Canberra Sem-
>   inar and any subsequent activities in any ways which may be
>   appropriate.
> (3) Reaffirmed the basic purposes and continued activities of PAFTAD
>   as an independent forum for policy-oriented discussions of Pacific
>   Basin economic issues on the basis of solid analytical, empirical
>   research ...
> (4) Indicated a strong desire to establish a permanent small secretariat
>   at the Australian National University, if feasible, to coordinate the
>   present national secretariats and related activities in PAFTAD
>   countries.
> (5) Agreed it would be desirable to have relatively modest ongoing
>   funding to cover secretariat costs, and for the initiation of the
>   future PAFTAD Conferences.
> (6) Regarded that one of the most useful functions of PAFTAD has been
>   and will continue to be to establish and strengthen contacts among
>   policy-oriented academic economists, government officials and
>   business leaders. The maintenance and strengthening of these link-
>   ages will be important for us all in the years ahead.[81]

By circulating these minutes, PAFTAD leaders were staking their claim
for a role in the regional cooperation movement and setting the course
for the future of PAFTAD. They believed that PAFTAD had 'provided the
foundation and the idea for the development of PECC, and its formation represents a concrete expression of the ideas generated by

PAFTAD.'[82] At PAFTAD 13 in 1983, Okita reaffirmed PAFTAD's role in the Pacific economic cooperation movement when he

> spoke of the vital role of the PAFTAD conferences and Steering Committee within the broader framework of policy discussions on economic cooperation in the Asia-Pacific region. He sees it as the main organization for bringing together academics for policy-oriented analysis of important trade and development issues; it has well proven itself over the years. PBEC performed the role of providing the input of private business in these policy discussions. [PECC] and its task forces provide an important forum for informal government-business-academic interchange. These activities in his view (and indeed of us all) are complementary and synergistic, and in no way competitive.[83]

Similarly, the discussion of PAFTAD and PECC in the inaugural *PAFTAD Newsletter* in 1985 depicted the ever-growing links between the two fora:

> The PECC provides a forum where policy issues brought forward by the PAFTAD Conferences and from other sources can be explained by those involved in policy decision making. PAFTAD and PECC are therefore integrally related and provide mutual support. Many of the influential participants in PECC have also been involved in the PAFTAD series, and the work of PAFTAD is a constant reference point at PECC meetings.[84]

Members of the PAFTAD-ISC now play key roles within many national PECC committees and the regional cooperation movement as a whole.[85] In a sense, the PAFTAD network has been expanded to encompass PECC. In 1987, six PAFTAD-ISC members (Okita, Drysdale, English, M. Hadi Soesastro of Indonesia, Lim Chong Yah of Singapore, and Narongchai Akrasanee of Thailand) were among the twenty members of the PECC-ISC and Coordinating Group. Ten other academics were also among the PECC leadership. In 1991, the addition of Noordin Sopiee of Malaysia and Tai-ying Liu of Taiwan brought the number of PAFTAD leaders listed as officers of PECC and its member committees (one of which is now PAFTAD itself) to eight. The impact of this sizable scholarly presence is broadened by the establishment of personal ties with business leaders and state officials, given that the corporate executives and bureaucrats appear willing to let the academics take the lead in PECC's research activities. The informality, flexibility, and, in most cases, speed of personal PAFTAD networking have also become major features of the PECC process.[86]

However, the arrival of PECC (and its 1989 agreement to work with the intergovernmental APEC forum) poses a potential threat to PAFTAD. Some resources (financial and human) have been shifted away from PAFTAD and towards PECC task forces. While this development may not trouble PAFTAD leaders (given the major roles they play in PECC, their view that the two groups are complementary, and the membership on the PECC-ISC which PAFTAD was granted following PECC V in 1986), it may become a problem if the level of support PECC and APEC receive from governments leads to PAFTAD's activities losing significance in the eyes of the non-academic sectors. It is possible that PAFTAD could disappear or be incorporated as the research wing of PECC, although moves to weaken or to alter PAFTAD's identity in this way are likely to be resisted by PAFTAD stalwarts should the organization's independent status be put at risk.[87]

The value of retaining an independent research organization has also been acknowledged by the leaders of PBEC, the international chairperson of which sits as a member of the PECC-ISC. Until the initiation of the PECC process, the relationship between PAFTAD and PBEC was not intimate, largely because of the differences in the interests of their participants and members. As English observed in 1982, PAFTAD and PBEC have 'evolved separately in part because [PAFTAD participants] have been primarily concerned with more fundamental applied research, often not directly related to the immediate concerns of individual businesses.'[88] Nevertheless, the relationships between PAFTAD and PBEC members have flourished within the PECC process. There is a high degree of contact on the PECC-ISC (where PBEC is also represented), in task force meetings, and on national committees. In 1985, this convergence of interests within PECC led two senior PBEC officials to commend the further institutionalization of the PAFTAD forum, noting that the 'increasing development of complementary interests in business and government policy circles requires closer coordination and, in turn, increases the need for a longer term strategy in the approach to PAFTAD's research planning.'[89]

Conclusion

The scholarly efforts embodied by PAFTAD have contributed to the diplomatic framework of the Asia-Pacific region in three ways. First, the stature and geographic breadth of participation indicates that the

PAFTAD leadership has been successful in efforts to engage prominent economic thinkers from all parts of the region in policy-oriented research and discussion. That it has been feasible to include these sometimes conflicting viewpoints in PAFTAD activities is again indicative of the forum's representative qualities.

Second, the PAFTAD research program has continually facilitated the forum's performance of the diplomatic function of providing information. From its early focus on alternative trading arrangements to its recent contributions to the study of topics such as industrial policy and trade in services, PAFTAD's academic yet policy-oriented approach has repeatedly demonstrated the link between scholarly research and official economic and political relations. An improvement in the publication and distribution of research findings and conference proceedings in recent years, the establishment of a central secretariat, and the production of a newsletter reflect steps towards institutionalization, which, in turn, are aimed at strengthening PAFTAD's information function.

These developments also highlight an effort to reinforce PAFTAD's third diplomatic function: communication. The PAFTAD network is now approaching 500 alumni, many of whom have been drawn from governments and international organizations. Several past participants have been senior state officials; others have had a wealth of government experience or have proceeded into high-ranking public service positions. For all who have passed through the PAFTAD network, the experience of exchanging (or monitoring the exchange of) views and information is likely to have been of some value (personal, professional, political, or otherwise) in a non-PAFTAD context. Without fulfilling the self-interests of many of its participants, while at the same time performing diplomatic functions, the PAFTAD network would not have persisted over the past two and a half decades. Nor, during that period, would it have enjoyed the financial assistance of governments, private foundations, and local institutions.

The range of governments and government agencies from which this support has come would tend to indicate that state apparatuses share the view that the research conducted by PAFTAD is valuable and that the pursuit of a symbiotic relationship is prudent. The key attributes which have allowed this INGO to gain such recognition and to engage in unofficial diplomacy include the expertise which has been accumulated in the PAFTAD research network, the societal prominence of participants, the politically significant contacts possessed by participants, the ability to provide an informal setting for policy discussions amongst scholars from a wide range of economies, and the dedication to the cooperation theme displayed by original and long-standing members of the PAFTAD-ISC.

Nowhere is PAFTAD's importance as a nongovernmental diplomatic actor more evident than in its relationship with PECC. Two early prime movers in PAFTAD, Crawford and Okita, were instrumental in the launching of PECC. Okita has remained a key figure in the PECC process, while Crawford's organizational genius lives on in the multi-sectoral, unofficial format of PECC conferences and task forces. Similarly, several PAFTAD academics sit on the PECC-ISC and maintain regular contact with business leaders and state officials at the regional and national levels. These factors have combined to form a close bond between these fora, with the PAFTAD research program increasingly being tailored to underpin the PECC task force activities, GATT negotiations, and APEC.

PAFTAD is not without problems and challenges. While the organization's capacity to perform representation, information, and communication functions has been addressed and strengthened by the PAFTAD leadership through the establishment of a consortium funding arrangement and an international secretariat, financial questions could still prove to be PAFTAD's Achilles' heel. A reliance upon external funding sets PAFTAD apart from the ideal form of an INGO and poses a direct threat to the forum's existence. It also allows PAFTAD's autonomy to be called into question. To date, the conditions set by philanthropic donors do not appear to have proven too onerous. But donations such as these are rarely permanent, and new donors must repeatedly be sought. More troublesome for PAFTAD's classification as an INGO is this forum's reliance upon funds from governments and government agencies. Often erratic, given the ebb and flow of government priorities and budgets, state funding may become distasteful for some should the Japanese government ever revert to being the 'ultimate backstop.'

Suspicions about government interference are also prevalent. Some authors go so far as to assert that the leaders of PAFTAD are participating in an act of 'academic brainwashing' as co-conspirators in a capitalist strategy which seeks to maintain and to reinforce the dependence of developing countries upon their industrialized masters.[90] One also finds suggestions that institutions such as the Ford and Rockefeller foundations are used to further the political objectives of a state, class, or individual.[91]

But have state links, real or imagined, been extended to meaningful interference in PAFTAD activities? It could be argued that this support and agreement amounts to consent, that states are interfering by assisting and prolonging PAFTAD activities, and that by accepting or seeking such support PAFTAD's claims to autonomy have been forfeited. Such arguments would carry more weight if a state's threat to refuse or to curtail funding could be shown to have forced the PAFTAD leadership to make a decision they would otherwise not have made – a decision desired by the state making the threat. This study has not revealed any such threats or detected any unusual PAFTAD actions which might have been due to state interference. Furthermore, it is unlikely that PAFTAD would have succeeded without state support. The leadership professes that the organization is policy-oriented. Therefore, positive reinforcement is desirable. Still, while negative effects are not apparent, a dependence on external funding does leave PAFTAD vulnerable. Its ability to defend itself against this financial dependence may well determine whether PAFTAD's nongovernmental contributions to the regional diplomatic framework are to be sustained.

5
The Pacific Basin
Economic Council

If a kingdom is divided against itself, that kingdom cannot stand. And
if a house is divided against itself, that house will not be able to stand.
                                                        Mark 3:24-5

The Pacific Basin Economic Council is the primary commercial component of the Pacific economic cooperation movement. This chapter
examines the Council's contribution to Asia-Pacific diplomacy by considering PBEC's origins and structure, its facilitation of diplomatic functions (representation, information, and communication), its relations
with governments, and its attitude towards the regional cooperation
concept.[1] The analysis suggests that the Council is in danger of becoming irrelevant as a regional actor.

Origins and Structure
The inspiration for the creation of PBEC was drawn from the activities
of a bilateral business cooperation committee linking commercial interests in Japan and Australia. Established in 1962 in response to a 1961
Japan Chamber of Commerce and Industry (Nissho) mission to Australia led by the chamber's vice-president, Shigeo Nagano (chairperson
of Fuji Iron and Steel), the Australia-Japan Business Cooperation Committee (AJBCC) sought to foster the development of economic relations
between the two countries. Personal contact between business executives was deemed necessary, though the support of the Japanese and
Australian governments was desirable. Supplementing government
efforts to encourage closer trading relations with other Asia-Pacific
nations and promoting opportunities for corporate interaction quickly
became additional objectives voiced by Australian and Japanese business leaders.[2]

The process of establishing PBEC was first discussed in detail at AJBCC II in September 1964 in Canberra, when a Japanese delegate suggested that AJBCC activities might serve as a model for a multilateral association involving participants from developing and developed countries. Following the presentation of position papers by the respective national committees, a formal discussion of the formation of a Pacific Basin Organization for Economic Cooperation and Development (PBO) was held.[3] The Australian paper, presented by R.W.C. Anderson (director-general of the Associated Chambers of Manufacturers of Australia [ACMA]) and I.R. Seppelt (chairperson of the Australian Wine Board), enthusiastically embraced the concept, expressed a desire to 'share the [AJBCC] experience with others,' and set out a three-phase strategy for achieving pan-Pacific cooperation: (1) consolidate and strengthen the AJBCC, (2) invite business leaders from other countries (initially New Zealand, Canada, and the U.S.) to form bilateral committees which would become national affiliates of a Pacific Basin Business Cooperation Committee, and (3) expand the membership of this regional business committee to include state and trade union representatives in a Pacific Basin Economic Cooperation Committee. A permanent secretariat to assist the performance of these tasks was also envisaged. The authors did not suggest a time-frame, acknowledging instead that phase three (during which they foresaw the integration of member country economies in mutually acceptable and beneficial fields) was 'a long way off,' and that it might be preferable to stop at phase two and to allow for business cooperation to bring about economic integration. The Japanese paper, presented by Nagano, was more reserved, stating the ultimate objective to be intergovernmental cooperation but stressing the daunting complexity of the task ahead, given the social diversity of the region, and suggesting that cooperation should first be undertaken at private levels.[4]

Emphasizing that businesspeople had a responsibility to promote relations on an informal basis and that a regional body should facilitate a systematic exchange of information aimed at relieving trade friction, AJBCC delegates subsequently agreed to invite business organizations in New Zealand, Canada, and the U.S. to send observers to AJBCC IV in 1966. Groups from Canada and New Zealand accepted and participated in a discussion of the PBO concept.[5] It was decided that any further action would have to be taken outside the context of the AJBCC. Participants also acknowledged that, although consultation between business leaders from the advanced countries would 'smooth the path

... for economic cooperation,' care must be taken 'to ensure that the less developed nations do not feel we are ganging up on them' and forming a 'rich man's club.'[6]

Suspicions about the true intent of the PBO's proponents remained. Unease about Japanese objectives was most pronounced, with Australian participants and observers sensing that the Japanese saw the PBO concept as a way of gaining market access around the region (especially in the U.S.), securing supplies of raw materials, and exercising political influence. Australian proposals for joint development projects in developing countries were treated with polite derision by their Japanese counterparts. Bryant's recollection of an American delegate's remark some years later illustrates these contending approaches: 'Japan was in PBEC to get its teeth into Australian iron ore and coal; Australia was in it to get the Americans to help get Japan off Australia's back and so on.'[7]

These differences notwithstanding, the birth of PBEC took place in Tokyo on 26-7 April 1967, following AJBCC V. Delegates from Australia, Japan, and New Zealand adopted temporary articles of association and elected Nagano (by then president of Nissho and chairperson of Nippon Steel Corporation) as the first chairperson. Business groups in Canada and the U.S. had declined invitations, and executives from other Pacific nations were to be invited to take up membership in due course.[8]

In an address to this organizational meeting, Nagano stressed that PBEC was initially to attempt to increase the flow of capital and goods among the five industrialized nations of the Pacific, to accelerate joint ventures in resource development in the region, and to enable advanced nations to cooperate with each other in expanding economic and technical assistance to lesser developed countries. The idea of eventually creating a 'European Economic Community of the Pacific' was eschewed, given the region's economic diversity, but initiatives such as the Asian Development Bank were noted as examples of government interest in regional cooperation schemes.[9] Nagano's immediate task was to sell the new organization to business communities in Canada and the United States, an objective he accomplished in time for a five-country steering committee meeting to be convened in Honolulu in February 1968. The Council's inaugural annual international general meeting was held in Sydney in May 1968 and was attended by 115 delegates and observers (39 Australian, 30 Japanese, 24 New Zealand, 6 Canadian, and 16 American).[10] A list of subsequent annual meetings, themes, and representation is provided in Table 5.1.

Table 5.1

Pacific Basin Economic Council: international annual general meetings

No.	Year	Place	Economies represented for first time (origin of firm or individual)	Theme
1	1968	Sydney	Japan, Australia, New Zealand, Canada, U.S.	International investment
2	1969	San Francisco		Problems of mutual harmony and competition
3	1970	Kyoto	Indonesia, South Vietnam, South Korea, Chinese Taipei, Philippines	Economic development in the 1970s
4	1971	Vancouver		Private investment in developing countries
5	1972	Wellington	Hong Kong, Fiji, Western Samoa, Peru	New international economic policies: challenges in the Pacific area
6	1973	Sydney	Malaysia, Mexico	Mutual prosperity and growth
7	1974	Washington	Thailand, Chile, Panama	Partners in Pacific progress
8	1975	Kyoto	France	Pacific resources: prospects for international cooperation
9	1976	Vancouver	Singapore	Priorities for Pacific progress
10	1977	Christchurch		An investment for Pacific progress: energy and food
11	1978	Manila	West Germany, England, Austria, Switzerland	The Pacific challenge: trade and investment growth
12	1979	Los Angeles	Italy, Kuwait	Pacific business in the 1980s: trade and investment
13	1980	Sydney	Colombia, Finland	The Pacific Basin in the 1980s: current issues
14	1981	Hong Kong	Papua New Guinea	Pacific Basin growth in the 1980s: prospects, problems, and priorities
15	1982	Nagoya	Sri Lanka	Pacific interdependence: the development of the Pacific Economic Community concept
16	1983	Santiago	Argentina, Brazil	Pacific cooperation: next steps
17	1984	Vancouver		Expansion of Pacific trade and investment

(continued on next page)

Table 5.1 (continued)

Pacific Basin Economic Council: international annual general meetings

No.	Year	Place	Economies represented for first time (origin of firm or individual)	Theme
18	1985	Auckland		Pacific cooperation: building confidence
19	1986	Seoul		Combatting protectionism
20	1987	San Francisco		High technology and Pacific cooperation
21	1988	Sydney		Towards 2000: succeeding in a changing world
22	1989	Taipei	Soviet Union	Asia-Pacific NICs: Pacific cooperation to the year 2000
23	1990	Tokyo		Pacific cooperation in the changing environment: growth and harmonization
24	1991	Guadalajara		The new Pacific model: development through open economies
25	1992	Vancouver		The Pacific Basin: a borderless economy?
26	1993	Seoul		Open regionalism: a new basis for globalism

Note: International and regional organizations represented at various sessions: FAO, General Agreement on Tariffs and Trade (GATT), South Pacific Forum Fisheries Agency, UN Centre on Transnational Corporations, ASEAN, ADB, World Bank.

Sources: PBEC Reports and PBEC Lists of Participants (1968-87); PBEC, *24th International General Meeting, Mexico, Guadalajara, May 4-6, 1991* (Mexico City: PBEC Mexico Member Committee 1991); *PECC Newsletter,* vol. 2, no. 3 (July 1992):6.

Today, PBEC's activities are overseen by an international president, a deputy international president, and a slate of vice-presidents drawn from the leaders of national committees (Figures 5.1 and 5.2). This International Steering Committee (PBEC-ISC) serves as the Council's primary governing body and meets semi-annually to set conference agendas, to sanction subcommittee terms of reference, and to make other major decisions. Decisions are made by consensus, the principle of unanimity having been abandoned in 1974. Corporate and individual participants agree to uphold the PBEC Covenant (Appendix B) and to pay fees set by national committees, which, in turn, remit dues to cover the international operating expenses, while a separate fee is levied against participants attending annual general meetings.[11]

Although the early Anderson/Seppelt blueprint cited the need for a permanent secretariat, the central office was shifted from country to country with the office of the international president during the

Figure 5.1

Pacific Basin Economic Council: organizational structure

Note: For an alternative depiction, see Norman D. Palmer, *The New Regionalism in Asia and the Pacific* (Lexington, MA: Lexington Books 1991), 138.

Figure 5.2

PBEC international officers, 1990-2

International President
Chen-Fu Koo
Board Chairman and President, Taiwan Cement Co.
Chairman, PBEC-Chinese Member
Committee in Taipei

Deputy International President
Pyong-Hwoi Koo
Chairman, Lucky Goldstar International
Chairman, PBEC-South Korea

International Vice-Presidents

Treasurer
Graham W. Valentine
Consultant, Coopers and Lybrand
  (New Zealand)

Pacific Economic Community
Frederick B. Whittemore
Advisory Director
Morgan Stanley and Co. (U.S.)

Australia
Russell J. Fynmore
Executive General Manager, Broken
  Hill Propriety Co. Ltd.
Chairman
PBEC-Australia

Canada
B. Vincent Kelly
Executive Vice-President (Corporate
  Banking), Royal Bank of Canada
Chairman
PBEC-Canada

Chile
Manuel Valdes
Chairman of the Board
Industria Metal-Mecanica Coloso
Chairman
PBEC-Chile

Chinese Member Committee in Taipei
Chen-Fu Koo (see above)

(continued on next page)

Fiji
C. Donald Aidney
Chairman
Williams & Gosling Ltd.
Chairman
PBEC-Fiji

Hong Kong
Helmut Sohmen
Chairman
World-Wide Shipping Agency Ltd.
Chairman
PBEC-Hong Kong

Japan
Rokuro Ishikawa
Chairman
Kajima Corp.
Chairman
PBEC-Japan

Malaysia
Tan Sri Basir Haji Ismail
Chairman
Petronas
Chairman
PBEC-Malaysia

Mexico
Julio Milan
President
Coraza Corporacion Azteca
Chairman
PBEC-Mexico

Figure 5.2 (continued)

PBEC international officers, 1990-2

New Zealand
Mike Robso
Chief Executive Officer
Independent Newspapers
Chairman
PBEC-New Zealand

Philippines
Jose Fernandez, Jr.
JBF Management and Investment
  Corp.
Chairman
PBEC-Philippines

South Korea
Pyong-Hwoi Koo (see above)

Peru
Gonzalo Garland
Senior Partner
Garland Attorneys at Law
Chairman
PBEC-Peru

United States
Robert S. Miller
Senior Partner
James D. Wolfensohn Inc.
Chairman
PBEC-U.S.

Past Presidents

Norton Clapp (1974-6)
  Chairman, Matthew G. Norton Co. (U.S.)

Kenneth H.J. Clarke (1972-4)
  Chairman of the Board, Simon-Carves of Canada Ltd.

Noboru Gotoh (1978-80)
  Chairman and President, Tokyu Corporation (Japan)

R.C. Macdonald (1976-8)
  Chairman, R.C. Macdonald Ltd. (New Zealand)

Sir James Vernon (1980-2)
  Director, CSR Limited (Australia)

J.H. Stevens (1982-4)
  Chairman of the Board, Canada Wire and Cable Limited

Frederick B. Whittemore (1984-6)
  Managing Director, Morgan Stanley and Co., Inc. (U.S.)

Sir Ronald Trotter (1986-8)
  Chairman, Fletcher Challenge Ltd. (New Zealand)
Noburo Gotoh (1988-9)
  (see above)
Rokuro Ishikawa (1989-90)
  (see above)

Sources: *PBEC Reports*; PBEC, *24th International General Meeting, Mexico, Guadalajara, May 4-8, 1991* (Mexico City: PBEC Mexico Member Committee 1991), 6-7; PBEC, *Pacific Basin Economic Council: Forum for Pacific Business* (San Francisco: PBEC International Secretariat 1990); *New Pacific*, no. 5 (Summer 1992):35

Council's formative years. Discussions about the utility of a permanent secretariat recommenced in the early 1970s, but little was done because of the perceived cost and a fear that PBEC's flexibility would be lost as bureaucratic control replaced the direction of elected officers. Organizational politics also tainted the deliberations, with concern about the autonomy of national committees set against the desire for collective action and central coordination.[12]

By 1973, reluctance had been overcome and the PBEC-ISC chose to enter into a contract with the World Business Division of SRI International (formerly Stanford Research Institute) in Menlo Park, California, for the provision of secretarial services on a temporary two-year basis. SRI's executive vice-president, Weldon B. Gibson (a participant at PBEC 1, member of the inaugural PBEC-ISC, and director-general of the U.S. national committee), became the first PBEC international director-general, though it was made clear that his role would be to assist, not to supplant, the efforts of national directors-general. It should be noted that the SRI's interest in things Pacific and, ultimately, in PBEC was evident well before the Council's founding. Gibson had discussed the PBO idea with Nagano in 1965 and had been one of the American observers at the preparatory meeting in Tokyo in 1967. Furthermore, the concept of a regional business association had been discussed and supported at SRI-sponsored meetings in Sydney and Jakarta earlier that year. These gatherings had been attended by several executives, who later became prominent PBEC leaders, including Julius Tahija (chairperson, Caltex Indonesia), Jose B. Fernandez (president, Far East Bank and Trust Company, Manila), and Yoshizane Iwasa (chairperson and president, Fuji Bank, Japan). It has also been stressed that some credit for the creation of PBEC must go to Eliot Mears, a Stanford University geographer and founding member of the IPR, who provided much of the impetus for the establishment of the SRI in 1946 (by the trustees of Stanford University at the request of American business leaders) and who later inspired many of Gibson's regional activities.[13]

Reservations about the International Secretariat have continued to plague the Council, with members citing problems with the distribution of correspondence and publications, the predictable contents of those publications, and the unilateral alteration of agreed positions. Dissatisfaction was becoming so acute that the suspicion in some government circles that PBEC was dominated by Japanese and/or American business interests had, by the mid-1980s, been replaced by the view that the Council may no longer be relevant to the regional economic policy-making process. It is thus not surprising that the PBEC/SRI relationship was placed under review by the PBEC-ISC in 1986, and that, as a result of discussions at PBEC 20 the following year, SRI International relinquished its secretarial responsibilities. The World Affairs Center in San Francisco undertook to coordinate PBEC matters on a temporary basis. R. Sean Randolph (a former U.S. State and Energy department official) was appointed international director-general, later moving to separate quarters. After yet another reassessment of its role and function, the secretariat was moved to the Honolulu office of the Center for Strategic and International Studies (a Washington-based think-tank) as of September 1992 and placed under the direction of a new international director-general, Robert G. Lees.[14]

Representation

Uncertainty about the motivations of participants from different countries and an uneasy relationship between national and central administrative bodies has made the performance of diplomatic functions difficult. In the case of PBEC's representative qualities, the limited geographic scope of its membership has posed a major problem.

The main event on the PBEC calendar is the annual general meeting held each May (Table 5.1), and it is at these gatherings that the Council's diplomatic potential becomes most apparent. Numbering 200-500 in recent years, delegates attend as company officials or private individuals – a feature which, on the surface, 'limits the diplomatic value of PBEC to [the] mutual exchange of unofficial policy and information.' Bryant has argued that PBEC participants 'are conscious of performing a supplementary role to their country's multilateral economic diplomacy but they do not represent their government or its official policy.'[15] However, it is by assuming representative qualities that participants fulfil this supplementary diplomatic role. For, while present in the first instance as representatives of their firms and local business communities, delegates are also required to represent their countries and governments. They may not agree with policy positions taken by their respective governments, but delegates from other countries will expect them to be able to present and to explain these policies. It is, therefore, by providing a forum in which businesspeople from different countries can share their policy concerns and can come to a mutual understanding of government positions that PBEC facilitates the performance of the diplomatic task of representation, which underpins the subsequent performance of information and communication functions.

The representation function is enhanced by activities within home countries. After participating in an annual general meeting, several national delegations report to their governments on the tenor and content of their exchanges with foreign business leaders. In effect, a symbiotic information exchange process has been established. PBEC participants act as their government's eyes and ears at annual general meetings and report to senior officials in post-conference briefings in exchange for pre-conference briefings on government policies and foreign service reviews of economic and political conditions in other countries. For example, detailed pre- and post-conference meetings between PBEC committee members and officials from the ministries/departments responsible for foreign affairs and/or trade in Japan, Canada, Australia, New Zealand, and the U.S. have been conducted for many years.[16]

This said, PBEC's capacity to facilitate representation has been limited by the Council's inability (or unwillingness) to attract (or accommodate) a significant number of participants from a broad range of countries. Some 850 fee-paying firms and individuals were members of PBEC in 1992, though estimates have ranged from 600 to 1,000.[17] For the Council's first two decades of operation the bulk of these came from just seven countries: Japan, Australia, New Zealand, Canada, the United States, South Korea, and Taiwan. The decision to limit membership to firms from Japan, Australia, New Zealand, Canada, and the United States at the time of the Council's founding was taken with the expressed intent of broadening the membership base once the organization 'got off the ground.' Yet, image problems were apparent from the outset, as Nagano reported to PBEC 1 in 1968 that 'the [PBEC] had received many enquiries from developing nations as to why only the five industrialized nations were invited to join.'[18] The danger of becoming known in the developing world as a rich man's club was recognized, but delegates chose to continue the restriction on new members and to place the onus on the countries of the prospective members to accept the principle of free enterprise.[19]

Business leaders from non-member countries first appeared at PBEC annual general meetings in 1970, when executives from Taiwan, South Korea, Indonesia, and South Vietnam accepted invitations to attend as observers. In 1971, executives from the Philippines came as observers, and, in 1972, 'guest participants' from Hong Kong, Fiji, Western Samoa, and Peru were present. Discussions on how to enlarge PBEC membership gathered momentum at PBEC 5, though ambivalence was still evident. Nevertheless, mounting dissatisfaction with the designations 'guest' or 'observer' and scepticism about the concept of 'associate membership' prompted PBEC leaders to seek a mechanism for the enlargement of PBEC membership. It was clear to many participants that businesspeople from non-member countries were 'treated like second class citizens.'[20]

Invitations were issued to more than eighty business executives from non-communist developing countries in advance of PBEC 6 in 1973, and it soon became clear that many of these 'special participants' were eager to become involved in standing committees. In 1974, an international committee (originally composed of company officials from the Philippines, Peru, South Korea, Hong Kong, Malaysia, and Indonesia) was created. This new committee was incorporated into the PBEC Covenant alongside provisions for the eventual rise of applicant member national committees.[21]

By the early 1980s the renamed Regional Member Committee (RMC) had fallen into disarray, and PBEC's image problem was reemerging. An ad hoc committee on the RMC's organization was formed in 1982, but efforts to realign its members into geographically, culturally, and economically similar subgroupings were destabilized in 1984 by the granting of full membership status to the most active RMC countries – South Korea and Taiwan. National committees from Mexico and Chile became full members in 1989, followed by Hong Kong and Peru in 1990, Malaysia in 1991, and Fiji and the Philippines in 1992. Colombia is to be admitted in 1993, with member committees from Singapore, Indonesia, and Brunei expected to enter soon thereafter.[22]

In the early 1980s, the most alarming trend in the eyes of PBEC officials had been the sharp decline in participation from the countries of ASEAN. In 1984, the PBEC-ISC was told by a Thai official of the ASEAN Chamber of Commerce and Industry (ASEAN-CCI) that it was incumbent upon PBEC leaders to explain the Council's purpose to the business communities of Southeast Asia. In response, SRI executives toured the ASEAN countries on behalf of PBEC in early 1985. Their report caused the PBEC-ISC to issue a policy statement which endorsed the organizational principles and aspirations of ASEAN and which sought a continuing liaison with the ASEAN-CCI. It was also decided that a senior business executive in each ASEAN country would be asked to become chairperson of a small PBEC-invited organizing committee and would be seconded to serve as a special member of the PBEC-ISC.[23] While there has been an increase in participation from within ASEAN in recent years, there remains a noticeable reluctance among Southeast Asian executives. A feeling that the PBEC approach is paternalistic, offensive, costly, and inconsistent persists.

In addition to its troubled profile within ASEAN, an inability to accommodate commercial interests from centrally-planned economies has detracted from PBEC's representational qualities. The initial PBEC view of Pacific affairs excluded communist nations. In the wake of moves by the governments of several PBEC member countries to reestablish formal diplomatic links with China, many delegates were, by 1972, urging the Council 'to keep our options open' and were suggesting that PBEC might be an appropriate forum for discussions between communist and non-communist countries. Some delegates sensed that the inclusion of China and the Soviet Union would be beneficial for PBEC (because it would widen its scope and population base), and that the Council's private nature offered the chance for informal ties between governments to arise out of business arrangements. Others believed that it would be suicidal for PBEC to invite both of these countries because of their political differences.[24]

In 1975, an expression of interest was received from the USSR, prompting Gibson, as PBEC international director-general, to meet with Soviet officials in Moscow prior to PBEC 8. However, obstacles to communist participation remained, the Chinese case having been complicated by the granting of full membership status to the Taiwanese in 1984. When the Taiwanese had applied for membership in 1982, the PBEC Covenant was amended in order to include standard references to 'member' rather than to 'national' committees – a reflection of a desire to refrain from alienating the Chinese. In 1985, the international president expressed hope that China would eventually participate in PBEC – a hope somewhat overtaken by China's decision to join the PECC at the same time as did Taiwan (as Chinese Taipei) the following year. Indeed, Chinese and Soviet (now Russian) participation in PBEC no longer appears to be an issue, given that both groups have already been accommodated within PECC (a forum the Soviets also attended for the first time, as observers, in 1986). This development tends to confirm PBEC's limited geographic scope and its limited ability to perform the diplomatic function of representation. However, the Gorbachev revolution and the establishment of a Soviet Far East Association for Business Cooperation with Countries of the Asia-Pacific Region in 1988 led to the reopening of discussions between PBEC and Soviet officials. Soviet observers attended the PBEC annual general meetings in 1989 and 1990, and three Soviet officials made formal presentations in May 1991.[25]

Information and Communication

Limited representation and organizational preoccupations do not bode well for the performance of information or communication functions. Yet participants in PBEC are primarily interested in collecting market information and making useful contacts with foreign business leaders. A key function of the Council's activities remains the provision of opportunities for individual business contacts to be renewed or enhanced. From this perspective, PBEC participants are 'no-frontiers men' driven by the profit motive and a conviction that commerce should not be impeded by political boundaries.[26]

But, given today's rapid communication and transport systems, corporate leaders may not need to spend their time attending PBEC meetings if they are merely interested in making deals and having contracts signed. Accordingly, company concerns have frequently been overtaken by enlightened self-interest and the personal objectives of participants, especially those PBEC members who have been or who remain actively involved in the multipartite, task force-oriented PECC process. Strict profit-seekers do not tend to remain members of the Council and are largely disinterested in PECC, whereas long-standing members often exhibit a sense of civic duty and international responsibility directly related to the diplomatic tasks of information and communication. As a result, the opportunities for input into the policy-making process afforded by interactions between national committees and governments have become another major focus of PBEC activities.[27]

The seeds of cooperation sown by this dual emphasis on business-business and business-government relationships have also caused dissension within the organization. The source of this tension has been the existence of two contending propositions about the degree to which the Council should pursue opportunities to influence the diplomatic framework of the Asia-Pacific region. The first proposition holds that PBEC should facilitate communication between businesspeople from different countries for commercial purposes only; the second proposition suggests that the Council should seek to develop a business consensus on matters of public policy and to express this regional consensus to the governments of member countries.

From the outset, participants questioned the utility of what seemed to be a philosophical talkfest which had little impact on the business climate the Council claimed to be influencing. Some hoped that PBEC would become an action- or project-oriented interest group which would lead by example and which would encourage governments to adopt policies favourable to the interests of its membership. Others, perhaps more concerned about raw material supplies and market access, felt that a *non-decision-making* forum designed to allow an exchange of views and to encourage mutual understanding was more desirable. They may have perceived participation in PBEC as a way of guarding against decisions which might have adversely affected their respective industrial sectors or specific business interests. Membership in such cases would thus be predicated on efforts to control the regional and organizational agenda in order to avoid the discussion of sensitive matters. At the time of PBEC's founding, the latter attitude prevailed, supported by the premise that members from the five founding nations would be able to agree on organizational objectives and activities.[28]

The lack of direction afforded by the business-business dialogue approach soon became apparent. According to one early account, PBEC started as 'a do-it-yourself organization of interested businessmen who think this effort worth their time, thought and expense.'[29] Yet neither talk of the need for members to 'strive toward the enrichment of spiritual life ... and the pursuit of human happiness' nor the stated intention of working in the public interest for mutually beneficial economic cooperation and social progress suggested anything about how PBEC might achieve its objectives.[30] In 1969, standing committees on tourism, transportation, human resources, natural resources, and economic development were established, but there remained concern about the 'delicate and practical balance between a debating society and a ponderous institution, between an exchange of ideas and a bureaucratic international agency.'[31] As Bryant later observed, in PBEC's early years the 'apparent lack of action projects had to do with inherent structural limitations' dictated by a preoccupation with procedures and priorities.[32]

As early as 1970, senior PBEC leaders urged members to look upon the Council as a multilateral catalyst for regional trade and development. They called for the formation of coalitions with other private institutions and collaboration with governments on development projects. Those businesspeople who saw PBEC as an example of private sector activism appeared to have gained the upper hand in 1971, when PBEC-ISC members unanimously agreed to forge a more practical modus operandi and to solicit governmental support for commercial goals.[33]

The claim that PBEC had by this time progressed from being 'an organization in search of a cause to one which [was] now prepared to play a positive role in developing the multilateral structure of economic cooperation in the Pacific' was open to debate.[34] Certainly opinions within the organization have differed on this matter, with many members continuing to question the level of interest in, and the nature of, the PBEC mission.[35] Over the past decade, the Council has been moving steadily in the direction advocated by the interest group/action-oriented school, still priding itself on being a unique meeting place for Asia-Pacific businesspeople but placing greater emphasis on business-government relations and the private sector's role in the enhancement of regional economies.

The Business and State of Business-Government Relations

The past, present, and future significance of PBEC's contribution to diplomacy in the Asia-Pacific should not be overstated. The rich man's club image remains, as do suspicions of Japanese and/or American domination and dissatisfaction with the Council's limited geographic scope.[36] Controversy over the central secretariat also reflects a preoccupation with basic organizational matters.

Perhaps most problematic is the perception within PBEC and government circles that the Council is becoming increasingly irrelevant as an actor in regional economic affairs. Many participants and observers now believe that PBEC's multilateral activities provide a less effective way of complementing commercial and diplomatic objectives than do the activities of bilateral business cooperation committees. The main reason for this view is the perceived ability of 'bilaterals' to be more transaction- and issue-oriented than a multilateral forum in which the presence of chief executive officers renders the content of discussions philosophical, nonspecific, predictable, and relatively unproductive. At the same time, PBEC's decline may be a product of its success. In its early years, participation in, and support for, PBEC was a useful way of promoting the familiarization process. But as familiarity and communications increased, the need to focus upon specific trade opportunities and problems became more important. Accordingly, the diplomatic relevance of PBEC has declined amidst the proliferation of bilateral fora, thereby robbing the Council of any remaining claim it might have had to being the primary voice of the regional business community and causing it to provide time within the context of its annual general meetings for bilateral discussions.[37]

Over the years, the PBEC Covenant has been augmented to encourage the consideration of more fundamental long-term commercial interests. By the mid-1980s, it encompassed three organizational objectives: (1) the provision of a 'forum for an exchange of views among businessmen' on Pacific affairs, (2) the provision of 'advice and counsel to governments and international agencies' on economic and commercial matters, and (3) the provision of private sector 'input to other organizations concerned with Pacific economic development and cooperation.'[38]

A useful window on the policy-making process has been afforded PBEC by the fact that some members are former senior state officials, and that some government officials have been PBEC members prior to taking up public office. Nevertheless, in 1982, the PBEC leadership set out to strengthen the organization's liaison and credibility with governments and other regional organizations. Local diplomats and up to five individuals representing either legislative or executive branches of governments were permitted to be affiliated with national delegations to PBEC conferences.[39] In addition, the idea of meeting with senior government officials was taken up, and, in 1985-6, members of the PBEC-ISC met with American, Japanese, Canadian, and South Korean political leaders. In the words of one PBEC participant: 'Our role is not to lobby in the narrow sense but to establish a clearer picture in the minds of the senior officials of the reality of Pacific commerce and finance, and from PBEC's viewpoint, desirable policy trends.'[40]

Concern about the organization's relations with governments is instructive, given that over the years praise for PBEC activities has come regularly from government leaders and senior representatives of intergovernmental organizations, many of whom have accepted invitations to address PBEC general meetings. One wonders whether concern about the organization's profile amongst politicians and bureaucrats has arisen because of a sudden realization on the part of PBEC leaders that actions speak louder than words and that members' commercial and political interests would be better served by the Council's adoption of an active, rather than a passive but oft-praised, approach to regional diplomacy.

PBEC and Regional Economic Cooperation

A final way of assessing PBEC's troubled contribution to the regional diplomatic framework is to examine the Council's overtly ambivalent attitude towards participation in the economic cooperation movement – an ambivalence which, since 1980, has been apparent in PBEC's maintenance of its own conception of regional economic cooperation.

Given the numerous organizational proposals put forward by participants in PAFTAD, it could be argued that academics have played leading roles in the cooperation movement, while most PBEC members have stood by amidst attempts to refine the Council's purpose, structure, and activities. Leaders of PAFTAD have noted that 'as a private organization, PBEC has been useful if low-keyed in promoting Pacific business interests, but it has neither the representation nor the prerogative to influence the broad framework of Asian-Pacific foreign economic policy,' and that 'what has been lacking [in the PBEC approach] has been in depth research to provide a solid empirical basis for policy positions.'[41] The tentative supporting role played by business interests in the promotion of Pacific cooperation is also the result of the corporate preoccupation with the profit/loss statements. This concern limits the freedom of business leaders to pursue such concepts in their formative stages – a limitation which is heightened by a corporate reluctance to promote ideas which might alter the status quo and/or impinge upon commercial interests. As a result, it is not surprising to find business leaders expressing caution about academic constructs.[42]

Although some early PBEC participants may have believed that they dealt with the practical realities of the regional economy while scholars tinkered with abstract and sometimes unrealistic cooperation models, it was not long before the need to explore the possibility of collaborating with PAFTAD participants was recognized. In 1971, the Japanese and Canadian member committees were asked by the PBEC-ISC to report on PAFTAD activities and to 'explore the feasibility of harmonising their efforts with those of PBEC.'[43] Two years later, R.W.C. Anderson (ACMA director general) suggested that his Australian committee strengthen ties with academic economists such as Peter Drysdale of the Australian National University, a prominent PAFTAD participant. Anderson proposed the commissioning of a research paper and a meeting with company economists, observing that 'it is time we started to get positive mileage out of our members' subscriptions.'[44]

Dissatisfaction with PBEC's position was still apparent in 1979, when the international president, Noboru Gotoh (vice-president of Nissho and president of the Tokyu Corporation), called upon the membership to move away from its preoccupation with organizational matters and to move towards active leadership with respect to the concept of regional economic cooperation. In Sydney, in 1980, the Japanese committee, claiming the support of the Japanese government, proposed the immediate launch of a Pacific Economic Community (PEC) study – a project which foresaw the creation of an intergovernmental organization.[45] The Canadian committee voiced support, stressing the potential for PBEC to be expanded into a 'Pacific Congress' or umbrella organization incorporating private sector leaders, academics, and government officials acting as private individuals. The American committee was less enthusiastic, observing that while the cooperation idea was economic at its core, the broader political implications must be appreciated. Nevertheless, delegates unanimously adopted a policy statement endorsing the pursuit of a Pacific Economic Community (PEC) and establishing a special committee to examine the idea.[46] In keeping with this position, Eric A. Trigg, a Canadian member of PBEC and senior vice-president of Alcan Aluminum, told the Pacific Community Seminar (PECC I) in Canberra in September 1980 that, with respect to the future examination of the regional cooperation concept,

> it is imperative that the private sector is kept directly involved in the process ... If we can move at a measured pace in this direction of involving both governments and the private sector, it would be a new and salutary approach in international relations, much in keeping with the mood of change which I believe is developing not only in the Pacific, but throughout the world.[47]

Ironically, Trigg was one of only five business leaders among the forty-seven participants and observers from the academic, business, and government sectors at the Canberra Seminar.[48]

The PBEC Special Committee on PEC, charged at the 1980 Sydney meeting with the task of suggesting how PBEC could relate to a tripartite (academic, business, government) body should one be initiated, reported to the 1981 Hong Kong meeting about the Canberra Seminar. James Vernon of Australia (international president, chairperson of the Special Committee, and director of CSR Ltd.) emphasized the need for PBEC to maintain its autonomy while supporting the Canberra recommendations by incorporating its examination of the PEC concept into the Council's overall program. This position formed the basis for the adoption of a resolution calling for continued study of the still-awkward concept, a balance between long- and near-term commercial objectives, and a recognition of the concerns expressed by ASEAN regarding threats to that organization's integrity.[49] In October 1981, the PBEC-ISC agreed that it

> may be useful for PBEC to use the term PEC to mean nothing more, at this stage, than improved forms of cooperation, communication, and consultation in the region and to pursue the clarification of the concept in an evolutionary manner. There should be wide participation in this process to ensure that the views of all interest groups be considered. The private sector and PBEC have a special role to play in this process, both to communicate views from business and to influence appropriately its evolution. If PBEC does not participate, developments inimical to private enterprise may emerge.[50]

The most detailed business perspective on regional cooperation was presented in 1982 by J.H. Stevens, chairperson of Canada Wire and Cable Company and the new chairperson of the PBEC Special Committee on PEC. In a paper circulated prior to PBEC 15, Stevens highlighted the need for a systematic examination of the concept, a determination of priorities, and a plan of action. He perceived a triangular relationship between corporate operations, commercial and financial opportunities in the Pacific, and the strategic business environment – a relationship which needed to be amended, given increased regional economic interdependence. Stevens suggested that 'a fourth set of interests needs to be added ... relating to the need to improve mechanisms and forms of cooperation, consultation and communication. That is to say, we need to address how to alter, in a positive manner, certain basic factors of the strategic business environment itself.'[51] For him, protecting and enhancing this 'environment' provided the most compelling reason for PBEC members to participate in the shaping of the tripartite PECC process by then under way.

The PEC concept served as the theme of PBEC 15 in Nagoya in 1982, where a consensus emerged in support of continuing to promote a step-by-step evolutionary approach towards the realization of a PEC as opposed to an immediate effort to create an umbrella organization.[52] The PBEC Covenant was amended the following year to reassert the Council's intention 'to ensure that private sector views play a role in the contemporary dialogue about Pacific affairs.'[53] Delegates at PBEC 16 in Santiago were able to reflect on the task forces which had been established at PECC II in Bangkok in June 1982. An improvement in business sector representation at the Bangkok session was noted, along with the corporate 'desire to participate if the activity remains worthwhile.' At the same time, members were reminded that the Council 'should not try to *out academic* the academics, nor should we confuse the tripartite process with our established government liaison programs.'[54]

In 1984 the PBEC-ISC reaffirmed the role of the Council's members in the regional dialogue and encouraged governments to declare their support for the tripartite Canberra process if they believed it to be a useful channel of communication. However, the need for PBEC to maintain its own exploration of the cooperation idea was again stressed by the Japanese committee, with Gotoh expressing his concern about the 'continuing conceptual ambiguity regarding PBEC, the PEC and the PECC.'[55] Nevertheless, Trigg (reporting on PECC III in Jakarta in November 1983, where seventeen of eighteen business participants were affiliated with PBEC) offered the following summation on behalf of the Special Committee on PEC: 'What seems to be emerging is that the PEC concept is not something separate from, but rather an extension of, all the activities of PBEC.'[56]

The contending positions taken by Trigg and Gotoh have come to reflect an ambivalent PBEC approach to regional cooperation and the PECC process. Those of Trigg's persuasion tend to equate *the PECC process* with the pursuit of what was earlier termed *the PEC concept* in Council circles, whereas adherents to the Gotoh line repeatedly state the need for PBEC to maintain the PEC concept as a separate pursuit. These two camps may be roughly divided into those PBEC members who willingly participate in the PECC process and those who believe that the business community's interest in regional cooperation would be better served by directing corporate energies elsewhere. Despite the obvious commitment to PECC shown by some PBEC members, such persons remain a minority, and a general malaise is apparent on the cooperation idea – a malaise which is consonant with Gibson's 1982 summary of the division within PBEC:

> Some thought addressing PEC issues offered the opportunity to contribute to broader Pacific affairs; others thought that the concept was vague and ambiguous and that it would be difficult to organize PBEC activities around the PEC concept. The latter position generally represents the view of most PBEC participants that emerged after extensive deliberations on the PEC concept.[57]

Those who are participating in PECC are likely doing so for reasons other than those strictly commercial considerations which may have first attracted them to PBEC. Some may see value in expanding the bounds of their business network to include other societal sectors, while others may be active in accordance with the dictum which holds that the degree of a company's involvement is commensurate with its stake in the region.

Prior to PBEC 18 in 1985, the international president, Fred Whittemore (managing director of the American firm, Morgan Stanley Co.), stated that 'in the United States, the Pacific Economic Community concept has captured the attention of the people to such a degree that no business activities can be done without the implication of the concept.'[58] In spite of such claims, active discussion of the cooperation concept within PBEC as a whole appears to be declining in favour of the consideration of more specific business-oriented issues. At the 1986 Seoul meeting of PBEC, the significance of the PEC concept continued to dwindle, with the discussion of global solutions dominating and the further examination of regional options being left to the International Secretariat. Almost as a concession, the meeting did agree to have a PBEC executive serve on the PECC-ISC if asked, and an invitation was forthcoming soon thereafter.[59] At subsequent general meetings the regional cooperation idea has been repeatedly overshadowed by the discussion of issues prominent in the Uruguay Round of GATT. As the chairperson of the Special Committee on PEC remarked in 1987, the 'general feeling seemed to be that PBEC [should] keep watch, [and that] members should advise their governments of the private-enterprise position on specific proposals that may come up [in the PECC process] ... PBEC now hasn't the resources to do much directly about it.'[60] The following year, delegates attending the annual general meeting in Sydney were urged to participate more actively in PECC in order to protect and to further business interests.[61] In 1989, six business leaders associated with PBEC (including Whittemore, Randolph, and International President Chen-Fu Koo) were listed as PECC officers.[62]

Conclusion

At first glance, the Pacific Basin Economic Council may appear to be a private sector body which complements regional interstate relations. However, organizational preoccupations, a limited geographic scope, and an internal ambivalence towards the regional cooperation movement have undermined PBEC's ability to contribute to or to facilitate diplomatic interaction. As a result, the statement of intent contained in the PBEC Covenant rings hollow. The degree to which PBEC is now able to facilitate an exchange of business views, to advise and to counsel governments, or to provide input to other organizations is questionable – in spite of the expertise, societal status, and political contacts possessed by its members. Its role in encouraging the elite contributions envisaged by theoretical perspectives such as neofunctionalism is thus a troubled one. This finding will not surprise critics of integration theory, who would be quick to note the Eurocentric roots of this literature and, given the cultural, political, and economic diversity of the region in which PBEC operates, to argue its inapplicability.[63] The Council retains its self-imposed image as a rich man's club, and its place in the Pacific economic cooperation movement has been that of a sectoral representative which responds rather than leads, defends rather than initiates, and moves cautiously to the beat of academic and state drummers. Organizations with broadly-defined, less ominous, project-oriented and/or multipartite objectives (such as PAFTAD and PECC) have found more room to manoeuvre amongst the developed and developing societies of the Asia-Pacific than has this business entity, in which the short-term pursuit of profit competes with the long-term perceptions of civic duty as a rationale for participation.

The creation of an intergovernmental organization was endorsed by PBEC at its May 1989 meeting, and, as discussed at its 1990, 1991, and 1992 conferences, the Council is seeking direct representation in APEC, an intergovernmental forum established in November 1989.[64] But before PBEC can fend off challenges from organizations such as the Confederation of Asia-Pacific Chambers of Commerce and Industry[65] and regain its status as a significant contributor to a regional cooperation movement in which governments have recently asserted themselves, its membership must resolve internal differences about the organization's role, lest the Council continue to be seen as a house divided.[66] It is unclear whether the almost U.S.$2.5 million endowment fund established at the Council's 1992 meeting will help PBEC recapture its diplomatic portfolio or reinforce its image as a rich man's club.[67] Indeed, if the business community is to play a greater part in regional diplomacy, it may have to utilize a channel other than PBEC.

6

The Pacific Economic Cooperation Council

The ability of the Pacific Economic Cooperation Council to facilitate the functions of representation, information, communication, and negotiation forms the subject of this chapter. Note the inclusion of *negotiation*. It is PECC's facilitation of this task which sets it apart from PAFTAD and PBEC and has made it the central nongovernmental element of the regional cooperation movement.

Origins and Structure

Discussion of the OPTAD proposal presented to the U.S. Senate by Drysdale and Patrick in 1978 marked the beginning of a new phase in the pursuit of Pacific economic cooperation. Responses to the OPTAD idea demonstrated again the difficulties inherent in creating an intergovernmental organization. Sceptics continued to allude to suspicions of a U.S./Japan conspiracy and to the repercussions of the Soviet fear of a Pacific version of the North Atlantic Treaty Organization (NATO). The cultural, economic, and political diversity within the region, it was argued, would also preclude meaningful intergovernmental cooperation. These reservations were not new, but their persistence throughout the 1970s led the proponents of Pacific economic cooperation to reconsider their objectives and to study the utility of pursuing a gradualist or organic approach to cooperation efforts. Attention turned to the possibility of establishing an informal, policy-oriented, and consultative regional forum displaying some of the attributes of the Trilateral Commission – a nongovernmental network bringing together state, business, and academic leaders from the United States, Japan, and Western Europe.[1]

Reaction to the *Pacific Commission* proposal was mixed, with many observers questioning the degree of influence a nongovernmental body would have upon state officials and the wisdom of designing an organization which might become dependent upon government funding and participation. Scepticism was particularly evident amongst commentators from Southeast Asia, who 'pointed out that in their countries private and governmental roles were less clearly separated than in the Western world.'[2] Despite these misgivings, it became clear to proponents such as Okita and Crawford that an informal and multisectoral forum would have to be established if the cooperation movement was to move forward. Okita's position as chairperson (at the 1978 request of Prime Minister Ohira) of a Pacific Basin Cooperation Study Group composed of Japanese bureaucrats, businesspeople, and academics symbolized the course to be followed.[3]

The organizational and diplomatic roots of PECC are usually traced to a May 1979 meeting between prime ministers Ohira of Japan and Fraser of Australia at UNCTAD V in Manila.[4] Their exploration of a vague concept of enhanced regional cooperation was renewed when Ohira (accompanied by his new foreign minister, Okita, and Mitsuro Donawaki, a senior member of the Japanese foreign ministry's European and Oceanic Affairs Bureau) visited Australia in January 1980.[5]

In choosing to pursue the regional cooperation theme, Ohira was no doubt heavily influenced by almost two decades of discussion within Japanese policy-making circles. It has also been suggested that he had taken up the issue upon coming to office in 1978 in response to American calls for Japan to play a larger role in world and regional affairs – a role commensurate with its economic standing. According to this line of argument, Ohira was in search of a foreign policy success – a desire which became evident when he enlisted Okita, a high-profile and well-respected former bureaucrat, as chairperson of the PBCSG and, later, as foreign minister.[6] Conceptualizing within Australian policy-making and academic circles had a similarly long history, and, in reaction to EEC protectionism, Fraser had been favourably predisposed to the idea for many years.[7]

It is generally accepted that the Pacific Community or Canberra Seminar, now referred to as PECC I, was organized 'at the request of the Australian and Japanese Prime Ministers' of the day.[8] Nevertheless, the manner in which the concept of an informal seminar series arose out of an intergovernmental initiative highlights the diplomatic utility of a nongovernmental approach to vague concepts or contentious issues. For, during the Ohira visit, Foreign Minister Okita asked Crawford, his long-time friend and the chancellor of the ANU, if he would agree to host a seminar (at the ANU) to examine the Pacific Community idea and the findings of the PBCSG report if asked by the prime ministers of Japan and Australia. In Crawford's words:

> My answer was 'Yes, provided that the two prime ministers do not attempt to give me instructions about it,' and this was accepted ... So this was a Japanese initiative in the sense of Dr. Okita's question to which both prime ministers responded very positively. There was one rider to my acceptance: this was that the Australian government alone provide the sinews of war, namely, the finance. And this was done.[9]

While the political masters did offer some quite acceptable suggestions regarding the need for the seminar to study the problems of market economies in the region, including the South Pacific Islands, no specific instructions about participants were given.

The organization of the Pacific Community Seminar (held 15-17 September 1980) was left to Crawford. A collection of recent papers on the subject was distributed to delegates prior to the seminar, and, during the breaks, meals, and five three-hour sessions, discussion centred around four questions: (1) What are the forces promoting the Pacific Community idea? (2) What are the issues for substantial cooperation? (3) Which countries are interested in participating and in what form? and (4) What step could be taken?[10] The main recommendation of the PBCSG report (i.e., that a private consultative committee of authoritative persons from around the Asia-Pacific region be established to coordinate the activities of working groups on subjects of common concern) was also given prime consideration.[11]

Crawford made the central feature of his organizational efforts the inclusion of what have been termed the three prominent 'stakeholder groups.' According to Earle and Trigg,

> the Canberra Seminar was unique in that Sir John had recognized the strengths and limitations of the various stakeholders in addressing such questions. The governments really had no political mandate to negotiate on any issue. Thus, senior officials were invited in non-official capacities. Businessmen were already part of a Pacific Regional business community by virtue of their trade and investment activities. Academics and specialists had been examining particular problems for many years, but generally in a detached environment.
>
> Sir John understood that if his four questions were to be addressed so

that he could report effectively to Prime Ministers Fraser and Ohira on the issues of cooperation, all three stakeholder groups would need to participate. Therefore, the concept of a series of meetings based on a tripartite format was conceived.[12]

At the Canberra Seminar, a consensus emerged around the following points and recommendations:

(1) the recognition that whereas economic interdependence suggests the need for cooperation, business and academic efforts have contributed to the growing, though fragile, sense of community which exists.

(2) that the need for better management of regional economic and political problems warranted the further exploration of consultative mechanisms.

(3) that existing bilateral, regional, and global cooperation mechanisms not be impaired by a pan-Pacific arrangement.

(4) that it was desirable for participation in the cooperation movement to be open and nonexclusive, with nations not represented at Canberra able to participate in the proposed task force activities of interest to them and to be considered for wider participation in due course.

(5) that existing models of cooperation should not be relied upon in the Pacific region.

(6) 'the need to avoid military/security issues to create a sense of community without creating a sense of threat.'

(7) 'that it was necessary to *hasten slowly*, to see the full blossoming of the Pacific Community idea as a longer term objective, and to proceed towards long-term goals step-by-step, with each intermediate step being useful in itself, not dependent for success on further steps being taken.'

(8) the need for an *organic* approach, and tripartite building upon the privately based efforts of groups such as PAFTAD and PBEC, and involving academics, businesspeople, and government officials.

(9) that any future arrangement be nonbureaucratic, flexible, and purposeful and concentrate on areas of mutual regional interest.

(10) to establish an *unofficial, private,* and *informal* tripartite standing committee of *considerable authority* from the countries represented in Canberra, with twenty-five persons to coordinate information exchange; to set up task forces on trade, direct investment, energy, Pacific marine resources, and international services; to transmit

findings to their governments; to appoint a contact institution in each country; to strengthen existing regional institutions such as PBEC and PAFTAD; and to hold another seminar within two years.

(11) 'that the Chairman of the seminar should, when he reports to governments, advise interested governments on arrangements necessary to establish the Pacific Cooperation Committee, its secretariat, and questions of funding, including their need to consult with nongovernmental groups.'[13]

Crawford later offered this retrospective on the format chosen for the pursuit of Pacific cooperation:

As to the mechanism, I want to make it clear that you can call it interim or not as you wish. If you believe there's ultimately going to be a major organization, the steps I'm outlining will be interim only. But a key principle applied by the seminar was that these steps, no matter how long or how briefly they last, should have a value in themselves, should produce worthwhile results regardless of the ultimate outcome of the movement toward a permanent form of intergovernmental organization.[14]

All that remained for the process to move forward was for the national governments and state apparatuses of the Pacific Basin to lend their support. In other words, 'the recommendations of the Canberra conference were not implemented immediately because of an implied need for official governmental endorsement and commitment'[15] – a need which starkly demonstrates the asymmetric nature of the relationship between state and nonstate actors in this context.

By asking governments to endorse a forum in which societal leaders and state officials appeared to participate on equal terms, the proponents of Pacific cooperation were putting at risk all previous efforts. For, as Kitamura has argued, a broad negative response to such suggestions could well have left the cooperation movement stalled indefinitely:

For some time after the gambit of the Canberra Pacific Community seminar ... it looked as if the pace of organizing the suggested Pacific Cooperation Committee ... had suffered a serious slowdown if not a complete stoppage.

... There is an element of paradox in the situation that deliberate attempts are made to minimize government involvement in a cooperative scheme in which government commitment is an essential precondition for success.[16]

Kitamura's commentary touches upon the main reason many governments were reluctant to respond positively to the Canberra Seminar recommendations: the attempt to garner government support for an activity over which these governments would not have direct control. The post-Canberra 'slowdown,' the reluctance of states, and the continuing doubts about feasibility and purpose have also been noted by Soesastro, though one is reminded that soon after the initial seminar the governor of Hawaii offered his state as the permanent site for a Pacific Community secretariat, and that, prior to the holding of a second seminar in 1982, tripartite national PECC committees were established, with government blessings, in Japan, South Korea, and Thailand.[17]

In the years since, many more governments have been persuaded by sentiments similar to those expressed by a veteran of the cooperation movement, General Ali Moertopo of Indonesia, during the 1980-2 interlude:

> The practice of meaningful consultation, on the basis of substantial issues of common concern, is believed to ultimately give birth to a greater sense of community. This is the ultimate objective of the present efforts. The creation of an intergovernmental body or other institutional set-up is only of secondary importance. Institutions, after all, are only a means and not the ultimate goal.[18]

Noting that governments were understandably hesitant to endorse the still-vague concept of regional economic cooperation, Moertopo argued that if private promotion of the idea was the only way forward at present, it should be undertaken in a systematic fashion: 'Not only will this be more meaningful than doing nothing, but as anywhere else a *grass-root* movement will always guarantee for a more solid basis for action.'[19] A chronology of what has since become known as the PECC 'process' is provided in Table 6.1.

Interestingly, it was within the countries of ASEAN that the calls for government support received perhaps their most sympathetic hearing – a hearing without which non-ASEAN countries would have hesitated even more – and plans to hold a follow-up meeting in Malaysia in 1982 were well advanced before being spurned by senior Malaysian state

Table 6.1

Pacific Economic Cooperation Council: conferences

No.	Year	Place	Economies represented for first time (delegates, observers, and guests)	Task forces, fora, working groups, study groups reporting – Coordinator (co-coordinators)
I	1980	Canberra	Japan, Australia, New Zealand, Canada, U.S., Indonesia, Malaysia, Philippines, Singapore, Thailand, South Korea, Papua New Guinea, Fiji, Tonga	The Pacific Community Seminar – Australia
II	1982	Bangkok	Chile, Chinese Taipei	Manufactures – South Korea
III	1983	Bali	Mexico, Peru, France	Agricultural products – Thailand
				Minerals – Australia
				Investment and technology – Japan
IV	1985	Seoul	Hong Kong, Solomon Islands, Brunei, Ecuador, Argentina, India, Iran, Turkey	Agricultural and renewal resources – Canada
				Minerals and energy – Australia (PBEC)
				Manufactured goods – South Korea
				Investment/technology – U.S. (Japan, Singapore)
				Capital flows – Indonesia (Japan, U.S.)
V	1986	Vancouver	China, USSR, Cook Islands, Kiribati	Fisheries development and cooperation – Canada
				Minerals and energy – Australia (Indonesia, S. Korea)
				Trade – South Korea (Japan, Malaysia, U.S.)
				Foreign investment – U.S. (Japan, Thailand)
				Livestock and feed grains – New Zealand
VI	1988	Osaka	Brazil, Colombia, Finland, West Germany, Italy, Netherlands, Norway, Switzerland, United Kingdom	Fisheries – Canada (Philippines)
				Minerals and energy – Australia (South Korea)
				Trade policy – Canada (Singapore, Chinese Taipei)
				Investment – U.S. (Thailand)
				Livestock and feed grains – New Zealand
				Economic outlook – Japan
				Funding – PECC-ISC

(continued on next page)

Table 6.1 (continued)

Pacific Economic Cooperation Council: conferences

No.	Year	Place	Economies represented for first time (delegates, observers, and guests)	Task forces, fora, working groups, study groups reporting – Coordinator (co-coordinators)
VII	1989	Auckland		Fisheries – Canada (Philippines) Minerals and energy – Australia Trade policy – Canada (Thailand) Agricultural policy/trade/development – New Zealand (U.S., S. Korea) Pacific economic outlook – U.S. (Japan) Transportation, telecommunications, tourism – Japan (S. Korea, Taipei, Thailand) Sustainable development of forest resources – Canada (Japan, Thailand, Indonesia) Pacific Island nations Science and technology – China, U.S. Institutional development – Indonesia, Canada
VIII	1991	Singapore		Fisheries – Canada (Philippines) Minerals and energy – Australia Trade policy – Malaysia (Canada, Indonesia, New Zealand) Agricultural policy/trade/development – New Zealand (U.S., S. Korea) Pacific economic outlook – U.S. (Japan) Transportation, telecommunications, tourism – Japan (S. Korea, Chinese Taipei, Thailand) Pacific Island nations – Chinese Taipei (U.S.) Science and technology – China (U.S.) Tropical forest cooperation – Malaysia (Japan) Human resources development – Singapore

IX 1992 San Francisco   Russia

Fisheries development and cooperation –
   Canada (Philippines)
Minerals and energy – Australia
Trade policy – Indonesia
Agricultural policy/trade/development –
   New Zealand (U.S., S. Korea)
Pacific economic outlook – U.S., Japan
Transportation, telecommunications, tourism –
   Japan (S. Korea, Chinese Taipei, Thailand)
Pacific Island nations – Japan, Indonesia,
   Chinese Taipei
Science and technology – China, U.S.
Tropical forest cooperation – Malaysia
Human resources development – Singapore
   (Brunei, Japan, Australia)

X 1994 Kuala Lumpur

Note: International and regional organizations represented at various sessions: PBEC, PAFTAD, OECD, ESCAP, South Pacific Forum, ASEAN, ADB, European Community, UN Development Program, International Monetary Fund, World Bank, Permanent South Pacific Commission, Asian and Pacific Development Centre.

Sources: Sir John Crawford and Greg Seow, eds., *Pacific Economic Co-operation: Suggestions for Action* (Selangor: Heinemann Educational 1981), 241-3; Michael West Osborne and Nicolas Fourt, *Pacific Basin Economic Cooperation* (Paris: Development Centre of the Organization for Economic Cooperation and Development 1983), 86-92; PECC, *Issues for Pacific Economic Cooperation: A Report of the Third Pacific Economic Cooperation Conference, Bali, November 1983* (Jakarta: Centre for Strategic and International Studies 1984); PECC, *Pacific Economic Cooperation: Issues and Opportunities: Report of the Fourth Pacific Economic Cooperation Conference, Seoul, April 29-May 1, 1985* (Seoul: Korea Development Institute 1985); PECC, *Report of the Fifth Pacific Economic Cooperation Conference, Vancouver, November 16-19, 1986* (Ottawa: Canadian Chamber of Commerce 1987); PECC, *Report of the Sixth Pacific Economic Cooperation Conference, Osaka, May 17-20, 1988* (Tokyo: Japan National Committee for Pacific Economic Cooperation 1988); PECC, *Report of the Seventh Pacific Economic Cooperation Conference, Auckland, November 12-15, 1989* (Wellington: New Zealand Committee for Pacific Economic Cooperation 1990); PECC, *PECC Work Programme 1991-1992* (Singapore: PECC Secretariat 1991).

leaders.[20] Nevertheless, the remnants of this planning provided a basis for a successful Thai initiative.

The gathering which eventually came to be called PECC II took place in Bangkok from 3-5 June 1982. Organized by the Thailand Pacific Economic Cooperation Committee and the John F. Kennedy Foundation (Thailand), with the assistance of ESCAP, it was the first meeting to utilize the title Pacific Economic Cooperation Conference. Thanat Khoman, deputy prime minister of Thailand, played host during sessions which discussed ASEAN's position in the Asia-Pacific economy and feasible forms for a new consultative arrangement.[21] Again, the role of academics (especially those who participated in a study coordinated by the Centre for Strategic and International Studies [CSIS] in Jakarta) in setting the course of the cooperation movement must be acknowledged, given that,

> prior to the conference, the academic group was invited to attend a two-day preparatory meeting at ESCAP, out of which came four papers drafted to reflect the consensus of their views on the main issues that face the Pacific region on trade, investment, commodity problems, and institutional structure for consultation and consensus-forming in the Pacific region.[22]

These papers were presented to the opening session of the Bangkok conference and effectively set the agenda for the ensuing three days of debate. Arguing in favour of the Pacific economic cooperation concept, they were also well-suited to Thanat's dual objective of clearly establishing the benefits of cooperation and, thereby, of refocusing the dialogue with and within ASEAN upon the positive aspects of improved and wider regional cooperation.[23] The conference reaffirmed the belief 'that Pacific economic cooperation at the intermediate stage should take the form of a series of tripartite consultative meetings to review matters of common concern to the Pacific Basin countries and to pass on recommendations to the respective governments and relevant organizations.'[24] Once more the failure of other intergovernmental fora to deal with issues of importance to the nations of the Asia-Pacific was seen as making imperative a tripartite nongovernmental approach, which the delegates maintained would serve to complement the subregional interests of, and enhance economic progress within, ASEAN.[25]

Even more significant was the decision to formally establish a standing committee and four task forces. The inaugural PECC International

Standing Committee (PECC-ISC), collectively referred to by some as the *Pacific Mafia*, was comprised of eight members: Crawford, Okita (who had become chairperson of the Japan Special Committee on Pacific Cooperation), Thanat, Moertopo (Indonesia's deputy head of intelligence, minister of information, minister of defence, and a personal advisor to President Soeharto), David Sycip (senior advisor to the Philippine firm, PCI Management Consultants), Eric Trigg (senior vice-president of Alcan Aluminium Canada), Ambassador Richard L. Sneider (vice-chairperson of the Washington-based Pan-Pacific Community Association), and Nam Duck-Woo (chairperson of the Korea Traders Association and a former prime minister and finance minister of South Korea).[26]

The task forces established were, in each case, to be managed by a lead institution: minerals and energy by the ANU, direct foreign investment and technology transfer by the Japan Special Committee for Pacific Cooperation, trade in manufactured goods by the Korea Development Institute, and trade in agricultural products by the Thailand Pacific Economic Cooperation Committee. Task force coordinators were responsible for convening fora for the examination of issues pertaining to the particular subject area and for preparing reports to be presented at the next conference.[27] Commenting on the role of tripartite task force activities, English noted that

it is hoped that propositions and policy suggestions they contain will have the added impact that can come from the criteria of relevance and feasibility arising out of the active participation of practical businessmen and politically-sensitive officials. It is an interesting experiment. Its success will depend on a number of considerations, of which two stand out:
(1) The effectiveness of the leadership of the group;
(2) The kind of policy ideas that emerge – in particular their appropriateness (including timeliness), and the size and distribution of expected benefits and costs (including perceived political costs).[28]

After a final review by the PECC-ISC, the task force reports were tabled at PECC III, which was held in Nusa Dua, Bali, Indonesia, on 21-3 November 1983. The meeting was sponsored by CSIS and hosted by the centre's chairperson, General Moertopo. Deliberations centred around four agenda items:

(1) a continuing call for the need to strengthen the process of tripartite consultation and to improve the exchange of information about national policies and market conditions.
(2) the belief that task force findings should be used to generate policy recommendations for governments, including the encouragement of a leading and collective role for Pacific countries in a new round of multilateral trade negotiations, the implementation of a moratorium on protectionist measures by Pacific countries, and the consideration of specific measures to curb protectionism and to coordinate economic policies as identified by the task forces.
(3) the review and endorsement of a five-part proposal for the institutionalization of the PECC process, covering the organization and operation of the conference, the PECC-ISC, task forces, a task force coordinating group, and national committees.
(4) the reorganization of the task force system.

As a result, the existing task forces underwent a variety of alterations: coordination of the Task Force on Agricultural Products and Renewable Resources was assumed by the newly formed Canada-Pacific Cooperation Committee, under the guidance of which it began to concentrate on fisheries cooperation and development; the focus of the Task Force on Trade in Manufactured Goods was shifted to trade policy and trade negotiations; American participants became responsible for the Task Force on Foreign Investment and Technology Transfer; and PBEC was formally charged with assisting the Australian coordinators of the Task Force on Minerals and Energy. Meanwhile, a new Task Force on Capital Flows was established under the direction of CSIS. A special group charged with examining the feasibility of cooperation in higher education was also launched.[29]

In advance of PECC IV in Seoul (29 April-1 May 1985), the PECC-ISC was joined by Brian E. Talboys (a senior executive of the Indo-Suez Bank and a former prime minister and foreign minister of New Zealand), Lim Chong Yah (head of the Department of Economics and Statistics at the National University of Singapore), and Noordin Sopiee (director of the Institute for Strategic and International Studies in Kuala Lumpur, Malaysia). The deaths of Moertopo in May 1984 and Crawford in October 1984 also saw the loss of two original committee members. Moertopo was replaced by the executive director of CSIS, Jusuf Wanandi, while Crawford was succeeded by his ANU colleague, Peter Drysdale.[30]

The Seoul conference was sponsored by the Korea Development Institute, hosted by the Korea Committee for Pacific Cooperation, and chaired by Nam. Portraying the Asia-Pacific as a region capable of setting examples which might reverse the protectionist trend, and citing PECC as a group ideally placed to set an example of North-South collaboration by developing a Pacific approach to a new round of global multilateral trade negotiations, delegates undertook to transmit the task force findings to the leaders of the seven major industrialized countries (including the U.S., Japan, and Canada) attending the upcoming Bonn summit.[31]

The tone of the debate which preceded this decision was set by Okita, who argued that economic growth in the Pacific region had benefited from the 'flying geese' pattern of development. According to this conception, the U.S., as the dominant industrialized country, was the lead goose at the head of a V-formation, with Japan and other East Asian economies working to catch up by utilizing it (the U.S.) as an engine of growth. Nevertheless, participants from the Philippines and Singapore continued to express reservations about the political will to foster substantive or mutually beneficial cooperation and about the perceived role of the state in such areas as the channelling of foreign investment. Delegates from Japan, Australia, New Zealand, Canada, and the United States responded that every consideration was being given to the concerns of the ASEAN nations, and (given that, in the end, ASEAN's support was a prerequisite) that the latter could set the pace of the cooperation movement.[32] As journalist Derek Davies later commented, the key role to be played by ASEAN in the future of the cooperation movement was very clear at the conclusion of PECC IV:

> While a healthy majority of the countries rimming the Pacific have staged dramatic recoveries from the after-effects of the second oil crisis and the resulting global recession, the cause of establishing a Pacific community is crawling along at a positively European rate. This may be no bad thing: instead of the rich industrialized countries setting a pace which creates worries and suspicions among their smaller, less-developed neighbours, ASEAN is today calling the tune ...
>
> The flying-geese theory thus makes a positive virtue of what had traditionally been regarded as an obstacle to Pacific cooperation – the huge variety in stages of development, endowment of natural resources and cultural, religious and historical heritages.[33]

Given participation from the North and the South, the need for moderation was emphasized in the planning of PECC V (sponsored by the Canadian government, hosted by the reconstituted Canadian National Committee on Pacific Economic Cooperation, and held 16-19 November 1986), which was intentionally run on a more modest scale than was PECC IV in order to set a precedent which would show that the hosting of a PECC general meeting should not be beyond the resources of less developed countries. The Japanese national committee suggested that PECC VI would fall between the Seoul and Vancouver conferences in grandeur and took the added step of initiating discussion of a common U.S.$20 million Pacific Cooperation Research Fund – a pool of resources upon which prospective conference and task force organizers and participants might draw, thereby reducing any inequalities in the abilities of nations to participate in the PECC process.[34]

Moves towards moderation were also intended to ensure that the most important aspect of the PECC process would be seen to be the activities of the task forces. In other words, the purpose of the conference is largely symbolic, periodically reaffirming the basic tenet of unity in diversity and providing the host country with an opportunity to show its support for PECC. Some interviewees believe that each host committee and/or country seeks a major achievement when hosting a conference. The signing of the Vancouver Statement on Pacific Economic Cooperation may be seen as an example of a successful Canadian quest for such symbolism, as might the research fund initiated by the Japanese and launched at PECC VI.[35]

The Vancouver conference saw discussion of the reports of the four task forces and one study group commissioned in Seoul (minerals and energy, trade policy and trade negotiations, fisheries development and cooperation, foreign investment, and livestock and feedgrains) and highlighted yet again the symbolic diplomatic value of the conference sessions. This was especially evident in the expression of overtly political, rather than economic, concerns. Comments on the Trade Task Force report stressed the substance of the meeting and the importance of PECC's role as a conveyor of ideas (e.g., on methods of monitoring tariff reduction, the need to counter agricultural subsidies, and the issue of trade in services) which were eventually taken up by governments in the agreement to begin a new GATT round. The presence of delegations from Taiwan and the People's Republic of China, each participating as full members for the first time, and of an initial observer from the Soviet Union similarly illustrated this shift in emphasis and the concomitant consolidation of the PECC process, as did the proclamation of a statement outlining the objectives and operating principles.

The politicization of PECC gathered speed prior to PECC VI in Osaka (17-20 May 1988), with the PECC-ISC's decision to move away from decision-making by informal consensus and to move towards 'formal votes to facilitate the anticipated growth in PECC activities.' Nine members would constitute a quorum, and unanimity would be required for the admission of new members or invitations to non-member guests. An 'overwhelming majority' would be sufficient to decide all other matters, although it was pledged that 'maximum efforts will be made to continue the present informal consultative style of decision-making in all issues before the Standing Committee.'[36] These moves allowed the Japanese to save face after losing the battle over Soviet observer status at PECC V. The Japanese (and PECC) were also spared further embarrassment by an earlier decision to place a moratorium on the admission of new members until after PECC VII in 1989, allegedly to allow for a period of organizational consolidation. Even so, a Soviet 'guest' was admitted to the Osaka meeting and was permitted to make an oral presentation. This speech and ten other addresses by regional political figures further highlighted the increasingly political nature and import of PECC. The Osaka conference (funded by the Japanese Ministry of Foreign Affairs and Japanese business organizations, hosted by the Japan National Committee for Pacific Economic Cooperation, and chaired by Saburo Okita) saw the release of the inaugural *Pacific Economic Outlook* volume (designed to provide an authoritative annual analysis of regional economies), the discussion of five other task force reports (trade policy, minerals and energy, private foreign investment, fisheries development and cooperation, and livestock and grains), and the creation of five new task forces (agricultural policy, trade and development, transportation/telecommunications/tourism, sustainable development of forests, Pacific Island nations, and science and technology). As for the issue of institutionalization, the formal establishment of the PECC Central Fund in March 1988 (with a budget of U.S.$1 million over three years) was announced. Although a larger outlay was envisioned in the future, the fund's main purposes were initially to assist developing countries to host and to participate in PECC activities and to finance special projects. Finally, amidst calls for the convening of an official Pacific Summit, member committees agreed to establish an ad hoc task force on PECC's own institutional development, the most pressing issue before which would be the desirability and feasibility of creating a permanent PECC secretariat.[37]

The primary concern of delegates gathered for PECC VII in Auckland

(12-15 November 1989) was, predictably, PECC's future role within the regional cooperation movement. The meeting was held immediately following the inaugural APEC ministerial session (in Canberra, 6-7 November 1989) and endorsed the recommendation to establish a permanent PECC secretariat in Singapore under Director-General Hank Lim (senior lecturer, National University of Singapore). The Auckland conference focused upon the PECC-APEC relationship, and, having received a message from APEC which 'sought PECC cooperation and [expressed] the need and reliance of the APEC Ministers on the PECC,' the PECC-ISC concluded that their organization 'should seek to coordinate information, analysis, and proposals which can be forwarded to APEC as well as helping to identify proposals for agenda items and policy initiatives.' As for improving the PECC process itself, the PECC-ISC sought to complement the new secretariat with efforts to strengthen the effectiveness of member committees, of the task force coordinating group, of task force organization, and of PECC's public relations.[38]

PECC VIII was held in Singapore (20-2 May 1991), with the admission of four new members (Mexico, Chile, Peru, and Hong Kong) being the dominant agenda item – the entrance of each having been facilitated by the May 1990 adoption of the following 'principles of membership.' These guidelines were subsequently included in a PECC Charter, which was promulgated at PECC VIII in order to formalize the organization's rules, procedures, and principles. (Later that year, APEC's Seoul Declaration was adopted to achieve the same goal.)[39] The Vancouver Statement is reaffirmed by, and appended to, the PECC Charter, which augments the earlier document by allowing a two-thirds majority vote for the passage of resolutions in the absence of a consensus and by creating a new category of associate membership for interested parties that have not met the criteria for full membership. Again arising out of Japanese concerns about Soviet involvement, these criteria state that applications from a Pacific economy can be considered provided that economy

(1) endorses the Vancouver Statement;
(2) is committed to economic cooperation in the Pacific based on free and open economic exchanges;
(3) has extensive economic activities in the region;
(4) has established a viable tripartite member committee; and
(5) has made a substantial tripartite contribution to a number of PECC works programs (excluding PECC general meetings) in the previous three years.[40]

Applications for admission were received at PECC VIII from Colombia, Mongolia, Papua New Guinea, and the USSR. The Soviet application was approved in September 1991, and, following the demise of the USSR, the formal admission of a Russian member committee was rescheduled for PECC IX the following year. Using the new membership criteria as a guide, the Mongolian application was declined and the others deferred indefinitely, pending further elaboration.[41] At PECC IX in San Francisco (23-5 September 1992), discussions addressed the theme, 'Open Regionalism: A Pacific Model for Global Cooperation.' Delegates explored the implications of the rise of regional and subregional economic entities in Europe, North America, Southeast Asia, and the Asia-Pacific with a view to grasping 'how they can fit together in the context of liberal global trade' and to formulating a 'San Francisco Declaration' outlining a consensual PECC position.[42]

As PECC has gained political recognition and importance, changes in its organizational structure (Figure 6.1) have followed. To review briefly, the conferences are now held at a different location every 18-24 months, with the international standing committee (PECC-ISC) and task forces operating continually. The intent of each conference is to receive and to review task force reports, to formulate policy recommendations to be transmitted to governments, and to confirm an ongoing research program.[43] The PECC-ISC is normally composed of one representative of each member committee (Figure 6.2). The international president of PBEC and the chairperson of PAFTAD have also been invited to sit on the PECC-ISC as non-voting institutional members. Chaired by the representative of the next host committee, the PECC-ISC is responsible for directing and monitoring task force activities, making decisions pertaining to membership and conference arrangements, securing funds to support the attendance of academic participants from the countries of ASEAN and delegates from South Pacific Island states, transmitting conclusions and recommendations as appropriate to governments (usually via member committees) and other interested organizations, and ensuring adequate media coverage.

The PECC task forces have been organized and coordinated by researchers and research institutions in different countries. Fora and workshops are held between PECC conferences. The participation of representatives from all interested economies is encouraged, in keeping with the principle of nonexclusiveness. Reports are sent to the PECC-ISC via a coordinating group, which is chaired by a representative of the current host committee of the upcoming conference. The international

Figure 6.1

Pacific Economic Cooperation Council: organizational structure

Note: For alternative organizational charts, see PECC, *PECC Handbook* (Singapore: PECC Secretariat 1989), 13; and Norman D. Palmer, *The New Regionalism in Asia and the Pacific* (Lexington, MA: Lexington Books 1991), 145.

director-general of PBEC has been invited to join the task force coordinating group, which, as a matter of convenience, has sometimes met in conjunction with PAFTAD conferences, given the preponderance of PAFTAD participants amongst the task force coordinators. The member committees or the ad hoc equivalent in each nation review the task force reports and submit relevant opinions for circulation prior to each conference.[44]

In the minds of many participants, this network of member committees and the institutes providing them with secretarial services (including the Japan Institute of International Affairs [JIIA], AJRC [Australia], the Institute of Policy Studies [New Zealand], the CCC and, as of 1991, APFC, the Asia Foundation [U.S.], CSIS [Indonesia], the Institute of Strategic and International Studies [Malaysia], the Korea Development

Figure 6.2

PBEC International Standing Committee, 1990-2

Chairperson
S. Chandra Das
Member of Parliament
Singapore

Director-General
Hank Lim
PECC Permanent Secretariat
Singapore

Members

Australia
Sir Russel Madigan
Chairman
Muswellbrook Energy and Minerals
Ltd.

Brunei
Pengiran Anak DSLJ Puteh
Permanent Secretary
Ministry of Foreign Affairs

Canada
William Saywell
President
Simon Fraser University

Chile
Amb. Octario Errazuriz
Ministry of Foreign Affairs

China
Li Luye
China Institute of International
  Studies

Chinese Taipei
Chen-Fu Koo
Board Chairman and President
Taiwan Cement Co.

Hong Kong
John Tsang
Trade Department

Indonesia
Jusuf Wanandi
Executive Director
Centre for Strategic and
  International Studies

Japan
Nobuo Matsunaga
President
Japan Institute for International
  Affairs

Malaysia
Noordin Sopiee
Director-General
Institute of Strategic and
  International Studies

Mexico
Andrés Rozental
Deputy Foreign Minister

New Zealand
Kerrin Vautier
Research Economist/Lecturer
University of Auckland

Pacific Island nations
Henry Naisali
Director
South Pacific Forum Secretariat

PAFTAD
Hugh T. Patrick
R.D. Calkins Professor
School of International Business,
  Columbia University

PBEC
Frederick B. Whittemore
Advisory Director
Morgan Stanley and Co.

Peru
Luis Piazon
Dean of Business Administration
College of Higher Studies

(continued on next page)

Figure 6.2 (continued)

Philippines	Thailand
S. Chandra Das	Thanat Khoman
Member of Parliament	Chairman
	Asian Institute of Technology
South Korea	*United States*
Nam Duck-Woo	Amb. Richard Fairbanks III
Chairman	Partner
Korean Traders Association	Paul, Hastings, Janofsky and Wallser

Sources: PECC, *Report of the Seventh Pacific Economic Cooperation Conference, Auckland, November 12-15, 1989* (Wellington: New Zealand Committee for Pacific Economic Cooperation 1990); PECC Secretariat, Singapore; *PECC Newsletter*, vol. 1, nos. 1-3 (1991).

Institute [South Korea], and the Centre for International Studies of the State Council [China]) underpins the overall cooperation process. For many years the network was also judged to preclude the need for a permanent central secretariat. Nevertheless, some delegates saw a need to go beyond the practice of rotating the functions of a central secretariat between host national committees in order to avoid discontinuity and to ensure the proper management of PECC activities (which had exceeded the means of some national committees).[45] This reasoning provided the major impetus for the establishment of a permanent central secretariat charged with coordinating the affairs of the PECC-ISC, administering the PECC Central Fund, acting as a liaison between member committees and with other organizations, and assisting in the organization of PECC conferences, task forces, and special projects such as high-level meetings. David Parsons, an Australian government official, succeeded Hank Lim as director-general at the beginning of 1993.[46]

A danger inherent in such institutional developments is that the search for financing may ultimately lead member committees and the PECC process to become even more dependent than they already are upon governments as sources of funding. Among the democratic polities involved, government funding has been cited as a prominent feature of PECC activities in Japan, Australia, Canada, and New Zealand.[47] A significant increase in such assistance may carry with it a significant cost if increased government involvement is accompanied by governmental attempts to control PECC activities. Like any other nongovernmental enterprise, therefore, member PECC committees must constantly defend the independence upon which their nongovernmental status rests.

The importance of PECC's nongovernmental status should not be understated, as this is its most valuable and its most vulnerable feature.

Formality of any kind tends to put the process under stress by provoking nationalistic responses. The real test will be whether or not the nongovernmental managers of the PECC process can continue to maintain control and to provide it with an even broader and firmer base of support in the face of increasing government interest and the November 1989 establishment of the intergovernmental APEC. To date, the PECC-ISC has been able to use the consensus-building ethic within the Council to its advantage, thereby retaining a modicum of independence from the machinations of state apparatuses. Continued recognition of this independence, real or perceived, will be critical,[48] as will be the need to demonstrate ongoing diplomatic utility.

Representation

Participation in Council conferences is determined by PECC-ISC members, who submit to the chairperson lists of prospective attendees from their respective states and organizations. As noted earlier, in 1988 consensual decisions on membership and the discretionary powers of host committees to admit observers and guests were replaced by a requirement for unanimity. Decisions on participation in task forces remain the discretion of the coordinating and host committees. The principle of nonexclusiveness espoused in the Canberra Seminar recommendations has traditionally been accepted as meaning that representatives from all nations or organizations wishing to attend should be welcomed by PECC, although membership criteria were adopted in 1990. Invitations may be extended to interested persons from non-member economies and institutions inside and outside the Pacific Basin in order to counter the perception that an exclusive regional bloc is being formed. Observers may only speak with the prior agreement of the conference chairperson, whereas guests (usually government officials of a ministerial rank) are allowed to make a brief formal presentation.[49]

The establishment of national PECC committees in the mid-1980s represented a critical phase in the institutionalization process. These committees serve both as a focal point in each economy and as a formal link between the process and the respective government ministries upon which they are often dependent for funding.[50] In countries such as Australia and Canada, the founding of a national committee has been given added legitimacy as a result of the appointment of committee members and the formal designation of advisory status by the state apparatus.[51]

Its tripartite format has enabled PECC to serve the diplomatic function of representation to a much greater extent than has been possible in PAFTAD or PBEC. Rather than continuing to push for the creation of an intergovernmental body (an aspiration traditionally troubled by questions of need, membership, financing, and purpose), Crawford saw greater value in a private tripartite group, which might avoid falling victim to obvious political disputes among or within states. At the same time, he sought to bring the activities of PAFTAD and PBEC closer to the realm of policy-making by involving state officials, thereby broadening the scope of participation in, and consolidating support for, the cooperation movement.[52]

Four operational considerations governed the decision to invite state officials in their private capacities. First, if academics and business leaders are to achieve their goal of policy coordination, the participation of state officials offers them a channel through which to gain information upon which policies are based and implemented. Second, significant political leadership and bureaucratic support will also be necessary in attaining this end. State participation can therefore be seen as part of an attempt to make state officials aware of the benefits of cooperation in the Asia-Pacific region. In addition, it was believed that academic and business input would act as 'a sort of leavening of reality,' which would tend to moderate 'government's wishful thinking.'[53] Third, it is important not to become prone to fixed patterns of political or bureaucratic thinking if progress is to be made. Despite the need to gain state approval, an unofficial tripartite format retains the flexibility of private groups because it keeps state involvement at arm's length. Governments and bureaucracies in all countries may try to use or to hinder the PECC process in accordance with their own interests, making the maintenance of an arm's-length relationship and an independent decision-making mechanism essential if the process is to sustain itself. Finally, a nongovernmental organization offers a way to avoid some of the political obstacles which often exist in the presence or absence of official diplomatic relations between states.[54]

It was decided that national representation at the Canberra Seminar would take the form of three-person delegations from eleven countries (the five OECD countries in the region – Japan, Australia, New Zealand, Canada, and the United States; the then five countries of ASEAN – Indonesia, Malaysia, the Philippines, Singapore, and Thailand; and South Korea). A twelfth delegation was to be comprised of representatives from South Pacific Island states.[55]

The governments concerned were asked 'to nominate a senior official to participate as a freely speaking member, that is, speaking in his own right.' In Crawford's view, these nominees 'proved to be an important element in the intense interest shown by governments – an interest which we also fostered by personal visits before the seminar.' The senior state officials who attended included Okita (who, in the wake of Prime Minister Ohira's death, had resigned as foreign minister but had been retained as a special ambassador for foreign economic relations), Thanat Khoman, and Richard Holbrooke (U.S. assistant secretary of state). All other seminar participants were chosen and invited by the conveners on the basis of their interest in the subject, although, as Crawford notes, 'we chose people known to be skeptical as well as people known to be rather positively inclined towards some future organization. It was not a one-sided selection.'[56] Nevertheless, it must be noted that many of the nongovernmental invitees were among the central proponents of the cooperation movement prior to the Canberra Seminar and have remained active. They include Peter Drysdale, Ross Garnaut, and Stuart Harris (Australia), H. Edward English (Canada), M. Hadi Soesastro (Indonesia), Seizaburo Sato (Japan), Mohammed Ariff (Malaysia), Lim Chong Yah (Singapore), Han Sung-Joo (South Korea), Narongchai Akrasanee (Thailand), and Lawrence Krause (U.S.).

The thirty-six participants at PECC I were joined by nine observers, while assorted special guests (including an official from the Chinese embassy in Canberra) were admitted to the opening and closing sessions. Four of these observers were additional state representatives from the U.S. State Department, the Gaimusho, and the Australian departments of foreign affairs and trade and resources. Two observers represented PBEC (International President James Vernon and Deputy Director-General M. Mark Earle, Jr.) and one attended on behalf of PAFTAD (PAFTAD-ISC Chairperson Kiyoshi Kojima), though it should be noted that the ADB (whose observer was Seiji Naya) and the ANU (whose observer was Heinz Arndt) were also represented by PAFTAD participants.

Given that PECC I was built upon the research efforts of PAFTAD and the commercial relations forged by PBEC, it is not surprising that many of the academic and business participants and observers were drawn from these two private sector organizations.[57] The fact that fifteen participants and observers had previous PAFTAD experience compared to just four with PBEC experience is perhaps less salient. For, while Crawford observed that there was 'no feeling of government versus the rest,'[58] it is likely that it may have seemed to be business versus the rest.

Although there may well have been a 'working community of interests' arising from the private efforts of PAFTAD and PBEC, which some hoped would underpin any future intergovernmental initiatives, the activities being promoted tended to be of the academic variety.[59]

The Bangkok conference in 1982 was attended by sixty participants, with tripartite delegations from the eleven countries represented at PECC I plus Chile. Taiwan was represented among the observers, as were the OECD, ESCAP, Asia Society, Pacific Forum, and Pan-Pacific Community Association.[60] The eleven founding countries were again represented among the sixty participants at the Bali conference in 1983. Officials from PAFTAD, PBEC, ASEAN, the Singapore-based Institute for Southeast Asian Studies (ISEAS) and the Hong Kong-based *Far Eastern Economic Review* (*FEER*) also attended as delegates, while Chile reverted to the ranks of a forty-person observer group, which included representatives from France, Mexico, Peru, Taiwan, and the OECD.[61] The 1985 Seoul conference drew together 162 persons, including tripartite delegations from twelve member economies (Brunei, as the newest member of ASEAN, having become the twelfth) and a composite delegation from the South Pacific Islands. Observers were also in attendance from Chile, Colombia, Ecuador, Hong Kong, Mexico, Peru, Taiwan, Argentina, France, India, Iran, and Turkey as well as from the ADB, ASEAN, ESCAP, *FEER*, ISEAS, OECD, PAFTAD, PBEC, the Asia Foundation, the Ford Foundation, the Friedrich-Ebert Foundation, the Rockefeller Brothers Fund, the Asian Pacific Development Centre, and the East-West Center.[62]

At PECC V, most of the 163 participants comprised member delegations from fourteen economies (China and Taiwan having recently been granted membership), the South Pacific Islands, PAFTAD, and PBEC. Observers from Chile, Peru, Mexico, France, the Soviet Union, OECD, the Permanent South Pacific Commission, the Asian Pacific Development Centre, the East-West Center, and the Rockefeller Brothers Fund were also in attendance, with the Soviet presence making the Vancouver conference the first high-level meeting in North America to be attended by American, Chinese, and Soviet representatives. Of the 862 attendees at PECC VI, 142 were participants from the existing member committees. Representatives from Brazil, Colombia, Finland, West Germany, Italy, the Netherlands, Norway, Switzerland, the United Kingdom, the European Community, and the UN Development Program joined the list of 'guests', illustrating rising levels of regional and extraregional interest and unease. At PECC VII in Auckland, the absence of the large host contingent on hand in Osaka dropped the attendance level to 364 – 197 of whom were full participants. A moratorium on admission precluded new members, although the range of the observer/ guest ranks was augmented by the inclusion of officials from the International Monetary Fund and the World Bank. More than 350 delegates, representing nineteen PECC member economies, attended PECC VIII in Singapore, while 600 participants and twenty member committees gathered for PECC IX in San Francisco.[63]

While the Soviets first expressed interest in joining PECC in 1986, countries from Latin America had sought membership for a much longer time. The Chilean government first sent observers to PECC II, and the desire of the Chilean and Peruvian authorities to be accepted in as many regional and international fora as possible was well known. Their calls for admission, like those of the Soviets, were routinely resisted by the PECC-ISC in order to avoid a potentially divisive debate on membership criteria. The Japanese, in particular, remained reluctant to admit Latin American countries about which little was known, whose participation in Pacific trade and the PECC process to date had been minimal, and whose entry would mean the introduction of the thorny issue of Third World debt.[64] Nonetheless, in the wake of the lifting of a membership moratorium following PECC VII, Latin American persistence paid off in September 1990, when formal applications for membership from Chile, Peru, and Mexico were accepted by the PECC-ISC. Mexico's recent admission to GATT, Latin America's growing use of Japan as a source of technology and capital, and an attempt by smaller PECC members to dilute or counter Japanese and American influence have been cited as reasons for this success. Hong Kong, which had sent observers since PECC V, was admitted at the same time, many of the qualms over its membership having been eased by the earlier admission of China and Taiwan and China's reluctance to raise objections amidst its attempts to overcome the diplomatic isolation it experienced following the 1989 Tiananmen Square massacre. Representatives from these four new member economies participated in PECC VIII in 1991. This gathering attracted more than 350 delegates, including twenty from nine non-member countries and three international institutions. Applications for membership were received from Colombia, Papua New Guinea, and the Soviet Union. The Soviets, in particular, continued to press their case prior to and during PECC VIII without success (largely due to an unresolved territorial dispute with the Japanese).[65] Ironically, as noted earlier, the Soviet application was finally approved in September 1991, just months before the dissolution of the USSR, paving the way for the admission of a Russian committee at PECC IX in September 1992.[66]

The growing diplomatic importance of PECC was highlighted, in 1983, with the attendance of an enlarged U.S. delegation, including four State Department officials.[67] Following this meeting, participants from Japan, Australia, New Zealand, South Korea, and the U.S. reported to their governments. These reports were made directly to the prime ministers of the first three countries and assisted in securing state support for the maintenance or establishment of national committees.[68]

The status of the PECC process within policy-making circles was further enhanced at PECC IV by the attendance of past and present state figures from throughout the region, including a former prime minister, five active cabinet ministers, three former cabinet ministers, and several junior ministers. The prominence of active state officials was increasingly seen as an illustration of the polite fiction being upheld within the PECC process with regard to the attendance of state officials in a 'private capacity – though at public expense.'[69] The chairperson of PECC V, Canada's Eric Trigg, openly acknowledged 'the difficulty which some government officials have found in trying to reflect viewpoints *in their private capacities*' and

> what seems ... to be an irrefutable conclusion that growing government participation will inevitably have some impact on the 'informal' nature of exchanges. Pragmatism requires acceptance of the fact that the ultimate success of the PECC process will be reflected in actions by governments and there should be no need for concern about further adaptive moves in the process if they help to take the region forward in economic cooperation. Paralleling such a conclusion, however, is the reaffirmation of the principle that the process should remain under non-governmental leadership to retain its tripartite nature.
>
> It is also worth noting that the tripartite approach has already become quadripartite in two National Committees with the decision to include legislators among the membership in both Canada and the USA.[70]

Indeed, following PECC VII in 1989, S. Chandra Das, a member of the Singaporean parliament, became PECC's chairperson. Finally, as another indication of expanding societal, sectoral, and political interest which has continued into the 1990s (U.S. vice-president Dan Quayle and Singaporean prime minister Goh Chok Tong addressed PECC VIII, followed by U.S. president George Bush and Philippine president Fidel Ramos at PECC IX), Trigg might also have observed that, by the mid-1980s, the PECC process had become quadripartite in Australia with the inclusion of labour, and in Japan and Indonesia with the inclusion of the media.[71]

Information and Communication

Assessments of the evolution of PECC's organizational structure and activities during its first decade vary, although most highlight the diplomatic functions of information and communication and its ability to engage 'government officials and other participants ... in constructive forward-looking discussion of policy issues ... in a way not possible via any other mechanism in the region.'[72] The format and structure of the PECC process may allow it to retain a nonpolitical and nonofficial appearance and to defy attempts to make it conform with existing models of intergovernmental cooperation. In the words of a Japanese scholar and participant, 'PECC is something of everything.'[73] Many interviewees have described PECC's most important function as the building of a Pacific perspective on trade and development issues. Though careful to avoid military security issues, participants routinely claim that the PECC process has strengthened the stability of the region by enhancing economic security and understanding, thereby implying that PECC's efforts in the economic sphere have had a significant political impact as well.[74] The PECC process supplements formal diplomatic channels by allowing for a wider range of options and ideas to be fully considered in a frank manner and for an external impetus to be given to the mobilization of a domestic constituency which will support policy innovations. Intergovernmental initiatives have also been stimulated by PECC activities. The establishment, in 1984, of the annual ASEAN-Pacific Dialogue (APD) between the foreign ministers of ASEAN and their counterparts from the five developed countries of the region (now frequently referred to as the ASEAN Post-Ministerial Conferences, given an expanded format incorporating European Community representation and other Asia-Pacific participants) has been cited as a case in point.[75] PECC deliberations on trade policy have, similarly, played a role in the initiation of Western Pacific Trade Ministers meetings, the Cairns Group of Fair Trading Nations in Agriculture, and APEC.

Even if minds are not changed, there is value to be found in the fact that PECC keeps people talking to each other and, like other elements of the regional cooperation movement, tends to promote the habit of cooperation through regular contact amongst policy elites and the scaling of social barriers erected by conflict and culture. Academics keep the spirit of the cooperation movement alive by generating the knowledge and expressing the ideas upon which others can build, while businesspeople inject an appreciation of commercial realities to the process. Alone, either sector would risk being biased or totally irrelevant. Finally, state input provides a necessary element of political complexity.[76]

Negotiation

With the exception of decisions on the admission of new members, which now require unanimity, a consensual approach to decision-making dominates the PECC process. This characteristic was reaffirmed at PECC IV. During the conference, an American resolution aimed at demonstrating the unanimity of Pacific countries about the need for further trade liberalization and the initiation of a new GATT round of multilateral trade talks was rejected. This was largely due to the fact that the act of presenting a motion during the protectionism debate overlooked the strong feeling, especially amongst ASEAN delegates,

> that to introduce the device of a resolution, and to vote upon it and seek a majority decision, was to go the way of the overlegalistic UNCTAD and all the other UN bodies. What was wanted in the Pacific was the more practical and workable device of consensus which would ensure public harmony, which would minimize divisions and which would maximize the resolve to implement whatever decisions were made.
>
> ... Anyone trained in the lore of Westminster-style procedure would find PECC debates vague, undefined and directionless. But the Asians and the old Pacific hands are insisting on consensus decisions, however slow, rather than the discredited majority voting.[77]

As Davies observed following the Seoul conference,

> It became plain that most of the delegates had come to terms with the fact that a Pacific community must grow by a process of accretion. It will slowly move forward through a morass of research, inter-

change, study groups, task forces and conferences, achieving *consensus positions* on a wide range of complicated issues, while setting up ad hoc groups and forums whenever possible in the hope that this process of Indonesian-style *musjawarat* will ultimately reach a stage where a community can be founded (though whether that community will ever be established as yet another international bureaucracy is still, triumphantly, in doubt).[78]

As the PECC process departed Seoul and set sail for PECC V in Vancouver in November 1986, the limited, oblique, consensus-driven *Asian* or *Pacific* approach to decision-making was well-entrenched, thereby strengthening the organization's ability to operate as a nongovernmental forum in which state officials could participate without their actions and statements being discerned as explicitly political.[79]

The lesson to be drawn from this example has to do with PECC's capacity to facilitate the diplomatic role of negotiation. As indicated earlier, the claim that state officials participating in the PECC process do so in a private capacity is regarded by many as a polite fiction. After all, they are only present because they are state officials. These persons are state representatives, though the state belief that they are attending as private citizens does allow them to attach a disclaimer to everything they say and ensures that their home governments will not be obliged to uphold any decisions taken. Nevertheless, state officials will endeavour to ensure that PECC operates in a manner compatible with the interests of their state, if only because that state might be funding some aspect of the process (i.e., a national committee, a conference) on the basis of an assessment which has suggested that PECC activities somehow complement official diplomatic efforts. State players will therefore seek to protect their investment should they have made one or, if they have not, to gain or maintain whatever benefits were foreseen upon agreeing to participate (i.e., information, added channels of communication, prestige).

Despite the recent introduction of formal votes, the main mechanism for the expression and protection of interests within PECC remains the consensual decision-making process. It is during the building of a consensus that diplomatic negotiation takes place. State participants express and defend state interests in deliberations with other PECC participants. The difference, as far as the traditional conception of diplomacy is concerned, is that not all of the other participants are state officials. The tripartite format has thus prevented a particular state or sector from running away with, or manipulating, the PECC process. Consensus decision-making in this context means that, in addition to the concerns of state representatives, the interests of academics and corporate leaders must also be satisfied. Though they may be expressing and defending state positions, academics and businesspeople are present because of their sectoral affiliation. In some cases they may also draw strength from their associations with PAFTAD or PBEC, but usually they have not been designated by these organizations and are therefore more appropriately considered as members of national academic or business communities. Often they have been invited because they are members of a national PECC committee (remembering that membership is sometimes conferred by a government appointment).

The presence of state officials and the stipulation that all participants must concur with a decision means that negotiation and compromise must be part of the PECC process if that process is to move forward. A state representative could refuse to accept a consensual position. However, dogged intransigence runs the risk of leaving one isolated and, eventually, of causing the collapse of an otherwise useful non-governmental forum through politicization. Thus, the weight of consensus can sometimes overcome reluctance.[80]

PECC and the Intergovernmental Option

Buoyed by the PECC process and academic blueprints, several regional leaders proposed the establishment of an intergovernmental forum in the early 1980s. For example, in 1982, South Korean prime minister Chun Doo Hwan called unsuccessfully for a regular Pacific Summit of heads of governments.[81] In 1983, Australian prime minister Bob Hawke floated an idea arising from PECC III, which led to the establishment of an ongoing series of annual meetings of Western Pacific trade officials. PECC is also credited with assisting in the development of the Australian initiative which led to the creation of the Ministerial Meeting of Fair Traders in Agriculture, popularly known as the Cairns Group.

The prominence of ASEAN has similarly presented an opportunity to go beyond the nongovernmental level. The annual ASEAN-Pacific Dialogue involving the foreign ministers of ASEAN, Australia, Canada, Japan, New Zealand, and the United States and a representative from the European Community was first convened in 1984 and follows the annual meeting of ASEAN foreign ministers. In 1991, South Korea attended as a full dialogue partner, and China and the Soviet Union were invited as guests. The Dialogue concept proposed by the leaders of ASEAN was initially suggested in 1981 by the Japanese economist, Kiyoshi Kojima, in an attempt to overcome the reluctance of some governments to show support for regional cooperation efforts such as PECC. The APD represented the first significant pan-Pacific intergovernmental arrangement, and adoption of this format indicated ASEAN's willingness to participate in shaping regional cooperation while, at the same time, controlling the pace of such efforts. However, substantive progress on cooperative programs and a set of proposed projects under the heading ASEAN-Pacific Cooperation has been plagued by differences amongst the countries of ASEAN.[82]

State ambivalence meant that PECC remained the focal point of the cooperation movement for most of the 1980s. Its ability to attract Chinese and Taiwanese membership, to allow informal diplomatic contact where formal diplomatic ties do not exist, to complement formal multilateral fora, and to gain the attention and support of national governments led many proponents and observers to suggest that the formation of a broadly based intergovernmental organization may not be a prerequisite for regional policy coordination.

Others insisted that recent developments in the global and regional trading environment (including the tentative progress of the Uruguay Round, the single market to be established in Western Europe in 1992, the Canada-U.S. Free Trade Agreement and the possibility of other bilateral free trade agreements between the U.S. and its trading partners, and the threats to market access posed by Section 301 of the U.S. Trade Act) made the creation of a regional governmental institution imperative. In their view, these developments had the potential to undermine the economic well-being of many Asia-Pacific nations. If these nations were to defend themselves or to set an example which might help to restore faith in the multilateral trading system, they would be well-advised to join together within a regional entity. Should global governmental solutions appear unattainable, Pacific nations must be prepared to consider regional solutions. These solutions, though second-best, might be easier to achieve, given the smaller number of players involved, and would serve as examples which might eventually be taken up at the global level.

The pace at which the idea of an intergovernmental institution began to take root in political circles quickened in 1988, with public endorsations coming from former Japanese prime minister Yasuhiro Nakasone and American leaders such as Secretary of State George Shultz.[83] Then, during a speech to a meeting of South Korean business associations in Seoul on 31 January 1989, Australia's Prime Minister Hawke launched what became known as the Hawke Initiative, proclaiming his belief that

> the time has come for us substantially to increase our efforts towards building regional co-operation and seriously to investigate what areas it might focus on and the shape it might take ... We want to assess what the region's attitudes are towards the possibility of creating a more formal intergovernmental vehicle of regional co-operation. A meeting of ministers from throughout the region would be a useful forum to investigate the question. What we are seeking to develop is a capacity for analysis and consultation on economic and social issues, not as an academic exercise but to help inform policy development by our respective governments. I see merit in the model provided, in a different context, by the OECD.[84]

Hawke suggested that it was appropriate to consider regional options at the governmental level in light of the failure to reach an agreement on textiles, intellectual property, safeguards, and agriculture during the Montreal mid-term review of the Uruguay Round in December 1988. Stressing Australia's commitment to achieving a successful conclusion to the GATT negotiations and denying that he was trying to found a Pacific trading bloc, the prime minister observed that creating a formal regional mechanism for policy consultation and coordination would enable Asia-Pacific countries to defend themselves through collective action should the multilateral trading system collapse and/or other countries be determined to conduct relations via trading blocs. By reviving the concept of a Pacific OECD, Hawke was outlining a regional strategy to cope with a worst-case scenario. Most of all, he was trying to foster the development of an institution which would go beyond the informal, nonpolitical, and nonbinding activities of the PECC process, possibly in response to PECC's own reluctance. The immediate goals of this new entity would be to improve the chances for success in the Uruguay Round, to provide a forum for the discussion of both the obstacles to trade and the scope for further dismantling of trade barriers in the region, and to enable the identification of common interests in a region where economies were extraordinarily complementary.

The fact that this proposal came from a current Australian prime minister was largely responsible for the relatively positive response it received, further illustrating the politics of Pacific cooperation. Initially, one of the most contentious aspects of the Hawke Initiative was the apparent Australian desire to restrict participation in an exploratory ministerial meeting in early November 1989 to representatives from a core group of Western Pacific countries (Australia, the six ASEAN nations, Japan, South Korea, and New Zealand) and to exclude the United States and Canada. But the omission of the U.S. and Canada probably was not a reflection of Australian intent: it is perhaps better seen as a ploy to make the initiative more palatable for officials from developing countries, given that a proposal from an industrialized country, which included all other industrialized countries in the region, could be seen as yet another paternalistic effort by the developed to preach to and to dominate the developing. By leaving out the U.S. and Canada in the first instance, the idea of expanding the list of participants could be promoted by the developing countries if they so wished. One should also note that the Japanese, though situated in the Western Pacific and actively considering the concept of a regional intergovernmental organization at the time, could not make the proposal because of suspicions extending back to the Second World War and beyond,[85] while the New Zealanders were busy preparing to host PECC VII in mid-November 1989. The Americans, though having voiced support for a regional forum several times over the past year, did not want to be seen as domineering; and the Canadians, like the Americans, preferred to wait for ASEAN to take the lead. If any of the industrialized countries of the Asia-Pacific were to act (and there seemed to be a working consensus between the Australians and the Japanese at the time that something should be done), it would appear that only the Australians were willing and able.

The response from other Western Pacific countries, including the members of ASEAN, was near uniform: we are willing to consider this idea further but serious consideration should be given to inviting the U.S. and Canada. By the time Australian diplomats crossed the Pacific in late May to explain the Hawke Initiative to officials in Canada and the U.S., it was evident that both countries, having lobbied for inclusion, would be welcome to attend the initial ministerial meeting as full participants – even if some Australian officials may still have seen their exclusion as appropriate in the wake of the Canada-U.S. Free Trade Agreement.[86]

The inaugural ministerial meeting was held in Canberra in November 1989, with the aforementioned twelve nations in attendance. The governments represented agreed to proceed with an initial work program under the title Asia Pacific Economic Cooperation and in accordance with a set of cautious principles, holding that cooperation should be pursued through 'non-formal consultative exchanges' and 'a commitment to open dialogue and consensus.'[87]

Several membership matters remained unresolved in the wake of a second ministerial gathering in Singapore in July 1990. The most pressing of these was the search for an amiable agreement allowing the participation of the 'three Chinas' (the People's Republic, Taiwan, and Hong Kong) – a search complicated by the international reaction to the Tiananmen Square massacre of June 1989. The status of the Soviet Union, the South Pacific Island states, and the non-ASEAN states in Southeast Asia was also at issue. For the time being these economies stood outside APEC. The European Community (EC) had expressed interest in becoming a member as well (or, as some might suggest, fear about being left out), but APEC leaders maintained that it was somewhat hypocritical for the EC to attack the initial proposal and then to ask to participate. Another major issue confronting APEC concerns the relationship between the new organization and existing bodies. ASEAN's misgivings and its insistence that its own organizational integrity not be impaired were repeated forcefully during the APD sessions in July 1989, when the Hawke Initiative was raised by the Australian foreign minister and endorsed by the American secretary of state. The Dialogue ended without a clear resolution on the matter, although ASEAN participants were willing to let a meeting of economic ministers discuss the idea later in the year. However, during the 1990 APD and the 1989 and 1990 APEC ministerial sessions, it was clear that the ASEAN states remained reluctant to let APEC overshadow or replace the APD as the premier intergovernmental forum in the region and to risk losing control over the pace of the cooperation movement.[88] This uneasiness, manifest in December 1990 in the Malaysian proposal of an East Asian Economic Grouping (later tempered to Caucus),[89] is destined to linger for some time and could, in the long run, pose an even bigger problem than the membership issues.

In addition to questions about the relationship between a new institution and ASEAN, the relationship between the Hawke Initiative and PECC quickly became a source of anxiety and debate – despite the prime minister's praise for PECC. Officials from New Zealand were upset with the Australian plan to hold a ministerial meeting in Canberra just prior to PECC VII in Wellington, perceiving this schedule to be part of an attempt to steal New Zealand's diplomatic thunder by drawing attention away from PECC. Protests by members of the PECC-ISC eventually brought assurances that the Australian proposal was not seeking to overshadow the PECC process or to create an organization which would replace PECC. Rather, the Australian government saw PECC becoming a leading component of a research network upon which a new intergovernmental institution could draw. The plan to hold a ministerial meeting prior to PECC VII was symbolic of what Australian officials hoped would become a close working relationship between PECC and an intergovernmental framework, given that this sequence of events would allow PECC to undertake immediately a discussion of the themes and proposals which might emerge from a ministerial exchange. Thus far, the pursuit of a symbiotic relationship between APEC and PECC has proven amenable to both sides[90] – a development which augurs well for the defenders of PECC and will placate those within APEC who fear the creation of a massive and unnecessary bureaucracy (the September 1992 decision to establish a permanent APEC 'support mechanism' in Singapore notwithstanding).[91]

For the time being APEC moves forward, albeit tentatively, amidst ASEAN reluctance. A third ministerial meeting was held in Seoul in 1991 and a fourth in Bangkok in 1992. The U.S. will host the 1993 meeting, followed by Indonesia in 1994. If Asian misgivings about a North American free trade agreement can be overcome[92] and fractious membership debates avoided, APEC's future may be bright. The main problem is that, in an intergovernmental setting, a consensus on questions such as the admission of new members is difficult to achieve because the political stakes are higher than is the case in a nongovernmental setting. Prospective Chinese and Soviet participation had posed major obstacles. The inclusion of references to economic rather than to foreign ministers from Taiwan (as Chinese Taipei) and Hong Kong enabled them to join APEC in 1991 alongside China,[93] while the demise of the USSR that same year may have provided APEC with yet further room to manoeuvre. In 1992, Prime Minister Paul Keating of Australia proposed that, every two to three years, regular heads-of-government gatherings be organized by APEC.[94] Still, the limitations of politics and protocol suggest that PECC has a better chance than has APEC of surviving and of serving as a constructive forum for regional cooperation. APEC may also be less able than is PECC to meet the challenges posed by more established bodies, such as ASEAN, the EC, and GATT, or by pressing issues raised by change and continuity throughout the world.

Conclusion

This chapter has highlighted PECC's role as an international actor by outlining its performance and/or facilitation of four diplomatic functions. The forum's representative qualities have been aided by a non-threatening and nonbinding format, which now brings together predominantly tripartite national delegations of academics, business leaders, and state officials from a wide variety of economies, including the ASEAN states, China, and Taiwan.

Participation from ASEAN has been of central importance, and attempts by PECC enthusiasts to placate the fears of this subregional grouping acknowledge that the pace of pan-Pacific cooperation is largely dependent upon the association's attitude towards the concept. The presence of Chinese delegates is desirable, given China's prospective economic impact on the Asia-Pacific region, whereas the presence of Taiwanese delegates permits informal diplomatic contact with representatives of a political entity which is a growing economic force, but with which many countries do not wish to maintain official relations.

Though state officials participate in an unofficial capacity, this distinction, while important to the maintenance of PECC's nongovernmental status, is widely recognized as a polite fiction perpetuated to circumvent protocol requirements. The question, 'How can a Chinese state official be present in a private capacity?' may be posed with equal validity to all other state officials. Each is present because he/she is a state official, and each has been permitted to attend by his/her employer because that employer apparently expects to benefit from such participation. The financial, technical, and moral support given to several national committees by governments and state agencies serves to reinforce the representative nature of PECC participation, whether one is considering the underlying interests of the state in question or of sectoral delegates.

The diplomatic functions of information and communication are facilitated as a result of national participation in standing committee meetings, conference sessions, and task force activities. During these interactions, participants are exposed to a broader range of policy ideas and options than would otherwise be available in an intergovernmental setting. The informal nature of PECC activities adds to the flexibility and depth of discussion. It also serves to promote a mutual understanding which has formed the basis for subsequent intergovernmental initiatives, thereby illustrating the utility of this unofficial diplomatic field of play, in which decisions are nonbinding and protocol can be breached.

The most significant feature of PECC's nongovernmental contributions to diplomacy is its capacity to facilitate negotiations between states and between sectors – a capacity not found in PAFTAD or PBEC. The decision to include 'unofficial' state officials as equal participants has ensured that state interests are expressed and defended alongside those of participants from other sectors. As a result, negotiations and compromises involving state officials and their societal counterparts are required at each stage of the process. An acceptance of a predominantly consensual decision-making approach has also placated ASEAN's fears of being divided by, or dominated within, a pan-Pacific forum and assisted the association in its attempts to control the pace of regional cooperation.

PECC's ability to engage in regional diplomacy has been aided by the collective expertise of those who have participated in this forum as well as by their societal prominence and by their access to policy-makers. The latter feature is reinforced by the involvement of active state officials. In addition, as in PAFTAD, the perseverance and dedication of a small group of national elites, who have participated in PECC activities since 1980, has given this forum the credibility and continuity required for successful unofficial diplomacy.[95] These qualities have also assisted in attracting the support offered by states for the establishment and operation of national committees in many member economies and for a cooperative APEC-PECC relationship – support which suggests that state participation in the Pacific economic cooperation movement remains predicated upon the pursuit of a mutually beneficial relationship with PECC and with other INGOs.

7
The PECC Process in Action

The utility of a nongovernmental approach to regional diplomacy may be further illustrated by examining four cases of consensus-building within the PECC process: (1) the activities of the PECC Trade Policy Task Force and Forum; (2) the efforts to secure the participation of the People's Republic of China (PRC); (3) the debate over Soviet observer status at PECC V; and (4) the evolution and contents of the Vancouver Statement on Pacific Economic Cooperation.

Trade Policy: Pursuing a Pacific Perspective

PECC's efforts to achieve regional economic cooperation appear to occur at a level just below that of state-to-state negotiations. However, a review of PECC task force reports suggests that sometimes these nongovernmental activities are part of, rather than merely a direct complement to, official negotiations.

Of the task force activities undertaken within the PECC process, perhaps those dealing with trade policy provide the most salient example of PECC's diplomatic role.[1] The present Trade Policy Forum has evolved from the Task Force on Trade in Manufactured Goods established at the Bangkok conference in 1982. In its report to the Bali conference in 1983, the original task force recommended: (1) measures to reduce the barriers to trade identified in the task force's review of trade patterns; (2) steps governments might take to increase opportunities for trade and to provide marketing assistance for firms; and (3) ways of improving 'the atmosphere for trade through consultation' among Pacific nations on economic prospects, macroeconomic policies, sectoral policies, and industrial planning. The failure of the 1982 GATT ministerial meeting to declare a standstill on the adoption of further non-tariff barriers was also noted, alongside a call for Pacific countries to become a separate and positive force within GATT in pursuit of global trade liberalization.[2] The harmonization theme was endorsed by the delegates to the Bali conference, and the PECC-ISC recommended 'that Pacific countries participate and take a leading role in a new round of multilateral trade negotiations (MTN) and in the interim make a commitment to a moratorium on further protectionist measures.' To emphasize this proposal, the title of the task force was changed from Manufactured Goods to Trade Policy and Trade Negotiations.[3]

The need for Pacific countries to play an exemplary role in creating the political will to begin a new MTN round was again stressed in the task force report presented to PECC IV in Seoul. As for PECC's role in the two-track pursuit of regional and global trade liberalization, the report also recommended that the existing task force be transformed 'into a trade policy forum to serve as a vehicle for discussing trade-related issues and for developing consensus positions.'[4] Among the issues highlighted for immediate attention in a new global round or a regional initiative were barriers to imports of manufactured goods from developing countries, agricultural protectionism, countervailing duties, safeguards, structural adjustment, trade in high technology products, trade in services, and trade-related investment regulations.[5]

The proposal for a trade policy forum was adopted by the participants at Seoul, and the pursuit of a 'Pacific GATT Agenda' continued to dominate PECC efforts through PECC V in 1986. During the Vancouver conference, delegates were able to reflect upon the September 1986 agreement amongst GATT contracting parties to launch a new MTN round (referred to as the Uruguay Round because agreement was reached at a meeting in the Uruguayan city of Punte del Este), which would include consideration of agricultural and services trade.[6]

Delegates were also able to review the contribution made by PECC in the effort to obtain the agreement on a new GATT round. Indeed, it had been clear since 1983 that the PECC process was playing an important role in supporting official diplomatic efforts of governments in the region. For example, as the Bali conference that year was concluding, Prime Minister Hawke of Australia launched a program which led to the establishment of 'a consultative process aimed at ensuring that issues of significance to regional states are addressed in the new [MTN] round.' This idea had its origins in discussions at PECC III and resulted in an ongoing series of annual meetings of trade officials from Western Pacific countries.[7]

Preparations for a new GATT round were also buttressed by the initiation of the Cairns Group of Fair Trading Nations in Agriculture in August 1986 – a ministerial gathering involving fourteen countries. These countries, nine of which were from the Pacific Basin, joined together in supporting the inclusion of agricultural trade issues in the new GATT round.[8] State officials and advisors from several Pacific nations have noted the link between PECC and the official fora mentioned above, agreeing that PECC activities 'continue to provide a useful complement ... to government-to-government negotiations with other countries.'[9]

Credit is also extended to these activities for their part in assisting the development of the 'specific issue coalition' of middle and minor powers embodied by the Cairns Group and the subsequent Pacific consensus, which successfully supported the placement of issues critical to the welfare of Pacific nations on the agenda of the Uruguay Round.[10] The pursuit of a specific issue coalition on agricultural trade matters is most apparent in Australian and Canadian diplomatic tactics. In the Australian case, a 'support generating strategy' launched by Prime Minister Fraser in 1982, following a failed attempt to secure a new GATT round, was continued by Prime Minister Hawke through his government's initiation and leadership of the Cairns Group. In the Canadian case, participation in the Cairns Group was first aimed at complementing the efforts to secure a bilateral free trade agreement with the United States. Thus, participation in the PECC process, the Cairns Group, and GATT illustrates the multi-level approach to trade diplomacy undertaken by state officials in Australia and Canada – an approach which once again highlights the polite fiction underlying any lingering claims that PECC's nonofficial status also renders it nonpolitical. For countries such as Australia, the inclusion of Canada in the Cairns Group and of Japan and the U.S. in PECC also raises the possibility of encouraging these countries to represent, or to be mindful of, the economic and political interests of smaller powers when their officials participate in major and exclusive fora such as the summit meeting of the Group of Seven Advanced Industrialized Nations.[11]

The First PECC Trade Policy Forum (held 20-2 March 1986 in San Francisco) was convened six months prior to the Punte del Este agreement on a new GATT round. During the forum, a comprehensive Pacific agenda for such a round emerged. This agenda included the following items: efforts to control and reduce agricultural protectionism; new approaches to remove trade barriers on processed natural products; the liberalization and removal of quantitative restrictions; a revision of policies towards preferences for developing countries; the rationalization of methods of temporary protection; a framework for policy on trade-related and investment-related services; reduced barriers affecting high technology goods and services and improved protection of intellectual property; a standstill commitment on new trade restrictions and a roll-back commitment on existing trade restrictions; and the strengthening of GATT machinery for monitoring protectionism and for dispute settlement (i.e., the establishment of a trade ombudsman).[12]

As noted earlier, this Pacific GATT agenda compares favourably with many of the subjects considered as part of the Uruguay Round, and many senior officials have acknowledged the PECC contribution to the effort which secured agreement on the initiation of a new round. Delegates at PECC V pledged that the PECC process would seek to maintain its contribution to the study of GATT-related issues from a Pacific perspective and would seek to expand its examination of the links between trade and investment issues. The meeting also adopted a proposal that 'small working groups be established to specify areas of consensus throughout the Pacific region on several of the highest priority sectoral and other issues on the proposed agenda for GATT negotiations.'[13] At the Second Trade Policy Forum, held in Singapore in January 1988, a PECC Trade Policy Statement (the Singapore Statement) was formulated, pledging continued support for trade liberalization, the search for temporary non-discriminatory safeguard provisions, and collective Pacific initiatives. This statement was reaffirmed at PECC VI in advance of the Uruguay Round Mid-Term Review and again at PECC VII amidst increasingly troubled GATT deliberations. The release of a Standing Committee Trade Policy Statement has become a standard feature of PECC meetings.[14] A commitment to pursue a Pacific trade perspective through the ongoing activities of the Trade Policy Forum and the subsequent focused effort of such meetings would appear to have ensured PECC's ongoing role as an informal complement to formal diplomatic negotiations considering and seeking global and/or regional policy coordination, especially given the symbiotic relationship which has since emerged between PECC and APEC.

Chinese Membership in PECC: What's in a Name?

China's participation in PECC has been complicated by Taiwan's desire to participate as well. From its formation in 1982 to the granting of full membership to the PRC (as China) and to Taiwan (as Chinese Taipei) in

1986, the PECC-ISC maintained that it would be desirable for China and Taiwan to enter at the same time or at least to gain membership in advance of the same conference. Priority was given to the entry of China; Taiwan would not be allowed to become a full member until China had agreed to do so, thereby avoiding any actions which might deter the Chinese.

Chinese interaction with the PECC process began in 1980, when an official from the Chinese embassy was invited to attend the final session of the Canberra Seminar. A delegation led by John Crawford (chancellor of the ANU and chief organizer of PECC I) visited China shortly thereafter to report on the proceedings, and Chinese leaders expressed interest in participating in future deliberations.[15] But the matter of Chinese membership did not become a major issue until 1984, when a Taiwanese group, which had sent observers to PECC II and III, applied for full membership in PECC as the 'Chinese Member Committee of the Pacific Economic Cooperation Committee in Taipei.' Despite a degree of support within the PECC-ISC, a response to this application was deferred on the grounds that Taiwan's entry as a full member should be undertaken in a way which would not hamper the participation of the PRC. In reaching a consensus against full membership at that time (due to delicate diplomatic circumstances), the PECC-ISC reaffirmed its position that Taiwan was welcome to send observers and to participate fully in task force activities. Saburo Okita (former Japanese foreign minister and chairperson of the Japanese national PECC committee) and Eric Trigg (senior vice-president of Alcan Aluminum, chairperson of the Canadian national PECC committee, and chairperson of the PECC-ISC) also agreed to raise the membership question informally with representatives of the PRC.[16]

The desire not to preclude Chinese membership is interesting for three reasons. First, it demonstrates recognition of China's potential role as a regional economic actor and the subsequent need to set a precedent which would indicate that the focus of the PECC process was not to be restricted to cooperation amongst free market economies. Second, it suggests a difference in attitudes towards China and the Soviet Union. Third, it highlights the role of a nongovernmental organization in engaging China in regional economic diplomacy.

The expectation that China's economic reforms and open-door policy would hasten its ascendancy as a significant player in the Pacific Basin economy made it a prime candidate for inclusion in the regional cooperation movement. This candidacy was propelled by China's desire to modernize its economic infrastructure, the expected impact of Chinese economic growth upon the trade and development of the ASEAN states, the size of the Chinese market, and the potential for a large-scale exchange of scholarly and commercial information.[17] These factors were also enlisted in support of attempts by many PECC enthusiasts to demonstrate this INGO's capacity to serve as a constructive meeting place for officials from free-market and centrally-planned economies. The leadership would thus be better able to refute characterizations of the PECC process as an attempt to create a capitalist economic bloc or to counter the aspirations of governments which might wish to preclude communist involvement.

Chinese membership would therefore set a precedent which would confirm PECC's professed status as a nonpolitical, nonofficial, nongovernmental organization. Its ability to circumvent and to complement formal diplomatic channels would be further enhanced if Taiwan was subsequently included, given that states which do not maintain formal relations with Taiwan could allow their officials to interact with Taiwanese officials on an informal basis within PECC without offending the PRC. The pursuit of a mechanism which would facilitate Chinese and Taiwanese participation, while preserving PECC's nongovernmental credentials, was thus undertaken in accordance with the view that 'the success or otherwise of the existing Pacific machinery [such as PECC] will depend on the resolution of this China/Taiwan question.'[18]

Whereas China's participation was clearly desired by many PECC members, more caution was shown towards the possibility of Soviet involvement. This was partly due to the fact that the Chinese, unlike the Soviets, had not voiced a strong anti-PECC position. Prior to 1986, the Chinese leadership had viewed the PECC process as primarily a Japanese-inspired effort to promote Japanese economic prosperity, national security, and political influence. Concern was also expressed about possible Japanese and American domination of the evolving institutional structures. Yet care was taken to refrain from enunciating an official policy on PECC. China no longer appeared apprehensive about joining a group composed of representatives from industrialized and developing countries, realizing the economic benefits which could flow to developing countries in the form of investment, technology, training, and market access. Cognizant of regional interdependence, improved relations with its Asia-Pacific neighbours were a prime foreign policy objective, and Chinese officials expected, eventually, to participate in the PECC process.[19]

A prudent position was thus maintained, in which the Chinese remained willing to examine the cooperation idea but were troubled by a lack of definition, the movement's free-market orientation, Japanese motivations, a desire to avoid being drawn into a special relationship with Japan or the U.S., and the search for a way to placate ASEAN fears about China's economic competitiveness. Though not yet ready to join PECC, it was evident that the Chinese officials did not want to be excluded, as Chinese delegates continued to participate in other informal discussions of regional cooperation.[20]

The 'wait and see' stance of the Chinese government and the belief that China was bound to play a key role in the regional economy provided the PECC-ISC with a better rationale for Chinese inclusion than could be mustered for Soviet participation. With its commentators having long described PECC as an imperialist ploy and less than 10 per cent of its trade being conducted with other Pacific countries, the Soviet Union, it was hoped, could be relegated to the periphery of the prospective membership debate without even having to consider the potential political tensions Soviet participation might create.

Efforts to facilitate China's entry into PECC began in earnest in August 1985 amidst the aftermath of PECC IV, when the new chairperson, Trigg, was commissioned with the task of mediation. It was noted that the Chinese had expressed a willingness to collaborate in resolving the China/Taiwan question – a tacit acknowledgement of PECC's diplomatic value to China. While they would protest strongly should Taiwan be granted full membership in China's absence, the search for a face-saving mechanism allowing simultaneous admission might be eased if China could be reassured about PECC's avowed nongovernmental status.[21]

Precedents for Chinese and Taiwanese membership in nongovernmental organizations had already been set. In most of these cases, Chinese participation depended upon Chinese acceptance of the title to be used by the Taiwanese delegation. Trigg noted that the 'Olympic Formula' of referring to Taiwan as 'Chinese Taipei' was followed by several sporting organizations, and that China appeared to be flexible as long as the name used by Taiwan did not imply the existence of 'two Chinas.'[22] Armed with an article from the journal *Pacific Affairs*, which outlined this formula and which he referred to as his 'bible' on the topic, Trigg proceeded.[23]

Demonstrating the importance of continuing elite interaction within the cooperation movement, Trigg's relationship with the leader of the

Taiwanese group, Chen-Fu Koo (board chairperson and president of Taiwan Cement Co.), proved to be a critical factor in resolving the China/Taiwan issue. Forged through their participation in PBEC,[24] this familiarity created a bond of trust between the mediator and one of the parties. In a sense, half of the problem was already solved. The Taiwanese were eager to become full members in the PECC process and, with Trigg and Koo being PBEC allies, would be willing to accept the mediator's decisions with minimal resistance.

The entire mediation period took fifteen months. At the request of the PRC, Trigg's correspondence was channelled through Ambassador Yu Zhan and the Chinese embassy in Ottawa. The designation of this channel instead of an academic institute indicated to some PECC participants that the Chinese, initially, had difficulty coming to terms with Trigg's nongovernmental credentials – a problem compounded by the lack of a written statement of PECC's purpose, principles, and organization. Indeed, upon being approached by Trigg, the Chinese embassy referred to the Canadian Department of External Affairs for clarification of PECC's intentions and Trigg's relationship with the Canadian government.

In his initial enquiries about Chinese interest in PECC, Trigg noted that observers from Taiwan had attended PECC sessions and that the Taiwanese had applied for full membership under a title which was in keeping with that adopted when the Taiwanese business community was granted membership in PBEC in 1984 (the Chinese Member Committee of PBEC in Taipei). But China was not a member of PBEC, and the Chinese ambassador responded that the use of a similar name in the PECC context was not acceptable to the PRC, as it could be interpreted as connoting the existence of two Chinese committees – one in Taipei and another on the mainland. He suggested the wording be changed to correspond with the name used by the World Energy Conference, which lists the Taiwanese member committee as being from 'Taiwan, China.'

Trigg reminded the Chinese officials that, unlike the World Energy Conference, PECC was not regarded by its members as an intergovernmental forum, and that the wording 'Chinese Taipei' had been acceptable to the PRC in the case of several nongovernmental organizations. He also noted that the names 'Pacific Economic Cooperation Committee of China in Taipei' or 'of China (Taipei)' would not imply that Taiwan is not part of China. In addition, either of these names would enable the PRC to establish a 'Pacific Economic Cooperation Committee of China.' Should such an arrangement be acceptable, the only problem still confronting China's entry into the PECC process would be reluctance within ASEAN.[25]

By late 1985, it appeared that Indonesian rather than Chinese objections were obstructing resolution of the China/Taiwan question. For example, in November 1985, a Canadian academic and PECC participant offered the following observations to the Canadian Department of External Affairs upon returning from a tour of Chinese research institutions: (1) Chinese academics appear well aware of the background and current status of PECC as a result of assessments made on behalf of the Chinese government, and 'it is very much on the front burner of their concern'; (2) the Chinese are willing to allow Taiwan to participate under the Olympic Formula; and (3) they are of the firm belief that only an Indonesian veto is preventing their involvement.[26]

Although this observer believed the Chinese were exaggerating the political influence wielded by the Indonesian PECC-ISC representative, Jusuf Wanandi, it was generally agreed that Wanandi remained the main stumbling block in reaching a consensus within PECC on China's admission. As an American Department of Energy official reported in December 1985, Wanandi had indicated that Indonesia wanted to defer a decision on the Chinese membership question until after PECC V on the grounds that immediate admission might hamper Indonesian efforts to improve official bilateral relations with China. However, Indonesia would not be averse to China's participation in PECC task forces or to the presence of a Chinese observer on the PECC-ISC. These exchanges illustrate the diplomatic importance placed upon the PECC process, as does the eventual withdrawal of the Indonesian objection to Chinese membership in PECC following talks between the Canadian foreign minister, Joe Clark, and the Indonesian foreign minister, Mochtar Kusumaatmadja, during the June 1986 ASEAN-Pacific Dialogue.[27]

By early 1986, China's position on Taiwan had softened to the point where participation alongside Taiwan was no longer a problem. Though an invitation to attend the first PECC Trade Policy Forum in San Francisco in March 1986 was declined by the Chinese Academy of Social Sciences, China was eventually represented by a scholar from the Institute of Contemporary International Relations, who was visiting an American university. A tripartite Taiwanese delegation also took part. In July 1986, Trigg met with the Chinese ambassador and agreed that, in accordance with the Olympic Formula, the Taiwanese participants in

PECC would be referred to as members of the 'Chinese Taipei Pacific Economic Cooperation Committee.' Following his report to the PECC-ISC in August 1986, Trigg was authorized to formally invite the Chinese to become full participants through what might be called the 'Pacific Economic Cooperation Committee of China' or the 'China Pacific Economic Cooperation Committee.' If and when China accepted this invitation, a membership offer would then be extended to the Taiwanese, thereby enabling both China and Taiwan to attend PECC V as full members. This sequence of invitations was important, for it recognized China's desire to be admitted as a member of PECC before Taiwan. It was also in keeping with the view of the foreign minister of the host country, who maintained that immediate attention should be given to China's entry and who stressed that Canadian government policy on the accession of the PRC to international organizations held that the solution should be in line with its (the PRC's) views. Accordingly, Taiwan's participation should be subject to a convenient arrangement with China.[28]

Trigg extended the appropriate invitation in September 1986. He was soon informed by the Chinese ambassador that China had accepted the invitation to join PECC as a full member, and that a delegation from the 'China National Committee for Pacific Economic Cooperation' would attend PECC V. The ambassador added that his country was accepting the invitation to participate on the understanding that, given PECC's nongovernmental status, on no occasion would the 'so-called' national flag, emblem, or anthem of 'the Taiwan region of China' appear during PECC activities, that the name 'Republic of China' would not be used, and that no references to 'two Chinas' would be condoned.[29]

Upon receiving this confirmation, Trigg extended an invitation to the Taiwanese via Koo, thanking him for his patience and noting the conditions accompanying the Chinese acceptance. Koo quickly accepted these conditions, prompting Trigg to announce the formal expansion of the PECC family to all members of the PECC-ISC with a telex which read: 'Pleased to advise that cousins have accepted invitations.'[30] This announcement came just five weeks prior to the opening of PECC V in Vancouver and reaffirmed China's recognition of PECC as a nongovernmental organization – a perception which tempered the Chinese response to the discovery that Taiwan and Hong Kong had been errantly referred to as 'countries' rather than 'regions' (of China) in materials distributed in advance of the conference. The PRC did not threaten to withdraw its delegation and was placated by the insertion of an erratum making references in the conference documentation to 'countries' inclusive of 'countries, regions or organizations.'[31]

Member delegations from China and Chinese Taipei have participated in all subsequent PECC conferences. Both committees have been active in task force meetings as well. China's recent involvement has been shrouded by changes within China and international criticism in the wake of the June 1989 Tiananmen Square massacre, although this criticism had been blunted by PECC's unofficial status.

Though maintaining PECC's nongovernmental appearance, the resolution of the China/Taiwan question illustrates that governments do play a role within the PECC process beyond the provision of financial support and the appointment of national committees.[32] Trigg's part in the mediation process was important and was enhanced by his PBEC association with Koo. However, the governments of at least two countries, China and Canada, were also key actors, the former by laying down conditions for Chinese and Taiwanese participation and the latter by working to ensure that all obstacles were removed in advance of a conference it was sponsoring. The nongovernmental coup embodied by the presence of Chinese and Taiwanese delegates during the Vancouver conference was thus heavily dependent upon governmental efforts to preserve and to extend PECC's diplomatic utility. It also paved the way for Hong Kong's admission in 1990.

Soviet Observer Status at PECC V: Seen But Not Heard?

The debate over the issue of Soviet observer status at PECC V provides yet another example of contending national approaches to regional cooperation. In the course of efforts to resolve the China/Taiwan question, one found the Chinese trying to ascertain and to ensure PECC's nongovernmental credentials, the Taiwanese happy to be considered for inclusion, the Canadians looking for ways to smooth China's entry, and the Indonesians conscious of the link between official bilateral relations and unofficial multilateral fora. In the dispute over Soviet participation, Canadian and Indonesian diplomatic concerns are again prominent, this time alongside those of the Soviets, the Japanese, and the Australians.

The roots of this controversy lie not only in the ideological gulf which separated Soviet and Western bloc political thinking but also in the long-belligerent Soviet attitude towards the PECC process. Prior to mid-1986, most Soviet commentators viewed PECC as a Japanese/American attempt to construct a Pacific version of NATO.[33] However, the impending entry of China, the apparent momentum being gathered by the PECC process, the Soviet desire to gain Western assistance for Siberian development projects, and the new diplomatic style of Soviet premier Mikhail Gorbachev caused the Soviet leadership to reevaluate, recast, and reassert Soviet interest in regional cooperation activities.[34] China's entry would also raise questions within PECC about the possibility of Soviet participation, although, as one commentator noted in 1985, 'surprisingly, the Soviet economic stake in the Pacific Basin seems to be declining as its military presence increases, and that is something again which would work against a Soviet membership.'[35]

In the months immediately before and after Gorbachev's Vladivostok initiative of 28 July 1986 (which included a call for an Asia-Pacific disarmament conference as well as a statement of the Soviet desire to participate in existing regional fora),[36] the Soviet foreign office campaigned to gain observer status at PECC V. Envoys visited the chairpersons of several PECC national committees, seeking support in advance of a written application lodged with Trigg (as chairperson of the PECC V host committee) the day before a PECC-ISC meeting in San Francisco in August 1986.

It was at this point that the controversy over Soviet participation began to unfold. Most oral accounts of the San Francisco meeting suggest that the Soviets had achieved their objective when a favourable consensus was reached on the granting of permission to the USSR to have one local (Canada-based) observer present for all plenary sessions of the Vancouver conference. However, the minutes of the meeting appear inconclusive on this point. They read as follows:

> Mr. Trigg reported on the approach he had received from the Soviet Embassy in Canada regarding possible Soviet participation as observers at the Vancouver PECC. There was division within the Standing Committee on inviting the USSR to participate at this time. It was suggested that the host Committee for PECC V consider including the USSR as one on a list of diplomatic and consular invitations, while at the same time suggesting that the USSR become involved in task force activities. It was agreed that Standing Committee members would consult further with their member committees and advise the Chairman of any further views, but that resolution of the China question should take priority over that of the USSR.[37]

It seems possible that at least some PECC-ISC members could have departed believing that no firm decision had been made on the Soviet observer issue – a perception reinforced when Trigg responded to the Soviet application by noting that, while some interest had been evident within the PECC-ISC, the matter had been referred to member committees in the hope that a decision could be made in four to six weeks.[38]

Even so, disquiet was apparent within days of the San Francisco meeting, indicating that there may have been an agreement which was not to the liking of some persons or governments engaged in the PECC process. The first signs of difficulty came in letters written to Trigg by Nobuyasu Abe, former director of the Policy Planning Division of the Japanese Ministry of Foreign Affairs (Gaimusho), and Edward Derwinski, a counsellor of the U.S. Department of State. Both men expressed reservations about the ability of the Soviet Union to make a positive contribution to PECC. While the American misgivings were quickly allayed by Trigg and the chairperson of the U.S. national committee, Ambassador Richard Fairbanks, the Japanese reluctance remained. One month after the San Francisco meeting, Okita informed Trigg that the San Francisco consensus was no longer acceptable to members of the Japanese national committee, although no objection would be raised to the presence of a Soviet consular official being present at the opening ceremony of the Vancouver conference or to Soviet participation in task force activities.[39] Other communications from the Japanese committee (sometimes relayed via the Gaimusho and the U.S. State Department) suggested that the U.S. national committee was of the same opinion – a claim which was promptly denied by American committee leaders.

Several members of the Japanese national committee have indicated that Okita (the only Japanese representative during the San Francisco session which reached the initial consensus) had either not interpreted the consensus the same way as had participants from other countries or was not certain that a consensus had been reached. Other participants in the meeting suggest that neither scenario is plausible. In their view, the agreement was clear to all present, and Japanese consent was only withdrawn when the Soviet desk of the Gaimusho became alarmed about nongovernmental meddling in affairs which could have a direct impact upon official Japanese-Soviet relations, particularly the long-standing Northern Territories dispute and the eventually unfruitful Japanese efforts to secure a visit to Tokyo by Gorbachev in January 1987. In addition, it was feared that the Soviets would send a high-ranking state official from Moscow as their observer, thereby forcing the

Japanese to drop their hard-line opposition to Soviet participation in Pacific affairs by setting a precedent and making it difficult for the Japanese, as hosts, to deny the Soviets admission to PECC VI in Osaka in 1988. The Soviet desk thus put pressure upon other bureaucratic elements and the leadership of the Japanese national committee in an attempt to revoke the San Francisco consensus.[40]

Scepticism about Soviet intentions, the need to avoid the political tensions which might result from Soviet participation, the necessity of first seeing through the entry of China and Taiwan, and the relatively low percentage of Soviet trade with other Pacific countries were among the reasons supplied by the Japanese national committee in the belated objection it raised to Soviet participation. But the delayed reaction of the Japanese committee, the suggestion that Okita was in disagreement with the San Francisco consensus, the transmission of communiqués through official diplomatic channels, and the lobbying of the host committee by the Japanese embassy in Ottawa indicate to many PECC enthusiasts that the Japanese bureaucracy had actively tried to interfere with the nongovernmental PECC process.

Prior to receiving Okita's communiqué, Trigg began to seek ways of restoring the San Francisco consensus or of adjusting it to suit all parties. A consensual resolution was desirable in order to avoid having to make a unilateral decision on the Soviet request in his capacity as chairperson of the host committee. He quickly found himself in the middle of a dispute which threatened to overtly politicize and, hence, to destroy the PECC process if not resolved in a manner which would retain PECC's integrity as a nongovernmental forum. The most vociferous responses to the apparent reversal of the Japanese position came from Peter Drysdale (executive director of the AJRC and chairperson of the Australian national PECC committee) and Jusuf Wanandi (executive director of CSIS and chairperson of the Indonesian national PECC committee), who staunchly defended the original consensus.

Having received a copy of the Abe letter from the Australian Department of Foreign Affairs in advance of Okita's report, Drysdale informed Trigg that the Australian national committee believed that if the PECC process was to be strengthened, participants must continue 'to recognise the sensitivities which can be raised by the concept of enhanced regional cooperation.' Of particular importance in this regard were fears of U.S./Japanese domination or of an eventual security arrangement which might exclude the Soviet Union and, thereby, violate the ASEAN policy of nonalignment. For these reasons, the principle of nonexclusiveness had been fundamental to the consensus upon which PECC was founded and to the Australian approach throughout. 'Without it,' Drysdale wrote, 'we invite interpretation of PECC motives which can only be diversionary and destructive.'[41] International organizations as well as interested Latin American and European countries had participated as observers at PECC conferences, so there was little reason to exclude the Soviets. Furthermore, it should be remembered by those who might object to a Soviet presence that observers can only contribute to discussions at the invitation of the chair. Accordingly, 'it remains the Australian Committee's hope that the consensus to accept local Soviet observer attendance at the Vancouver meeting not be disturbed. Certainly we would want exposure to a wider range of arguments than those that have been so far advanced in order to be persuaded otherwise.'[42]

The Australian position had at its core a desire to protect the integrity of what was seen as a useful diplomatic forum. To deny Soviet observer status and to bow to a dissident element of a state apparatus would violate the principle of nonexclusiveness which had, to that point, preserved PECC's nonofficial, nonpolitical appearance. Such a violation ran the risk of causing the process to collapse under its own weight. The Soviets could not be excluded without endangering PECC. Prudence dictated that they be given the opportunity to prove their sincerity.[43]

Drysdale's response was relayed to Trigg by the Australian Department of Foreign Affairs and was circulated to Okita and Wanandi. Though concurring with those who suggested that the minutes of the San Francisco meeting did not accurately reflect the understanding reached at that time, Wanandi was quick to support Drysdale's position. Placing special emphasis on the need to avoid a breach of ASEAN's nonaligned foreign policy stance, he also highlighted the inherent ambiguity of inviting China but not the Soviet Union and of trying to exclude the Soviets when even Iran had been granted observer status at PECC IV. In later communications, Wanandi went on to threaten the withdrawal of the Indonesian delegation to the Vancouver conference if a Soviet observer was not admitted and to take the remaining ASEAN delegations with him.[44]

But the willingness to compromise shown by other ASEAN members of the PECC-ISC indicates that continuing tension in the China-Indonesia relationship may have added to the Indonesian desire to see Soviet participation act as a counterweight against Chinese entry into PECC. It has also been observed that Wanandi's stubborn support for the Soviets may have been due to a rapprochement in Indonesian-Soviet relations begun when Mochtar Kusumaatmadja visited Moscow in 1984 (becoming the first high-ranking Indonesian to do so since 1974) and continued when his Soviet counterpart, Eduard Shevardnadze, visited Indonesia in 1987. Like the Soviet attempt to join PECC, these interactions can be seen as part of a multidimensional foreign policy approach which the Soviets adopted in an effort to be recognized as a legitimate actor in Southeast Asia and the Pacific. By acknowledging ASEAN's political concerns and by portraying cordial relations with the Soviet Union to ASEAN as a way of defusing the rise of a superpower rivalry in Southeast Asia, the Soviets hoped to foster a sense of 'strategic ambivalence' within the association towards Soviet military capabilities in the region.[45]

Still facing the prospect of having to make a unilateral decision, Trigg enlisted the support of Canada's foreign minister, Joe Clark, in an attempt to restore the San Francisco consensus. Prior to the San Francisco meeting, the Canadian government's position had mirrored that of the now hesitant Japanese: get the Chinese in and worry about the Soviets after PECC V. But, given the possibility of a diplomatic failure on Canadian soil at a conference financed and sponsored by the Canadian government, the Department of External Affairs chose to promote Trigg's position, even though he had acted somewhat independently during the affair (and not always the way the department would have preferred).[46]

A compromise proposal limiting attendance of the Soviet observer to the opening ceremony but permitting a TASS reporter to remain was rejected by Drysdale and Wanandi, while a scheme to ensure that the Soviet observer would be a consular official posted in Vancouver was set aside when it was discovered that no such consulate existed. Finally, mediation by Trigg, Fairbanks, and the Canadian Department of External Affairs achieved the result desired by the host committee. With the weight of consensus against it, the Gaimusho was forced either to set aside its misgivings or to risk being blamed for the collapse of an otherwise useful nongovernmental forum – a forum in which many Japanese resources had already been invested. The Japanese national committee met in a special session on 23 October 1986 and agreed to accept the original consensus.[47]

The Canadian organizers subsequently instructed the Soviet observer, Minister-Counsellor Alexey P. Makarov, not to speak during the PECC V plenary sessions, as to do so might prove disruptive. He acted accordingly. Indeed, the uninformed bystander might have remained unaware of either the fact or the significance of Makarov's attendance. His presence was noted only twice – by Clark during his keynote dinner address and by Thanat Khoman (former deputy prime minister of Thailand and chairperson of the Thai national PECC committee) during discussion of the Vancouver Statement on Pacific Economic Coopera- tion.[48] These acts of omission and commission provide further evidence of the diplomatic tensions underlying proceedings at the Vancouver conference.

It has been suggested by senior PECC participants that the Gaimusho mishandled the Soviet observer status issue by attaching great signifi- cance to it, forgetting or choosing to overlook that it was observer status and not membership which was at issue, and precipitating strong sup- port for a Soviet presence. Discussion of membership expansion was deferred until after PECC VII in Auckland in November 1989, and the Japanese were subsequently placated by the adoption of membership criteria and a unanimity requirement for admission decisions. Even so, a staunchly defended precedent regarding Soviet involvement had been set.[49] Having forced others to support the Soviet application, it would be much more difficult to deny Soviet attendance in the future. This constraint manifested itself in the decision to invite a Soviet academic to attend as a 'guest' in response to the Soviet request for observer status at PECC VI and the admission of Soviet observers to PECC VII and PECC VIII. The Soviets were also active in several subsequent PECC task force sessions.[50] While the Soviet pursuit of membership in PECC con- tinued to be plagued by Japanese misgivings, the Soviet burden was much lighter and the Japanese dilemma much greater. In September 1991, the PECC-ISC voted to admit the Soviet National Committee for Asia-Pacific Economic Cooperation as a full member. With the collapse of the USSR in December 1991, membership was transferred to a Rus- sian committee.[51]

Even more interesting is the way in which resistance from within the Japanese state apparatus was overcome by a nongovernmental organi- zation, albeit in the company of state support. Wanandi, Drysdale, and Trigg defended the original consensus with the knowledge that it was probably not their PECC associate Okita to whom they were directing their arguments, and, in the end, it was the network of close and nonbureaucratic contacts together with the diplomatic importance attached to the PECC process by state apparatuses which won the day. In the eyes of some analysts, the politics surrounding the resolution of the observer status issue and the regional role being played by PECC helped the Soviets gain another ominous diplomatic toehold in the Pacific. Others saw Soviet participation in the PECC process as a diplomatic step forward, assuming that the Soviets could be constructively engaged in this nongovernmental forum which had previously moved in their shadow. Both sides will now observe Russian involvement with interest.

The Vancouver Statement: Explicit and Implicit

One of the major problems encountered by the promoters of the PECC process prior to PECC V was the lack of a document outlining the organization's objectives and operating principles. The reliance upon individual leaders and participants to disseminate news of PECC and its activities in the absence of a written set of guidelines had sometimes resulted in confusion. Some difficulties encountered in the efforts to resolve the China/Taiwan and Soviet observer status issues discussed above may have been due to such misunderstandings.

Before the Vancouver conference in 1986, PECC activities were conducted in accordance with the principles enunciated by John Crawford in his summary of the Canberra Seminar. But, following PECC III, it became clear to PECC-ISC members that if state support (often required for the funding of national PECC committees) was to be obtained and/ or sustained, then PECC participants and state officials should be able to refer to a written statement of principles, objectives, structures, procedures, and activities.[52] The flexible, word of mouth approach was no longer sufficient to maintain PECC's nongovernmental integrity.

The process of formulating what would become the Vancouver Statement on Pacific Economic Cooperation (Appendix C) began at the January 1985 PECC-ISC meeting, when 'on behalf of Dr. [Thanat] Khoman, Dr. Narongchai [Akrasanee] proposed that efforts should be made to formalize the PECC and that implementation of a specific measure such as the adoption of a charter or the creation of a formal commission should be agreed to at the Seoul Conference.'[53]

However, when Thanat 'called for a Pacific declaration which would summarize the goals of PECC, his trial balloon was embarrassingly shot down from the floor' during a debate on the subject at PECC IV, although an agreement to circulate a draft 'Statement on the PECC Process' among national committees was reached.[54]

Thanat's proposal was refloated by the PECC-ISC following the Seoul conference in the hope that acceptance of such a document might be achieved at PECC V in Vancouver. Responsibility for drafting what was initially called a 'Pacific Declaration' was given to Trigg and to the Canadian host committee. Spurred on by the difficulties encountered while trying to ensure Chinese participation, the text of this document was revised five times in response to the comments of national committees before finally being ratified by all PECC-ISC members and endorsed by PECC V participants as the 'Vancouver Statement.' According to Trigg, while this document might be interpreted as a cautious endorsement of motherhood issues, the significance of the Vancouver Statement lies in the list of signatories.[55]

The diplomatic symbolism imparted by the signatories is, as Trigg hints, complemented not only by the contents of the document they have agreed to uphold but also by the absence of an explicit restatement of the principle of nonexclusiveness. The significance of this omission was highlighted by the clarification sought by an Australian state delegate at PECC V. While commending the adoption of the statement, Stuart Harris (secretary of the Australian Department of Foreign Affairs) queried Trigg as to why a clear expression of the principle of nonexclusiveness had not been included. Noting that much of PECC's success to date had been due to the enunciation of this principle by Crawford at the close of the Canberra Seminar, Harris observed that its omission risked allowing the PECC process to collapse under the weight of politicization. Echoing the sentiments expressed by the Australian national committee on the Soviet issue, he sought Trigg's assurance that the principle of nonexclusiveness 'is still in fact accepted as a principle and is implied in the Statement we have before us.'[56] An assurance to this effect was received and accepted, but not before Harris had aptly demonstrated yet again the delicate nature of PECC's consensual decision-making approach. At some point during PECC's voyage to Vancouver, an explicit reference to nonexclusiveness had been negotiated away in exchange for an agreement on an implicit and weaker compromise position, which allowed specific membership criteria to be adopted in 1990 and to be enshrined as part of the PECC Charter (to which the Vancouver Statement was appended) in 1991. Indeed, by PECC VI in 1988, member committees had already agreed to abide by the principle of unanimity when admitting new members.

Conclusion

One of the most salient examples of PECC's diplomatic utility is provided by the trade policy deliberations which take place within this forum. The success of the PECC process in laying the groundwork for a Pacific perspective on the new Uruguay Round of MTN under the GATT has been dependent upon the facilitation of all four diplomatic functions: (1) its ability to attract multipartite representation from a broad range of developing and developed economies; (2) its ability to engage delegates in a detailed information exchange; (3) its ability to organize an ongoing policy discussion on trade matters; and (4) its ability to facilitate the building of a consensus on a Pacific GATT agenda. These functions have been particularly useful to middle and minor powers of the region, as they have supplemented the formation and maintenance of official interstate coalitions on trade policy (e.g., the Cairns Group).

The resolution of the China/Taiwan membership question, in which China agreed to become a full member of PECC after accepting the terms for Taiwanese participation specified by the Olympic Formula, illustrates yet another state's recognition of PECC as a nongovernmental diplomatic channel. China's desire to enhance its regional relations through participation in PECC has been accommodated. At the same time, China has been required to condone Taiwanese membership as long as PECC's nongovernmental credentials are upheld by discreet nuances (such as the reference in the documentation for PECC V to 'countries, regions and organizations' as participants). The personal relationship forged between Trigg and Koo via PBEC also assisted in achieving satisfactory resolution, thereby confirming the diplomatic value of private elite interaction in the various nongovernmental elements of the Pacific economic cooperation movement. It should be noted that the solution arrived at in PECC became a model for components of the agreement which, in 1991, allowed China, Taiwan (as Chinese Taipei), and Hong Kong to enter APEC.

The issue of Soviet observer status has also helped to demonstrate PECC's role in facilitating diplomatic negotiations. First, the objections raised by elements within the Japanese foreign ministry on this issue and the role played by the Canadian government in its resolution indicate that bureaucracies and governments do play an active role in the PECC process. Second, the capitulation of the Japanese demonstrates the dynamics of building and defending a consensus within PECC. The weight of consensus proved critical in this case by successfully countering an effort by state officials which threatened to corrupt PECC's integrity as a nongovernmental forum and to rob it altogether of its innovative diplomatic value.

This said, it must be acknowledged that the principle of nonexclusiveness upheld by those who saw little reason to block Soviet participation is, itself, a political construct: it is just as political to want representatives from one country included as it is to want them excluded. Nevertheless, this principle has helped to overcome the fears and suspicions of various participants, such as those from the ASEAN states, China, and the Soviet Union. Whether its now implicit acceptance will be sufficient to allay conceptual fears similar to those which the drafting of the Vancouver Statement sought to address remains to be seen, given the subsequent adoption of membership criteria, the proclamation of the PECC Charter, and the deferral or rejection of membership applications from Colombia, Papua New Guinea, and Mongolia. Ironically, the theme of PECC IX in September 1992 was 'open regionalism.'

As the PECC process moves forward, the identification of ways in which it has been or can be of use to states will become more significant. For with success will come not only increased government interest and support but also more government attempts to control a diplomatic forum in which they may have made an investment. The institutionalization of the PECC process, which in January 1992 caused the PECC-ISC to change the organzation's name from Pacific Economic Cooperation Conference to Pacific Economic Cooperation Council, will increasingly require states to make a firm commitment of support – a commitment which, while strengthening its foundations, will increase the probability of this INGO collapsing under the weight of state interference. The issue of control versus access gains added prominence, given the observation that, in 1992, seven member committees were coordinated by government offices, while several others were managed by institutions with close government connections.[57] Only by continual vigilance in defence of principles designed to ensure the integrity of a theoretically nonpolitical structure, and by constantly demonstrating the utility of that structure, will such interference be deterred. The maintenance of a suitable balance between state interest and state involvement will therefore prove critical to PECC's future as the central nongovernmental element of the Pacific economic cooperation movement.

Finally, an appreciation of the need for the aforementioned balance between state interest and state involvement will be required if an ongoing academic and bureaucratic attempt, to which the PECC process is similarly vulnerable, is to be overcome – the attempt to make it conform to an existing model of international organization. Despite a summary observation at PECC I, which sought to preempt such attempts, some analysts and enthusiasts continue to characterize the PECC process as part of an effort to form an EC or OECD of the Pacific.[58] In seeking the replication of existing models, they have failed to perceive that PECC is different, and that being different from other nongovernmental and intergovernmental forms of cooperation is its main diplomatic advantage.[59] They have also failed to comprehend that much of the tripartite and consensual PECC process has been aimed at accommodating the pursuit of a risk-aversion approach to diplomacy – an approach in which interstate relations are developed and conducted cautiously and patiently through nongovernmental channels and networks which are relatively inexpensive to support and which require minimal political commitment.[60]

It will be difficult to accommodate all of the economies which presently participate in the PECC process in an official forum in the near term. It is similarly unlikely that the reluctance exhibited by the ASEAN states, and which has thus far forced the industrialized countries of the region to adhere to a primarily informal, consensual approach, will soon dissipate. Pushing for further institutionalization of the PECC process may therefore produce a negative reaction instead of a positive result.

On the other hand, the suggestion that 'to the degree that ministries of foreign affairs get involved in issues of Pacific cooperation, cooperation itself declines' is equally misguided. While one might agree with the concomitant observation that 'much of the cooperation that already exists in the Pacific does so only because it occurs outside official channels,'[61] it does not necessarily follow that state involvement should be proscribed. For, just as proposals for intergovernmental action ignore the diplomatic significance of the nongovernmental activities discussed in this study, warnings against state involvement fail to acknowledge the possibility that mutually beneficial relationships between states and INGOs may develop. Indeed, without the attention and support given to PAFTAD, PBEC, and PECC during the past twenty years by state officials from a wide range of economies countries, the Pacific economic cooperation movement would not have gathered the momentum now apparent in the PECC process. Calls for the transformation of PECC into a Pacific OECD (including a proposal from former Japanese prime minister Nakasone) and the convening of a Pacific Summit to be held under the auspices of PECC (made by Okita) received little support from delegates attending PECC VI in Osaka, although it was agreed that ways of strengthening PECC's institutional structure should be studied and that the report of PECC's Pacific Economic Outlook study group would become the Pacific equivalent of the OECD annual report.[62] As it turned out, the Australian initiative which led to the creation of APEC in 1989 preempted further efforts to raise PECC beyond its nongovernmental status.

The desire to facilitate new standards of global cooperation through regional initiatives has also been understated in attempts to model PECC after existing intergovernmental organizations and warnings against state involvement. At the same time, it must be acknowledged that this two-pronged regional/global pursuit has produced some tension within the process itself and, in 1986, caused former PECC-ISC member, David Sycip, to ask, 'Is regional economic cooperation PECC's goal?':

> Five years after the Canberra conference was convened to consider the Pacific Economic Community Concept it seems odd that the Pacific Economic Cooperation Committee (a product of that conference) has yet to come forth with a goal statement that stresses *regional* economic cooperation. In fact, PECC statements about economic cooperation *non-exclusive* to the Pacific imply that this cooperation, although initiated by Pacific region countries, is meant to be multilateral in a global rather than regional arena.[63]

This query illustrates the tension between those who see participation as a way of eventually achieving global policy coordination and those who seek tangible results which are not dependent upon extraregional players. PECC's 1992 San Francisco Declaration praising 'open regionalism' as a model for global cooperation upholds the preferences of the former group.[64] Should the effort to reform the multilateral trading system at the global level fail, PECC (given its evolving relationship with the intergovernmental APEC) may play a critical part in the development of an Asia-Pacific option. But, as previously expressed in PAFTAD and PBEC deliberations, the closed regional alternative remains a second-best solution.

8

Conclusion:
Asia-Pacific Diplomacy,
INGOs, and Regional Economic
Cooperation

The Pacific Trade and Development Conference, the Pacific Basin Economic Council, and the Pacific Economic Cooperation Council contribute to the regional diplomatic framework in three ways: (1) influencing state action through the provision of constraints and opportunities; (2) making it advantageous for states to pursue symbiotic state/INGO relationships; and (3) performing and/or facilitating the diplomatic functions of representation, information, communication, and, in the case of PECC, negotiation. Drawing upon the example set by the Institute of Pacific Relations, these organizations have earned their status as international actors by attracting state recognition of their roles as unofficial agents of diplomacy. This study has demonstrated that use of the term *nongovernmental*, in this context, remains appropriate. Governments sponsored the inaugural meetings of PAFTAD and PECC and supported the efforts of the Japanese businesspeople who were among the founding members of PBEC, but in each case the decision to launch an ongoing conference series was taken on the basis of an agreement reached between private individuals and institutions, not by their respective governments.

Some aspects of funding and participation do cause PAFTAD, PBEC, and PECC to diverge from the ideal conception of an INGO, which holds that the activities of such organizations should be free of state ties in order to ensure an autonomous decision-making process. However, a desire to participate in public policy development has meant that the groups under study here need to gain the confidence and support of governments. PAFTAD and PECC do not have fee-paying individual members and are therefore forced to seek funding from governments and state agencies. States have also contributed funds to PBEC activities in countries such as Canada and Japan. Similarly, state participation is a feature of all three organizations, albeit in what is astutely described as an unofficial capacity. Government officials have been invited to participate in PAFTAD conferences when the theme has made their presence particularly useful and have attended PBEC meetings as guests and members of national delegations. Moreover, a state presence has become an integral element of the PECC process, thereby strengthening the interaction between academe, the business community, and state apparatuses. Governments in some countries have also begun to appoint members of national PECC committees.

Should state involvement be translated into total state control, an organization's nongovernmental status would be compromised. The evidence examined here suggests that a significant degree of autonomy has been retained. It is acknowledged that a withdrawal of government support would severely limit the scope and import of the cooperation movement; in the case of PECC, operations in some countries might cease altogether. Yet no government has been able either to manipulate PAFTAD, PBEC, or PECC for its own purposes or to achieve foreign policy objectives against the weight of consensus. Even in the most obvious cases of state pressure (e.g., the Chinese government's pronouncement of conditions governing Chinese and Taiwanese membership in PECC and the Japanese bureaucracy's attempt to prevent a Soviet observer from attending PECC V), the state apparatuses applying pressure were forced to recognize the nonofficial, nongovernmental status of the organization in question and to amend their positions accordingly.

As for the typologies introduced in Chapter 2, the INGOs discussed here conform to the functional categories of *forum*, *service organization*, and *pressure group*. The term 'forum' depicts one of the main purposes of each of these INGOs: the provision of opportunities for the discussion, development, and exchange of policy ideas and positions amongst academics, business leaders, and state officials.

Each of these organizations also services the interests of those involved in its activities: of the PAFTAD leadership, many of whom have been involved in the conference series since it began and who have proceeded to establish themselves as leaders of the cooperation movement as a whole; of PBEC's corporate members, who seek to defend the free enterprise system and to ensure the implementation of public policies which favour the expansion of their commercial activities; and of state officials seeking to reap the benefits of unofficial diplomacy via PECC.

PAFTAD, PBEC, and PECC may also be characterized as pressure groups. PBEC's stated intention is to provide advice and counsel to governments, although the pressure applied in the pursuit of improved forms of regional cooperation, communication, and consultation in policy-making has been less significant than has been the pressure exerted by the ideas emanating from PAFTAD. The placement and maintenance on the regional diplomatic agenda of the cooperation theme is directly attributable to the early organizational modelling efforts of PAFTAD enthusiasts such as Kojima, Drysdale, and Patrick and the relationship between Crawford and Okita, which was instrumental in the launching of the PECC process. While PBEC has gained recognition as the voice of the regional business community, its contributions to the cooperation movement have been, and continue to be, plagued by organizational preoccupations and ambivalence, the leadership offered to PECC by individuals such as Trigg notwithstanding. The ideas promoted within PAFTAD, on the other hand, have taken root within the broader context of the PECC process and in official fora such as the ASEAN-Pacific Dialogue, the Cairns Group, and the Asia Pacific Economic Cooperation forum.

PECC is also a pressure group, in as much as its presence and policy discussions have exerted pressure upon states to participate or to risk becoming isolated, to offer support and, thereby, to demonstrate sincerity towards regional affairs, to bow to the weight of an otherwise objectionable consensus, and to consent to or to insist upon the maintenance of a symbiotic relationship between APEC and PECC.

Consequences and Responses

State action may be adjusted in response to five consequences of *transnational* relations involving nongovernmental forces: (1) changes in attitudes; (2) the spread of policy ideas via interactions between national elites; (3) constraints placed on policy-making and implementation by attitude changes and international pluralism; (4) the use of nongovernmental interactions by states in an effort to influence other states; and (5) the emergence of politically significant nonstate and nongovernmental organizations possessing and pursuing their own foreign policies. Each of these consequences has been observed in this study, reaffirming the validity of assessing PAFTAD, PBEC, and PECC as international actors.

First, the regional cooperation theme is now more significant than ever, as is indicated by the increase in state participation in, and support for, PECC and the 1989 establishment of APEC. The 1986 involvement of China and the Soviet Union in PECC presents a particularly revealing example of attitude change. Although reluctant to join following PECC I, Chinese concerns and Soviet disdain were overcome by the desirability of taking part in an increasingly important diplomatic forum. Second, as interest has increased so has the spread of policy ideas and the effort to link discussions within PAFTAD, PBEC, and PECC with other regional and global economic fora.

Third, as the desire and need to be involved in informal yet supplementary multilateral policy discussions has increased, the costs of unilateral policy initiatives has also risen – a feature poignantly illustrated by the Japanese capitulation on the Soviet participation issue within PECC. Constraints upon unilateral state pursuits may also account for the Chinese and Soviet desire to participate in the PECC process. The momentum attained by the regional cooperation movement has gradually made it less viable to remain a bystander, to downplay its significance, or to stand by one's own cooperation scheme. The opportunity to engage in decision-making and nondecision-making, to determine which ideas are examined, and to control the pace at which ideas are pursued is more easily obtained if one is present when these ideas are discussed.

Fourth, attempts by states to influence other states via nongovernmental interactions have long been a prominent feature of the Pacific economic cooperation movement. Japanese foreign ministry support for the activities which led to the founding of PAFTAD, PBEC, and PECC was predicated upon the ability of such interactions to bolster Japan's regional image and economic objectives. The interest in the OPTAD proposal shown by American legislators in the late 1970s, state interaction with the U.S. national PBEC committee, and state support for the PECC process have also been forthcoming for similarly symbolic and functional reasons (e.g., the need to demonstrate America's interest in the region and to keep Pacific countries in a friendly orbit), as has Chinese interest in PECC. In the latter case, the Chinese agreement to participate was, in part, predicated upon China's desire to set the terms governing input from Taiwan.

But the use of an INGO to gain leverage over other states is not an option only available to major powers. For, in agreeing to offer support for, or seeking to participate in, such organizations, lesser powers have perceived certain benefits as well, as is aptly demonstrated by the converse of the Chinese case invoked above (i.e., the attempt by Taiwanese officials to conduct external relations via nongovernmental fora, given the reluctance of many countries to maintain official relations with Taiwan for fear of offending China). Another salient example involves the opportunities provided within each forum to engage representatives from the major powers in debate (as in Australian initiatives aimed at fostering and promoting a Pacific perspective on trade matters) and to affect the pace of that debate (as in the case of participation from within ASEAN). A trade-off is apparent: major, middle, and minor powers alike are seeking to secure diplomatic advantages by participating in nonofficial, nongovernmental fora, in which there is a risk of being overwhelmed by those they seek to influence. Presumably, the informal nature of these organizations means that the implications of being overwhelmed are not seen as making the potential costs of participation greater than the benefits.

The fifth consequence of cross-border nongovernmental activities (i.e., the emergence of INGOs possessing their own foreign policies and the resources to pursue those policies) has also been apparent in this study, particularly in the case of PECC. The establishment of a permanent PAFTAD secretariat indicates that this research network is consolidating its ability to raise and to examine new policy ideas. However, it is questionable whether any unified conception of an organizational foreign policy exists within PAFTAD (aside from a common desire amongst long-standing PAFTAD-ISC members to see the conference series continue to play a role in supplementing national, regional, and global policy deliberations). A private foreign policy is implicit in the statements emanating from PBEC activities concerning the maintenance and enhancement of a favourable commercial environment, but, beyond agreement on this general theme, there are likely to be as many policy preferences on specific issues as there are participating executives and companies. Indeed, disagreements on purpose and direction have helped to rob PBEC of what was supposed to be its greatest political resource: its ability to speak on behalf of the regional business community.

Differences of opinion on policy are also evident within PECC, but there would appear to be at least one private foreign policy position upon which a healthy consensus remains: the value of maintaining PECC as a nongovernmental forum and, thereby, retaining a nongovernmental approach to regional cooperation. Calls for PECC to be transformed into a Pacific version of the OECD have so far been resisted, and PECC's greatest political resource in mounting a defence continues to be its nongovernmental status and diplomatic value. The former has been challenged by attempts to further institutionalize PECC, and the latter has been challenged by the creation, in November 1989, of APEC, an intergovernmental focal point. Just as PBEC's decline might be partly attributable to the Council's having outlived its usefulness as a forum in which businesspeople from around the region can meet each other, so, too, might the PECC process lose favour if the states supporting it perceived diminishing returns from their investment or the possibility of a better return via a forum in which governments play an even greater role. The agreement between APEC and PECC participants to foster a symbiotic relationship between the two organizations suggests that states involved in APEC do see value in retaining rather than abandoning PECC.

This observation is relevant to an assessment of the ways states have responded to the consequences of these nongovernmental activities. One case of unilateral defensive action against domestic activities has been noted. This occurred indirectly during the dispute over Soviet participation at PECC V, when the Japanese foreign ministry attempted to reverse the position evidently taken by Okita at the August 1986 San Francisco meeting of the PECC-ISC. One of the reasons given for the Gaimusho's reluctance was the fear that a Soviet observer would have to be admitted to the subsequent Osaka conference as well – a matter in which the Japanese national committee was to have the final say. The efforts of the Gaimusho fell victim to the weight of consensus; representatives of other countries vehemently defended the principle of nonexclusiveness, and the Japanese were forced either to back down or to risk damaging the by then central component of a regional cooperation movement from which they had derived diplomatic benefits.

Unless the aforementioned Japanese action is interpreted as having been aimed at influencing a decision to be taken in another country (i.e., the Canadian national committee's decision on the Soviet application for observer status), no cases of defensive actions being projected extraterritorially have been detected. Nor have any instances of cooperative defensive reactions to nongovernmental activities been observed, with the possible exception of the collective reluctance of the ASEAN states to support national participation in PBEC and early PECC activities. A collective state response may be forthcoming if elements within the PECC leadership are perceived as being overly protective of the organization's nongovernmental status or as acting like selfish political entrepreneurs trying to defend their personal stake (i.e., the time and energy they have invested) in a process which may have outlived its usefulness from the state viewpoint. Though now, in some cases, appointed to national PECC committees by governments, persons who have been associated with the cooperation movement since or prior to 1980 remain influential because of their contacts and experience. The continuity which has been so important to the pursuit of regional cooperation over the past two decades would be lost if these leaders were removed by government decree. Thus, long-standing Pacific enthusiasts continue to hold somewhat protected positions within PECC. Even so, should they be judged to be obstructing the objectives of several states, these positions of power could be usurped by the creation of an IGO. It is possible that the creation of APEC represents this form of collective defensive response by states.

Attempts by individual states or groups thereof to coopt an INGO or to derive benefit from an INGO with blatant disregard for the well-being of the INGO itself are often similar to defensive reactions. In seeking to coopt an INGO, a state may be attempting to defend its role as a primary unit of international relations. Unless the APEC-PECC arrangement is viewed in this way, the only evidence of a cooptation attempt involving a component of the Pacific economic cooperation movement appears in the Japanese bureaucracy's objections to a Soviet presence at PECC V. In the end, concern about the possibility of these objections causing the collapse of the PECC process loomed larger for the Japanese than did the Soviet threat.

By far the most frequently detected type of state response to the activities of PAFTAD, PBEC, and PECC has been the pursuit of a symbiotic relationship. Although Foreign Minister Miki's support of Kojima's PAFTA idea and the forum which eventually became PAFTAD could be interpreted as part of a cooptation effort, the ongoing funding of PAFTAD by the Gaimusho would suggest that a mutually beneficial relationship has been fostered. The same could be said of the support offered by other governments through state agencies and research institutions. A symbiotic relationship is also evident in countries where PBEC delegates are briefed by, report to, and advise officials of their respective governments, where governments have agreed to let state officials participate in PECC and/or supported the establishment and operation of a national PECC committee, and where the leaders of PECC and APEC have agreed that their organizations should complement one another.

The prevalence of symbiotic relationships tends to confirm Keohane and Nye's observation that, in the interdependent world of the late twentieth century, the use of multiple diplomatic channels (official and unofficial) is a prominent feature of international relations. The exploration of new ideas from as many perspectives as possible and efforts to place these ideas on the international agenda via informal discussions aimed at facilitating the formation of a coalition of policy elites characterize what has been termed complex interdependence. This is especially evident in cases in which middle and minor powers have adopted a strength-in-numbers strategy aimed at overcoming the asymmetry inherent in interdependent relationships with major powers, such as the U.S. and Japan, by engaging them in multiple multilateral examinations of policy. If interested parties can be engaged in a constructive dialogue via PAFTAD and PECC, then the dangers posed by the lingering unease which exists between major military and economic superpowers of the region may, from the perspective of the middle powers, minor powers, and nongovernmental actors, be positively defused as well. The proponents of APEC appear to have heeded this logic in their decision to work with, rather than without, PECC.

Diplomatic Contributions

The use of nongovernmental diplomatic channels illustrates another primary theme of this study: the inadequacy of the traditional conception of a diplomatic agent as an officially accredited state representative. One way of demonstrating the shortcomings of a narrow conception is to assess potential diplomatic agents by their performance of diplomatic tasks such as representation, information, communication, and negotiation. The suggestion that classifications of diplomatic agents should be expanded to include actors other than those officially designated by states builds on the observation that much of what is considered traditional diplomatic practice was originally inspired by a desire to extend trade links. Merchants and traders have long played diplomatic roles – roles which have been accentuated in the twentieth century as economic and trade policies have reasserted themselves as essential elements of foreign policy.

Regional and global economic interdependence, the complexity of policy issues, and rapid technological improvements in communication have also brought to the fore the diplomatic utility of nongovernmental academic experts as participants in scholarly fora and interstate conferences. The state may remain the prime unit of analysis in the study of international relations, but the complexity of the world it now confronts has made the use of unofficial agents an important aspect of late twentieth-century diplomacy. The traditional conception of diplomacy is, itself, the product of an era in which the scope of diplomatic interaction was redefined to suit the needs of a changing state system. The contemporary use of nongovernmental actors today reflects yet another process of adaptation – a process in which the pursuit of diplomatic objectives through as many channels as possible is desirable for major, middle, and minor powers. In the Asia-Pacific region, this pursuit will often require an informal, consensus-seeking approach to international interactions in order to facilitate the accommodation of contending cultural traits and values. Just as the rise of Japan as an economic superpower and the emergence of ASEAN and China have challenged American hegemony in the Pacific, so, too, are such forces precipitating a change in the way bilateral, regional, and global diplomacy is conducted.

Amidst the social diversity of the region lies a common interest in the development of economic relations. Accordingly, it is not surprising to find economists and businesspeople examining and promoting the idea of Pacific economic cooperation. It is even less surprising that INGOs should play leading roles in these deliberations. Official diplomatic channels (many of which have only a short history and are tainted by suspicion and/or unfamiliarity) tend to be rigid, understandably exhibiting caution and abiding by accepted rules of protocol. The flexibility of nongovernmental networking thus becomes attractive to anyone seeking to address new ideas in a milieu consisting of a wide variety of cultures, historical experiences, languages, economies, and political systems. A nongovernmental approach may also be adopted by states as part of a risk-aversion strategy. When one needs to interact with persons who are unfamiliar, or with the representatives of countries which have in the past been fickle or unfriendly, ways of reducing risk are desirable. Enter the INGO as a diplomatic actor.

The IPR, as one of the first INGOs engaged in the promotion of regional cooperation, may be conceived as a precursor. When one pauses to compare the IPR with PAFTAD, PBEC, and PECC, it becomes evident that the Institute provided a useful and proven model of a nongovernmental yet diplomatic forum, bringing together policy-relevant *constituencies* or groups of persons without whose support cooperative policies would have had less chance of success. Participants usually attended IPR conferences as members of multipartite national delegations made up of active and retired state officials, academics, businesspeople, labour leaders, journalists, and philanthropists. Cognizant of the Institute's once-revered research efforts, the Japanese proponents of what has become PAFTAD set about reconstituting a regional academic constituency. Although somewhat narrower than the research constituency within the IPR (given that PAFTAD is dominated by economists), the PAFTAD constituency has embraced other societal sectors via PECC and has established for itself a role within the regional cooperation movement which is as prominent as that previously maintained by academic participants in the IPR.

The SRI's interest in PBEC was also inspired by the IPR model and the involvement in the IPR of Stanford University academics such as Eliot Mears. SRI's ties with the North American and Southeast Asian business communities played a significant role in the early development of PBEC and complemented the Japanese and Australian efforts to establish a regional business association.

In the case of PECC, recent moves to augment its tripartite format by including legislators, labour leaders, and media representatives on national committees have brought it even closer to the IPR model of multipartite participation. However, it should be noted that there is no reluctance on the part of PECC to stress its policy-oriented objectives – something the IPR leadership took pains to disavow prior to the Institute's conferences during the Second World War.

The explicit policy-oriented approach inherent in the PECC process might also explain the lack of a permanent PECC secretariat prior to 1990 – a structural omission which effectively preempted claims that control was being exercised by one country, group, or ideology and may, therefore, have alleviated possible government reluctance to support the PECC process. Though a permanent secretariat has now been created in Singapore, participants should pay heed to the IPR experience (in which the secretariat eventually became the prime target of the anti-communist witch-hunt that precipitated the organization's downfall) and the reasons underlying the recent upheaval in PBEC's secretarial arrangements. One should at the same time be cautious about using the successful launch of a PAFTAD secretariat as a precedent to justify a PECC central office, remembering that PAFTAD does not possess the network of formal national committees which characterizes the PECC process. Fears of undue influence being exerted by a central secretariat and the vagaries of the intraorganizational politics which may ensue would, therefore, have been much less of a consideration in the PAFTAD case than they would in the PECC case, as national committees learn to deal with a similar office. Accordingly, the PECC leadership may have been wise to defer calls for central coordination until the outset of the organization's second decade, thereby preventing internal and external detractors from being given an opportunity to attack the activities of a permanent secretariat. Certainly, the new Singapore secretariat will be observed with interest.

Although the suggestion that the IPR contributed to the regional diplomatic framework would have been denied by the Institute's leadership, many participants and observers were cognizant of its performance and of its facilitation of at least three diplomatic functions: representation, information, and communication. The misgivings expressed by Chinese and Japanese delegations in the 1930s, the public status of individual delegates from all participating countries, the maintenance of a well-respected research program, the interaction between some national delegations and foreign offices, the decision to include active state officials in wartime conferences, and the tenor of the discussions at those conferences illustrate some of the major reasons for the perception that the diplomatic functions of representation, information, and communication were being served by the Institute in a way which brought it very close to the facilitation of interstate negotiations.

PAFTAD's contributions to regional diplomacy are derived from this forum's performance of the same set of diplomatic functions which were evident in the case of the IPR. First, the participation of leading economists and policy advisors from developing and developed countries and from capitalist and centralized economies has facilitated PAFTAD's representative qualities. Second, from the perspective of policy-makers, the research findings on carefully selected topics are often timely. Third, the PAFTAD research program frequently leads to the development of a better understanding of different analytical approaches, and, in some cases, agreed definitions and conceptual frameworks are derived. This feature has been complemented by the development of an extensive network of researchers and institutions, which serves to ensure that channels of communication are widespread, well-placed, and in keeping with the organization's efforts to influence attitudes towards regional economic affairs. The diplomatic value attached to these activities by other international actors can be seen in the ongoing financial support from the Japanese government, other state agencies in the region, intergovernmental organizations, and private foundations. The establishment of an international secretariat at the ANU in 1984 highlights the increasingly important role

PAFTAD plays in maintaining the intellectual foundations of the Pacific economic cooperation movement.

The diplomatic functions performed by PBEC and its members are similarly threefold. National delegations to the annual general meetings are often expected to represent not only the interests of individual participants and the local business community but also those of their respective governments. It is by facilitating the explanation and discussion of commercial conditions and government policy positions that the Council serves the function of communication. Added significance is imparted by the absence or tenuous nature of formal diplomatic relations between some countries represented in PBEC. Council members also serve as conduits for communication by reporting to their governments on the mood and substance of conference deliberations in return for pre-conference briefings from senior bureaucrats.

PBEC's diplomatic qualities and the appearance of a healthy business-government relationship are promoted by the inclusion of state officials as members of national delegations to annual meetings and the addresses made by government leaders, foreign ministers, and other senior officials. However, PBEC executives have recently been forced to reaffirm their quest for effective communication between business and government by arranging meetings with politicians. In addition, an effort has been made to improve the Council's profile within the countries of ASEAN – a profile long hampered by organizational divisions and PBEC's image as a rich man's club.

PECC's ability to facilitate negotiation provides the initial and most important distinction between its diplomatic contributions and those made by the IPR, PAFTAD, and PBEC. Arising from a decision taken in preparation for the Canberra Seminar (and which sought to include state officials as full participants), this ability has been augmented by the adoption of a consensual approach to decision-making. Accordingly, negotiations and compromises involving state officials as well as academics and businesspeople are often required.

The organization of delegations on the basis of nationality and sectoral affiliation enhances PECC's facilitation of diplomatic representation. The research, discussion, and debate taking place under the auspices of this organization (e.g., the filtering of policy ideas, the identification of areas for possible intergovernmental action, and the setting of priorities for further deliberation and study) conform to the tasks of information and communication – a feature which is particularly noticeable in the effort to use PECC deliberations on trade policy as a direct supplement to GATT proceedings. The signing of the Vancouver Statement on Pacific Economic Cooperation at PECC V (an act which committed the signatories to supporting a set of operating principles) also provides an illustration of diplomacy being conducted via an INGO, as do the events surrounding, and precedents set by, Chinese, Taiwanese, and Soviet involvement.

The factors which have allowed these organizations to perform diplomatic tasks and the reasons for success or failure of such activities may be assessed by utilizing the criteria derived from the work of Berman and Johnson introduced in Chapter 2. The first three requirements for the success of unofficial diplomacy (acknowledged expertise, the participation of prominent societal figures, and the possession of politically significant contacts) are characteristics shared by each nongovernmental component of today's regional cooperation movement. Yet, the fourth element of success, a clear statement of intent, is not apparent in the case of PAFTAD. While this lack does not appear to have seriously hampered PAFTAD's progress, the adoption of the Vancouver Statement, and its subsequent inclusion in the PECC Charter, has allowed the PECC leadership to refer to a written set of guidelines whenever the objectives and organization of the PECC process come under scrutiny, thereby removing some of the conceptual difficulties which have plagued attempts to secure state support. On the other hand, PBEC's possession of a statement of intent since its founding does not seem to have prevented disagreements about the Council's purpose, suggesting that, if an INGO is to make a lasting contribution to diplomacy, then, in addition to being clear, an organizational statement of principles must also be meaningful and unambiguous. As a result, given the subsequent decision requiring unanimous consent for the admission of new members, it is to be expected that the omission of a reference to the principle of nonexclusiveness in the Vancouver Statement, and the claim that this principle has been accepted implicitly, may continue to be a source of difficulty for the PECC process.

As for the ability to offer privacy and confidentiality, each of the INGOs under study prides itself on maintaining an informal or unofficial setting for policy discussions. The publication of conference papers and proceedings is an important part of each forum's activities, but a large amount of interaction takes place away from the conference floor. Media attention has been sought by PAFTAD, PBEC, and PECC in order to garner public support, and a major objective of each body is the dissemination of policy ideas. Operating under strictly private or confidential guidelines would not further this goal. However, for the purposes of facilitating a free and wide-ranging exchange of views and the formation of a broad consensus on policy matters, informality remains an important attribute of INGOs.

Perhaps the most revealing criteria governing the success or failure of the unofficial diplomacy undertaken within the regional cooperation movement are those which pertain to an INGO's ability to deliver a constituency of supporters and to create an environment in which competing approaches and attitudes to policy matters can be reconciled. PAFTAD has successfully delivered a constituency of economists, while PECC, designed to ensure that academics and businesspeople were able to engage state officials in the discussion of economic policies, has gradually managed to broaden the interest and support of these constituencies. These INGOs have succeeded in engaging participants from a wide range of nations and cultures in policy discussions, thereby illustrating an ability to accommodate competing viewpoints. PBEC, on the other hand, has had difficulty attracting members from developing countries and is competing with bilateral business committees for the support of companies based in industrialized countries. These difficulties have, consequently, impeded the Council's ability to deliver the constituency it seeks to represent and have demonstrated PBEC's failure to accommodate competing perspectives on the role of the business community in national and regional development.

The qualities of dedication, sophistication, and perseverance stipulated by Berman and Johnson are obvious in the efforts of PAFTAD leaders, some of whom have been actively promoting the concept of regional economic cooperation for almost three decades and who continue to be prime movers within the PECC process. PBEC's interest in the cooperation concept prior to 1979 was muted by organizational preoccupations, and even recent corporate involvement in the cooperation movement is reminiscent of a disinterested or, at best, ambivalent business sector when compared with the high degree of academic input.

Although participants in the Pacific economic cooperation movement seek to improve regional economic policy-making, this general goal must be seen as part of each participant's own set of objectives. Many different reasons have led people to take up the cooperation theme. Nevertheless, the nongovernmental fora discussed here provide participants with an opportunity to influence the regional diplomatic framework and with a means to achieve their collective and individual objectives.

Has cooperation improved as a result of such activities? This question can be answered in the affirmative, although the contributions made by PBEC have been plagued by organizational problems and the uncertainty about the Council's regional role which these preoccupations have imparted. This said, some business leaders have joined with academics and state officials in PECC. Building upon the groundwork laid by PAFTAD and PBEC, the PECC process has been able to engage elites from developed, developing, market-oriented, and centralized economies in policy deliberations. It has also been able to act as a catalyst or supplement for regional intergovernmental mechanisms.

These concrete diplomatic achievements have not been gleaned from lists of successfully launched and completed development projects. Rather, the achievements arise from an assessment of efforts to encourage elite interaction on policy issues. It is through the INGO promotion of such contact that cooperation, communication, and consultation have been enhanced. PECC's Vancouver Statement serves as a symbol of progress. The signing of an informal, nonbinding agreement may not, at first glance, appear to have been a momentous event in the history of international affairs, but it does represent a major advance in the development of diplomatic relations in such an economically, politically, and culturally diverse region. The Vancouver Statement might also be viewed as a necessary step en route to the intergovernmental agreement which established APEC.

The Future
If one was asked to rank the INGOs within today's Pacific economic cooperation movement by the relative effectiveness of their diplomatic contributions, the assessments presented in this study would tend to require the following response (in descending order): (1) PECC, (2) PAFTAD, and (3) PBEC. What is instructive about this order is that the organizations at either extreme are in danger of losing their ability to make such contributions. Whereas the development of an extensive research network, efforts to regularize funding from state and private sources, and the establishment of a permanent secretariat have enabled PAFTAD to consolidate its ability to act as the research wing of the Pacific economic cooperation movement, PBEC and PECC have had their diplomatic capabilities challenged – one as a result of organizational shortcomings and the other as a result of organizational successes.

In the case of PBEC, the presence of a challenge is not surprising. Any diplomatic utility the Council might once have been able to claim has been rapidly dissipating because of a divisive internal debate about purpose, structure, and direction, because of the stigma of its rich man's club reputation, and because of an ambiguous organizational attitude towards the regional cooperation. Therefore, as PBEC's decline continues, businesspeople genuinely interested in regionalism should be encouraged to participate in the activities of national PECC committees instead.

However, whereas PBEC is increasingly ascribed limited diplomatic significance by state officials because of organizational difficulties, the positive momentum gained by PECC may also cause this innovative nongovernmental process to lose its ability to contribute to diplomacy. The rise and fall of the IPR reveals this lesson only too well by illustrating how a successful INGO can become a target or scapegoat for elements within a state apparatus. The main threat today is posed by calls to transform the PECC process into an IGO. Inspired by earlier academic attempts to apply existing models of state-led international cooperation, these calls exhibit both a bureaucratic penchant for creating bureaucracies and a governmental penchant for governing. As state interest and involvement in PECC has increased, so has the expectation that state control will eventually follow, the underlying assumption being that cooperation will be improved by the creation of an intergovernmental institution. For the time being, the establishment of APEC and the decision within that forum to build upon existing nongovernmental bodies appears to have saved PECC from the potential destruction of a nongovernmental to governmental transformation.

The task facing PAFTAD, PBEC, and PECC is thus the task confronting any INGO seeking to contribute to the conduct of diplomacy: the need to attract and to maintain state interest, state support, and state involvement, while at the same time discouraging state control and interference. At stake is each INGO's status as an international actor. The IPR's experience should not be forgotten. For each of the nongovernmental components of today's Pacific economic cooperation movement, the best way of defending this status amidst the debate over, and evolution of, intergovernmental mechanisms will be by continually demonstrating and drawing attention to the utility of a nongovernmental approach to regional diplomacy. PAFTAD and PECC remain in a position to meet this challenge; PBEC's capacity to do so is in serious doubt.

While these INGOs have precipitated the establishment of intergovernmental fora, it is important to note that the intergovernmental and nongovernmental options are not mutually exclusive. The APD and APEC have benefited from, and now parallel the activities of, PAFTAD, PBEC, and PECC. Furthermore, with the prospect of irreparable politicization, insurmountable political obstacles, and/or competing political agendas looming large within and between regional and subregional intergovernmental bodies, the value of the nongovernmental approach to Asia-Pacific diplomacy outlined above has risen further. Accordingly, even if governments continue to interact directly via the APD, APEC, or another official mechanism, they would be ill-advised to abandon the nongovernmental route already travelled, lest it whither away, leaving them stranded should the intergovernmental path become impassable.

Appendixes

Appendix A

PAFTAD: Guidelines on Conference Organization[1]
On 28-29 August 1985 the International Steering Committee met in Tokyo to consider a set of guidelines drafted by the International Secretariat for the organisation of future PAFTAD Conferences. The following were some of the matters raised by members.

Final responsibility for organising Conferences lies with each Host Organising Committee, with the International Steering Committee acting on occasion in an advisory capacity. The issuing of invitations to persons to participate in Conferences is the responsibility of each Host Organising Committee, but the International Steering Committee, welcomes in principle, participation from any country in the Pacific region, and by people from countries which have never or only infrequently supplied participants. In June 1985 two of the consortium funding bodies, the Ford Foundation and Rockefeller Brothers Fund, had themselves indicated a preference for the broadest possible regional participation, including some from Vietnam when that becomes appropriate.

Papers submitted by Conference participants are being more rigorously edited under new arrangements to have the volume arising out of each Conference published commercially, the volume no longer being a simple reproduction of Conference proceedings. Accordingly, the publication of all papers is no longer automatic but depends upon the writer's acceptance, when necessary, of editorial guidance.

In future, the number of papers formally presented at Conferences will be reduced to allow more time for discussion. Some additional papers might be commissioned but not formally presented, or alternatively, paper-writers might talk on their papers for five minutes and dispense with a formal presentation altogether. This system, however, will depend on sound organisation in getting Conference papers printed and circulated to participants in advance to allow adequate time for reading. In this context, the retention of a reading day prior to each Conference is regarded as very important.

The Host Organising Committee is to consider in advance whether a communique is to be issued at the conclusion of Conferences so that a drafting committee can be set up beforehand. International Steering Committee members for their part have the responsibility of publicising the results of each Conference, particularly to policy makers, and are to make use of material provided by the International Secretariat for this purpose.

Appendix B

PBEC Covenant (excerpt)[2]

Preamble
We, the Member Committees of the Pacific Basin Economic Council (PBEC), recognizing the importance of the Pacific Basin in the world economy, and realizing the need for business enterprises to cooperate with each other and with governments and international agencies in the overall development of the Pacific Basin and in improvement of the people's livelihood as well as in promoting peace and prosperity, join in constituting the Council as a unique international institution. We take this action to encourage further cooperation among business communities of the Pacific Basin, thereby strengthening economic ties and contributing to economic and social advancement in the Pacific Region.

The Member Committees of PBEC recognize the growing community of interest among business people within and bordering the Pacific Ocean as well as their individual and collective relationships with countries in other parts of the world. Thus, while dedicated primarily to regional objectives, PBEC assumes a worldwide perspective in its deliberations and activities.

Article I: Purpose
(a) PBEC will engage in consultations and an exchange of views on a multilateral basis among business people in the Pacific Basin and elsewhere. Its principal objectives are to:

- Strengthen the business enterprise system
- Improve business environments
- Generate new business opportunities and relationships
- Increase international trade and investment.

These particular objectives will be pursued within a broad purpose aimed at actively fostering mutually beneficial economic cooperation and social progress throughout the Pacific Region.

(b) The unique role of PBEC will be implemented by providing an international forum for participating executives and by maintaining close liaison with governments and international agencies.

(c) The international consultations within PBEC will be focused on the objectives in (a) above, but also will include a wide spectrum of related subjects as may be selected from time to time in response to interests of its Members.

(d) Each Member Committee within PBEC ... will engage in such implementing activities as it may consider appropriate within guidelines adopted by the international PBEC organization.

Appendix C

Vancouver Statement on Pacific Economic Cooperation (excerpts)[3]

Preamble

Participants in the Pacific Economic Cooperation Conference (PECC) from business and industry, government, academic and other intellectual circles, believe that realization of the full potential of the Pacific Basin depends on enhanced economic cooperation based on free and open economic exchanges and in a spirit of partnership, fairness and mutual respect.

We are mindful of the shared interest in promoting economic cooperation among the economies in the region to bring about greater economic and social benefits and well-being for our respective peoples and contribute to the stability, prosperity and progress of the entire region.

Participation in the PECC process will depend upon a commitment to economic cooperation in the Pacific. PECC participants, who have extensive economic activities in the Pacific, will seek to achieve increased regional economic cooperation and interaction, while recognizing both the realities of and the benefits accruing from global inter-dependence and continuing to encourage increased economic cooperation and interaction with other nations and regions ...

Premises

The PECC process is based on the following premises:

(1) The respective strengths of business and industry, government, academic and other intellectual circles can be better focussed to promote the acceleration of economic growth, social progress and scientific and technological development in the region.

(2) Trade, joint ventures, mutual aid and other forms of linkage, when developed in a spirit of partnership, fairness, respect and genuine cooperation, strengthen the foundation needed for a prosperous, progressive and peaceful Pacific region.

(3) Promotion of active collaboration on matters of common interest in economic, social, scientific, technological and management fields will contribute significantly to the realization of the Pacific's economic potential.

(4) Human resources development through the provision of training and research assistance by Pacific countries to their regional neighbours is especially significant in enhancing development.

(5) Increased cooperation in trade and development of natural resources (agriculture, fisheries, minerals and energy), industrial adjustment, expansion of free and open trade and investment, and the improvement of transportation and communication capabilities, will contribute to raising the standard of living throughout the Pacific Region.

(6) Development of the Pacific Region cannot take place in isolation from the rest of the world economy and should be consistent with the objectives of improving global growth and trade performance. The PECC should liaise with other international and regional organizations having complementary aims and purposes and ensure that duplication of activity is avoided.

Structure

The structure of the PECC has developed several unique features:

– It is **tripartite**, with representatives from business and industry, government, academic and other intellectual circles all participating in their private capacities.

– It is **consultative, consensus-seeking and policy oriented.**

– It is **pragmatic**, responding to problems as they develop, and
– It is **anticipatory**, looking to emergent issues and events ...

Activities
(1) Examination of key problems and issues influencing regional economic growth.
(2) Provision of opportunities for identifying regional interests and consensus.
(3) Stimulation of efforts to solve common problems through regional cooperation, reduce economic tensions and encourage new actions and creative development among Pacific nations.
(4) Development, dissemination and sharing of materials and analyses to encourage greater Pacific economic cooperation and demonstrate how regional economic potential can be realized.
(5) Promotion of a Pacific voice in other multilateral organizations.
(6) Promotion of greater awareness and understanding of the increasing interdependence of the Pacific economies.

Notes

Chapter 1: The Pacific Economic Cooperation Movement

1 See, for example, James W. Morley, ed., *The Pacific Basin: New Challenges for the United States* (New York: Academy of Political Science 1986); Peter Drysdale, 'Building the Foundations of a Pacific Economic Community,' in Toshio Shishido and Ryuzo Sato, eds., *Economic Policy and Development: New Perspectives* (Dover, MA: Auburn House 1985), 46-58; Staffan Burenstam Linder, *The Pacific Century: Economic and Political Consequences of Asian-Pacific Dynamism* (Stanford, CA: Stanford University Press 1986), 1-20; David Aikman, *Pacific Rim: Area of Change, Area of Opportunity* (Toronto: Little, Brown and Company 1986); Endel-Jacob Kolde, *The Pacific Quest: The Concept and Scope of an Oceanic Community* (Toronto: Lexington Books/D.C. Heath 1976); E. Gough Whitlam, *A Pacific Community* (Cambridge, MA: Harvard University Press 1981); and Hadi Soesastro and Han Sung-Joo, eds., *Pacific Economic Cooperation: The Next Phase* (Jakarta: Centre for Strategic and International Studies 1983), 91-103. Less sanguine conclusions are reached by Christopher Coker, 'The Myth or Reality of the Pacific Century,' *Washington Quarterly* 11 (Summer 1988):5-16 and Chung-in Moon, 'Conclusion: A Dissenting View on the Pacific Future,' in Stephen Haggard and Chung-in Moon, eds., *Pacific Dynamics: The International Politics of Industrial Change* (Boulder, CO: Westview 1989), 359-74.

   The terms Pacific, Pacific Basin, Pacific Rim, Pacific Asia, Asia-Pacific, and Asian Pacific are understood to refer to a region encompassing those countries which border upon, or lie within, the Pacific Ocean. It is acknowledged that some authors apply a narrower or broader definition.

2 Masahide Shibusawa, Zakaria Haji Ahmad, and Brian Bridges, *Pacific Asia in the 1990s* (London: Routledge 1992); Alan Bollard and David Mayes, 'Regionalism and the Pacific Rim,' *Journal of Common Market Studies* 30 (June 1992):195-209; Cal Clark and Steve Chan, eds., *The Evolving Pacific Basin in the Global Political Economy: Domestic and International Linkages* (Boulder, CO: Lynne Rienner 1992); Gérard Hervouet, ed., *Asie-Pacifique: Les Nouveaux Espaces de Coopération et de Conflits* (Sainte-Foy: Les Presses de l'Université Laval 1991); Steve Chan, *East Asian Dynamism: Growth, Order, and Security in the Pacific Region* (Boulder, CO: Westview 1991); H. Edward English, *Tomor-*

row *the Pacific* (Toronto: C.D. Howe Institute 1991); Norman D. Palmer, *The New Regionalism in Asia and the Pacific* (Lexington, MA: Lexington 1991); Reinhold Drifte, *Japan's Foreign Policy* (New York: Council on Foreign Relations Press 1990), 92-102; Peter Drysdale, *International Economic Pluralism: Economic Policy in East Asia and the Pacific* (New York: Columbia University Press 1988); Martin H. Sours, 'Transpacific Interdependencies,' in Gavin Boyd, ed., *Region Building in the Pacific* (New York: Pergamon 1982), 103-42; United States, Joint Economic Committee, Congress of the United States, ed., *Pacific Region Interdependencies: A Compendium of Papers* (Washington: U.S. Government Printing Office 1981); *Asia-Pacific in the 1980s: Toward Greater Symmetry in Economic Interdependence* (Jakarta: Centre for Strategic and International Studies 1980); and Lawrence B. Krause and Sueo Sekiguchi, eds., *Economic Interaction in the Pacific Basin* (Washington: Brookings Institution 1980). The term *interdependence* is understood here to mean a circumstance in which the actions of one party have an impact upon the other parties in the same system or region and vice-versa, although this mutual dependence is not necessarily symmetrical, in as much as each party may display a varying degree of *sensitivity* and *vulnerability*. See Robert O. Keohane and Joseph S. Nye, *Power and Interdependence: World Politics in Transition* (Toronto: Little, Brown 1977), 8-19 and Robert O. Keohane and Joseph S. Nye, Jr., 'Power and Interdependence Revisited,' *International Organization* 41 (Autumn 1987):725-53. For analyses which dispute claims of increasing economic interdependence in the Pacific Basin or the need to address such interdependence on a regional basis, see R.T. Robertson, 'From Community to Cooperation to Self-Reliance: Death of the Pacific Basin Concept,' *Journal of International Relations* (Japan), no. 17 (July 1986):66-80; J.K. Johansson and Robert K. Spich, 'Trade Interdependencies in the Pacific Rim Basin and the E.C.: A Comparative Analysis,' *Journal of Common Market Studies* 20 (September 1981):41-59; and Alfred Reifman, 'An Asian-Pacific Regional Economic Organisation: A Skeptical View,' in John Crawford and Greg Seow, eds., *Pacific Economic Co-operation: Suggestions for Action* (Selangor: Heinemann Educational 1981), 205-6.

3 M. Mark Earle, Jr. and Eric A. Trigg, 'Pacific Economic Cooperation and an Overview of the Canberra Process,' *PBEC Papers, 1985*, 1. See also Crawford and Seow, eds., *Pacific Economic Co-operation*, 28. This conception of cooperation is similar to that posited by Arnold Wolfers, *Discord and Collaboration: Essays on International Politics* (Baltimore: Johns Hopkins Press 1971), 27. The logic of cooperation in international affairs is reviewed in Bruce M. Russett and John D. Sullivan, 'Collective Goods and International Organization,' and Mancur Olson, 'Increasing the Incentives for International Cooperation,' *International Organization* 25 (Autumn 1971):845-65 and 866-74, respectively.

4 See Donald Crone, 'The Politics of Emerging Pacific Cooperation,' *Pacific Affairs* 65 (Spring 1992):68-9; Grant Battersby, 'APEC Moves Another Step,' *Insight* (Department of Foreign Affairs and Trade, Australia) 1 (24 July 1992):4-5; Australia, Department of Foreign Affairs and Trade, 'APEC Ministers Meet in Bangkok,' *Insight* 1 (21 September 1992):3; Australia, Depart-

ment of Foreign Affairs and Trade, 'APEC Comes of Age,' *Backgrounder* 2 (8 December 1991):1-7; Andrew Elek, 'The Challenge of Asia-Pacific Economic Cooperation,' *Pacific Review* 4 (1991):322-32; Andrew Elek, 'The Evolution of Asia Pacific Economic Cooperation,' *Backgrounder* (Department of Foreign Affairs and Trade, Australia) 1 (15 June 1990):4-8; James Cotton, 'APEC: Australia Hosts Another Pacific Acronym,' *Pacific Review* 3 (1990):171-3; Richard A. Higgott, Andrew Fenton Cooper, and Jenelle Bonnor, 'Asia-Pacific Economic Cooperation: An Evolving Case-Study in Leadership and Co-operation Building,' *International Journal* 45 (Autumn 1990):823-66; and English, *Tomorrow the Pacific*, 13-21.

5 Lyman Cromwell White, *International Non-Governmental Organizations: Their Purposes, Methods, and Accomplishments* (New Brunswick, NJ: Rutgers University Press 1951), 3. For surveys of intergovernmental and nongovernmental cooperative arrangements in the Pacific region, see Evelyn Colbert, 'Regional Cooperation and the Tilt to the West,' in Morley, *The Pacific Basin*, 46-57; Richard L. Sneider and Mark Borthwick, 'Institutions for Pacific Cooperation,' *Asian Survey* 23 (December 1983):1,246-9; Paul F. Hooper, 'Pacific Regional Organizations,' in Paul F. Hooper, ed., *Building a Pacific Community* (Honolulu: East-West Center 1982), 139-54; and George S. Kanahele and Michael Haas, 'Prospects for a Pacific Community,' *Pacific Community*, no. 6 (October 1974):83-93.

6 Richard M. Fairbanks III, 'Networking in the Pacific: Private Actions with a Public Purpose,' *Speaking of Japan* 7 (November 1986):30.

7 Crone, 'The Politics of Emerging Pacific Cooperation,' 69-71; Drysdale, *International Economic Pluralism*, 209-22; David Arase, 'Pacific Economic Cooperation: Problems and Prospects,' *Pacific Review* 1 (1988):128-44; Linder, *The Pacific Century*, 114-15; Palitha T.B. Kohona, 'The Evolving Concept of a Pacific Basin Community,' *Asian Survey* 26 (April 1986):399-400; Michael West Osborne and Nicolas Fourt, *Pacific Basin Economic Cooperation* (Paris: Development Centre, Organization for Economic Cooperation and Development 1983), 8-9; Han Sung-Joo, 'The Pacific Cooperation Concept: Scope and Limitations,' *Korea and World Affairs* 7 (Summer 1983):189-90; Estrella D. Solidum, 'The Pacific Community in Search of a Form,' *Asian Perspective* 9 (Fall/Winter 1985):184-219; and Hadi Soesastro, 'Institutional Aspects of Pacific Economic Cooperation,' in Soesastro and Sung-Joo, eds., *Pacific Economic Cooperation: The Next Phase*, 3-52.

8 The term *movement* is used here in a collective sense and refers to 'organizations which carry ideas across borders.' See W.J.M. Mackenzie, *Politics and Social Science* (Harmondsworth, UK: Penguin 1967), 376. This term has been invoked in the context of Pacific cooperation by Jusuf Wanandi, 'Pacific Economic Cooperation: An Indonesian View,' *Asian Survey* 23 (December 1983):1,271 and John Bresnan, 'Strengthening Human Ties,' in Morley, *The Pacific Basin*, 88, 99-100.

The designation of groups such as PAFTAD and PECC as *organizations* is not beyond dispute. For example, PAFTAD is often referred to as a *research network* and *conference series*, while PECC is now described as a *process*. See Peter Drysdale, 'The Pacific Trade and Development Conference Series:

A Brief History,' *Pacific Economic Papers*, no. 112, Australia-Japan Research Centre, Research School of Pacific Studies, Australian National University, June 1984, v and Earle and Trigg, 'Pacific Economic Cooperation,' 10-15. Nevertheless, PAFTAD, PBEC, and PECC will be considered here as *international organizations* in accordance with the definition supplied by Cox and Jacobson: '[cross-border] systems of interaction including all of those who directly participate in decisions taken within the framework of the organization, and in addition all officials and individuals who in various ways actively determine the positions of the direct participants.' See Robert W. Cox and Harold K. Jacobson, 'The Framework for Inquiry,' in Robert W. Cox and Harold K. Jacobson, eds., *The Anatomy of Influence: Decision Making in International Organization* (London: Yale University Press 1974), 16. The criteria used in designating these organizations as *nongovernmental* will be reviewed in Chapter 2 and will remain a matter of analytical concern throughout.

9 Hank Lim, 'Pacific Rim Economic Cooperation in a Changing Global Environment,' *Asia Horizon* (Canadian Asian Studies Association) 12 (November 1990):23-7 and Elek, 'The Evolution of Asia Pacific Economic Cooperation,' 6. This relationship is explicitly recognized in the Seoul APEC Declaration of November 1991, reprinted in Australia, Department of Foreign Affairs and Trade, 'APEC Comes of Age,' 6-7.

10 This debate focuses upon the roles of, and relationships between, PECC, APEC, the intergovernmental ASEAN-Pacific Dialogue (APD, also known as, or forming part of, the expanded ASEAN Post-Ministerial Conferences) begun in 1984, and the East Asian Economic Caucus (EAEC, formerly Grouping), an official body arising from a proposal by Malaysian prime minister Mahathir in December 1990. See Stuart Harris, 'Varieties of Pacific Economic Cooperation' and Lawrence T. Woods, 'Non-governmental Organizations and Pacific Cooperation: Back to the Future?' *Pacific Review* 4 (1991):301-11 and 312-21, respectively. On APD, see Michael B. Yahuda, 'The Pacific Community: Not Yet,' *Pacific Review* 1 (1988):119-27; Jusuf Wanandi, 'The Role of PECC in the 1990's and Pacific Institutions,' in PECC, *Report of the Seventh Pacific Economic Cooperation Conference, Auckland, November 12-15, 1989* (Wellington: New Zealand Committee for Pacific Economic Cooperation 1990), 21-8; and Shiro Saito, *Japan at the Summit: Japan's Role in the Western Alliance and Asian Pacific Co-operation* (London: Routledge 1990). On EAEC, see Nigel Holloway et al., 'An Insurance Policy,' *Far Eastern Economic Review*, 25 July 1991, 52-3 and Linda Low, 'The East Asian Economic Grouping,' *Pacific Review* 4 (1991):375-82.

11 A brief comparative analysis is offered by Palmer, *The New Regionalism in Asia and the Pacific*, 133-47.

12 Stephen D. Krasner, 'Structural Causes and Regime Consequences: Regimes as Intervening Variables,' *International Organization* 36 (Spring 1982):186.

13 See, for example, Drysdale, 'Building the Foundations,' 46; Drysdale, *International Economic Pluralism*, 229-55; and Palmer, *The New Regionalism in Asia and the Pacific*, 12-15.

14 For a critique of the concept of regime analysis, see Susan Strange, 'Cave! hic

dragones: A Critique of Regime Analysis,' *International Organization* 36 (Spring 1982):479-96.

15 Wolfers, *Discord and Collaboration*, 23. Although the terms *state* and *government* will be used interchangeably here, it must be acknowledged that they are not true synonyms. *State* normally refers to a set of persons and institutions recognized to have the authority to legislate and to enforce rules and laws within a society. *Government* usually refers to that part of the state which legislates, though this reference is sometimes broadened to include the administrative activities of the bureaucracy and other components of the public service. Those entities which are not singular states, or the official representatives thereof, are referred to as *nonstate*, while those nonstate entities which are not predominantly composed of official state or governmental representatives are termed *nongovernmental*.

16 While this study will focus on diplomatic contributions, such a restriction is not meant to imply that diplomacy is the only type of activity in which these organizations may be engaged.

17 Adam Watson, *Diplomacy: The Dialogue Between States* (London: Methuen 1982), 11.

18 Kanahele and Haas, 'Prospects for a Pacific Community,' 87. For differing American perspectives of the rise and fall of the IPR, see John N. Thomas, *The Institute of Pacific Relations: Asian Scholars and American Politics* (Seattle: University of Washington Press 1974) and Frederick Vanderbilt Field, *From Right to Left: An Autobiography* (Westport, CT: Lawrence Hill 1983), 116-33.

19 For an introduction to the origins, purpose, structure, and activities of PAFTAD, see Drysdale, 'The Pacific Trade'; PAFTAD, *The Pacific Trade and Development Conference: The First Twenty Years* (Canberra: PAFTAD International Secretariat, April 1989); H.E. English, 'PAFTAD – A Quiet Success,' *PAFTAD Newsletter*, no. 7 (July 1992):4-6; and Palmer, *The New Regionalism in Asia and the Pacific*, 133-7.

20 For a brief review of PBEC's origins, purpose, and structure, see William E. Bryant, *Japanese Private Economic Diplomacy: An Analysis of Business-Government Linkages* (New York: Praeger 1975), 71-5; *PBEC Report: Seoul Meeting – 1986* (Menlo Park, CA: SRI International 1986), ii; Earle and Trigg, 'Pacific Economic Cooperation,' 5-6; and Palmer, *The New Regionalism in Asia and the Pacific*, 137-40.

21 *PECC Newsletter*, vol. 2, no. 2 (April 1992):5.

22 An overview of PECC's history and activities (including a survey of the regional economy, PECC task forces, the Pacific economic cooperation idea, related organizations, and PECC publications) was recently released by PECC. See M. Hadi Soesastro, Han Gwang Choo, and Robert A. Armstrong, *Pacific Economic Development Report 1992-1993* (Singapore: PECC Secretariat 1992). For a review of the 1980 Pacific Community Seminar, see Crawford and Seow, *Pacific Economic Co-operation*, 1-32. For a review of PECC II in Bangkok, 3-5 June 1982, see Osborne and Fourt, *Pacific Basin Economic Cooperation*, 84-92. Reviews of PECC I-V and task force activities are also contained in PECC, *Issues for Pacific Economic Cooperation: A Report of the Third Pacific Economic Cooperation Conference, Bali, November 1983* (Jakarta:

Centre for Strategic and International Studies 1984); PECC, *Pacific Economic Cooperation - Issues and Opportunities: Report of the Fourth Pacific Economic Cooperation Conference, Seoul, April 29-May 1 1985* (Seoul: Korea Development Institute 1985); PECC, *Report of the Fifth Pacific Economic Cooperation Conference, Vancouver, November 16-19 1986* (Ottawa: Canadian Chamber of Commerce 1987); PECC, *Report of the Sixth Pacific Economic Cooperation Conference, Osaka, May 17-20 1988* (Tokyo: Japan National Committee for Pacific Economic Cooperation 1988); and PECC, *Report of the Seventh Pacific Economic Cooperation Conference, Auckland, November 12-15 1989* (Wellington: New Zealand Committee for Pacific Economic Cooperation 1990). These reports are hereafter cited as *PECC III Report, PECC IV Report, PECC V Report, PECC VI Report,* and *PECC VII Report,* respectively. See also Palmer, *The New Regionalism in Asia and the Pacific,* 140-7; Kumao Kaneko, 'A New Pacific Initiative: Strengthening the PECC Process,' *Japan Review of International Affairs* 2 (Spring/Summer 1988):67-90; and *PECC Newsletter,* vol. 2, no. 2 (April 1992) and vol. 2, no. 3 (July 1992).

23 A categorization of the reasons people participate in the Pacific economic cooperation movement is attempted in J. Stephen Hoadley, 'Dimensions of Pacific Cooperation,' paper prepared for the First Indonesia-New Zealand Seminar, Auckland, New Zealand, 17-18 February 1981, 13-15.

24 Sherif El-Hakim, 'The Structure and Dynamics of Consensus Decision-Making,' *Man* 13 (March 1978):55-71.

Chapter 2: INGOs, International Relations, and Diplomacy

1 White, *International Non-Governmental Organizations: Their Purposes, Methods, and Accomplishments* (New Brunswick, NJ: Rutgers University Press 1951), 3.

2 Harold K. Jacobson, *Networks of Interdependence: International Organizations and the Global Political System* (New York: Alfred A. Knopf 1979), 8.

3 J.J. Lador-Lederer, *International Non-Governmental Organizations and Economic Entities: A Study in Autonomous Organization and Ius Gentium* (Leyden: A.W. Sythoff 1963), 60; Lyman Cromwell White, *The Structure of Private International Organizations* (Philadelphia: George S. Ferguson 1933); Samuel P. Huntington, 'Transnational Organizations in World Politics,' *World Politics* 25 (April 1973):333-68; Werner Feld, 'Nongovernmental Entities and the International System: A Preliminary Quantitative Overview,' *Orbis* 15 (Fall 1971):880, 884; Werner J. Feld, *Nongovernmental Forces in World Politics: A Study of Business, Labour and Political Groups* (New York: Praeger 1972), 5, 175-6; and Kjell Skjelsbaek, 'The Growth of International Nongovernmental Organizations in the Twentieth Century,' in Robert O. Keohane and Joseph S. Nye, Jr., eds., *Transnational Relations and World Politics* (Cambridge, MA: Harvard University Press 1973), 70-3.

4 Feld, *Nongovernmental Forces.*

5 Huntington, 'Transnational Organizations in World Politics,' 334-5.

6 Phillip Taylor, *Nonstate Actors in International Politics: From Transregional to Substate Organizations* (Boulder, CO: Westview 1984), 20-3.

7 Jacobson, *Networks of Interdependence,* 13.

8 White, *International Non-Governmental Organizations*, 3.

9 Feld, 'Nongovernmental Entities,' 879.

10 Cox and Jacobson, 'The Framework for Inquiry,' in Robert W. Cox and Harold K. Jacobson, eds., *The Anatomy of Influence: Decision Making in International Organization* (London: Yale University Press 1974), 5-7.

11 Richard W. Mansbach, Yale H. Ferguson, and Donald E. Lampert, *The Web of World Politics: Non-State Actors in the Global System* (Englewood Cliffs, NJ: Prentice-Hall 1976), 37-9.

12 White, *International Non-Governmental Organizations*, 10-16.

13 Peter Willetts, 'Pressure Groups as Transnational Actors,' in Peter Willetts, ed., *Pressure Groups in the Global System: The Transnational Relations of Issue-Oriented Non-Governmental Organizations* (London: Frances Pinter 1982), 1-2.

14 Willetts, *Pressure Groups in the Global System*, xiii-xiv. See also Lador-Lederer, *International Non-Governmental Organizations and Economic Entities*, 379-80.

15 Lador-Lederer, *International Non-Governmental Organizations and Economic Entities*, 64.

16 Frederick Sherwood Dunn, *The Practice and Procedure of International Conferences* (Baltimore: Johns Hopkins Press 1929), 34-8.

17 Wellington Koo, Jr., *Voting Procedures in International Political Organizations* (New York: Columbia University Press 1947), 19-20.

18 Peter Willetts, 'The Impact of Promotional Pressure Groups on Global Politics,' in Peter Willetts, ed., *Pressure Groups in the Global System*, 190-1.

19 Joseph S. Nye, Jr. and Robert O. Keohane, 'Transnational Relations and World Politics: An Introduction,' in Robert O. Keohane and Joseph S. Nye, Jr., eds., *Transnational Relations and World Politics* (Cambridge, MA: Harvard University Press 1973), xxiv-xxv.

20 Wolfers, *Discord and Collaboration: Essays on International Politics* (Baltimore: Johns Hopkins Press 1971), 23.

21 Lador-Lederer, *International Non-Governmental Organizations and Economic Entities*, 60.

22 P.A. Reynolds, 'Non-state Actors and International Outcomes,' *British Journal of International Studies* 5 (July 1979):91-2.

23 Jacobson, *Networks of Interdependence*, 8 and White, *International Non-Governmental Organizations*, 10-11.

24 Nye and Keohane, 'Transnational Relations and World Politics: An Introduction,' xvi-xxii.

25 Nye and Keohane, 'Transnational Relations and World Politics: An Introduction,' xi.

26 David A. Baldwin, *Economic Statecraft* (Princeton, NJ: Princeton University Press 1985), 12-14.

27 Nye and Keohane, 'Transnational Relations and World Politics: An Introduction,' xxi.

28 Options 1-3 correspond to those suggested in Joseph S. Nye, Jr. and Robert O. Keohane, 'Transnational Relations and World Politics: A Conclusion,' in Robert O. Keohane and Joseph S. Nye, Jr., eds., *Transnational Relations and World Politics* (Cambridge, MA: Harvard University Press 1973), 394-5.

29 Karl Kaiser, 'Transnational Politics: Towards a Theory of Multinational Poli-

tics,' *International Organization* 25 (Autumn 1971):804-8 and Andrew M. Scott, 'The Logic of International Interaction,' *International Studies Quarterly* 21 (September 1977):429-60.

30 Bryant, *Japanese Private Economic Diplomacy: An Analysis of Business-Government Linkages* (New York: Praeger 1975), 3 and Trevor N. Matthews, 'Business Associations and Politics,' PhD Dissertation, University of Sydney 1971, 361.

31 Henry S. Albinski, *Canadian and Australian Politics in Comparative Perspective* (New York: Oxford University Press 1973), 345.

32 Donald K. Crone, *The ASEAN States: Coping with Dependence* (New York: Praeger 1983), 184.

33 Keohane and Nye, *Power and Interdependence: World Politics in Transition* (Toronto: Little, Brown 1977), 24-9.

34 Keohane and Nye, *Power and Interdependence*, 29-36.

35 Lador-Lederer, *International Non-Governmental Organizations and Economic Entities*, 59-60.

36 Charles Doran, 'U.S. and Canadian Pacific Perspectives,' in Gavin Boyd, ed., *Region Building in the Pacific* (New York: Pergamon 1982), 177-8.

37 See Mahathir bin Mohamad, '*Tak Kenal Maka Tak Cinta*,' in John Crawford and Greg Seow, eds., *Pacific Economic Co-operation: Suggestions for Action* (Selangor: Heinemann Educational 1981), 41-5 and Fairbanks, 'Networking in the Pacific: Private Actions with a Public Purpose,' *Speaking of Japan* 7 (November 1986):30-2.

38 The concepts of *interest groups* and *political entrepreneurs* in international relations are discussed in Robert O. Keohane and Joseph S. Nye, eds., *Transnational Relations and World Politics* (Cambridge, MA: Harvard University Press 1973); Peter Willetts, ed., *Pressure Groups in the Global System*; and Robert O. Keohane, 'The Demand for International Regimes,' *International Organization* 36 (Spring 1982):339. For Marxist analyses, see Greg Crough and Ted Wheelwright, *Australia: A Client State* (Harmondsworth, UK: Penguin 1982), 58-81; Jim Hyde, *Australia: The Asia Connection* (Melbourne: Kibble 1978), 12-27; Philip Resnick, 'BC Capitalism and the Empire of the Pacific,' *BC Studies*, no. 67 (Autumn 1985):40-6; and R.T. Robertson, 'From Community to Cooperation to Self-Reliance: Death of the Pacific Basin Concept,' *Journal of International Relations* (Japan), no. 17 (July 1986):51-66.

39 John Naisbitt, *Megatrends: Ten New Directions Transforming Our Lives* (Sydney: Futura-Macdonald 1984), 112-17.

40 Hans J. Morgenthau, *Politics Among Nations: The Struggle for Power and Peace*, 4th edition (New York: Alfred A. Knopf 1967), 135.

41 Ernest Satow, *A Guide to Diplomatic Practice*, edited by Neville Bland, 4th edition (London: Longmans, Green 1957), 1-3. For related definitions, see Morgenthau, *Politics Among Nations*, 135, n. 9; Martin Wight, *Power Politics*, edited by Hedley Bull and Carsten Holbraad, 2nd edition (Harmondsworth, UK: Penguin Books/Royal Institute of International Affairs 1986), 113; and R.B. Mowat, *Diplomacy and Peace* (London: Williams and Norgate 1935), 16.

42 Harold Nicolson, *Diplomacy*, 3rd edition (London: Oxford University Press 1963), 14.

43 Watson, *Diplomacy: The Dialogue Between States* (London: Methuen 1982), 14.

44 Watson, *Diplomacy*, 122-4.
45 Wight, *Power Politics*, 115.
46 Satow, *A Guide to Diplomatic Practice*, 115.
47 Elmer Plischke, 'The Optimum Scope of Instruction in Diplomacy,' in Smith Simpson, ed., *Instruction in Diplomacy: The Liberal Arts Approach* (Philadelphia: American Academy of Political and Social Science 1972), 20.
48 Plischke, 'The Optimum Scope of Instruction in Diplomacy,' 20.
49 Plischke, 'The Optimum Scope of Instruction in Diplomacy,' 20-1.
50 Wight, *Power Politics*, 120. See also D.P. Heatley, *Diplomacy and the Study of International Relations* (Oxford: Clarendon 1919) and Gordon A. Craig, 'On the Nature of Diplomatic History: The Relevance of Some Old Books,' in Paul Gordon Lauren, ed., *Diplomacy: New Approaches in History, Theory, and Policy* (New York: Free Press 1979), 21-42.
51 Satow, *A Guide to Diplomatic Practice*, 3-4.
52 Richard Langhorne, 'The Regulation of Diplomatic Practice: The Beginnings to the Vienna Convention on Diplomatic Relations, 1961,' *Review of International Studies* 18 (January 1992):3-17 and Grieg, *International Law* (London: Butterworth 1970), 95 and chs. 4, 12-15.
53 Nicolson, *Diplomacy*, 16-35, 50-1. See also Garrett Mattingly, *Renaissance Diplomacy* (London: Jonathan Cape 1955).
54 Reynolds, *An Introduction to International Relations*, 124-6.
55 Nicolson, *Diplomacy*, 31-3.
56 Clifton E. Wilson, *Diplomatic Privileges and Immunities* (Tucson: University of Arizona Press 1967), 1-25.
57 Clifton E. Wilson, *Diplomatic Privileges and Immunities*, 21-2, 154-5, 219-21, 269-71; Paul Gordon Lauren, *Diplomats and Bureaucrats: The First Institutional Responses to Twentieth-Century Diplomacy in France and Germany* (Stanford: Hoover Institution Press 1976), 219-28; and Maureen R. Berman and Joseph E. Johnson, 'The Growing Role of Unofficial Diplomacy,' in Maureen R. Berman and Joseph E. Johnson, eds., *Unofficial Diplomats* (New York: Columbia University Press 1977), 1-3, 30-3.
58 K.J. Holsti, *The Dividing Discipline: Hegemony and Diversity in International Theory* (Boston: Allen and Unwin 1985), 3-4.
59 Nicolson, *Diplomacy*, 52-3.
60 Nicolson, *Diplomacy*, 54.
61 Nicolson, *Diplomacy*, 162-3. See also Russel Madigan, *Of Business and Foreign Policy* (Canberra: Australian Institute of International Affairs 1985), 7-11.
62 Lauren, *Diplomats and Bureaucrats*, 155-74 and Satow, *A Guide to Diplomatic Practice*, 102.
63 Lauren, *Diplomats and Bureaucrats*, 176.
64 Gordon Osbaldeston, 'Models for the Future: Canada,' in A.C. Milner and Trevor Wilson, eds., *Australian Diplomacy: Challenges and Options for the Department of Foreign Affairs*, Occasional Paper No. 5, Australian Institute of International Relations, Canberra, August 1986, 18-25 and Alan Burnett, 'Australia's Trade Diplomacy,' paper presented to a seminar in the Department of International Relations, Research School of Pacific Studies, Australian National University, 12 May 1988.

65 Nicolson, *Diplomacy*, 50.
66 Satow, *A Guide to Diplomatic Practice*, 303, 307-8 and Watson, *Diplomacy*, 127-8, 151-2, 188-9.
67 Watson, *Diplomacy*, 190-4.
68 Herbert Butterfield, 'The New Diplomacy and Historical Diplomacy,' in Herbert Butterfield and Martin Wight, eds., *Diplomatic Investigations: Essays in the Theory of International Politics* (London: Allen and Unwin 1966), 181-92.
69 See Martin Wight, 'Why Is There No International Theory?' and 'Western Values in International Relations,' in Butterfield and Wight, eds., *Diplomatic Investigations*, 22 and 92-3, respectively.
70 Watson, *Diplomacy*, 11, 223-4.
71 Mattingly, *Renaissance Diplomacy*, 11-13, 55.
72 Andrew M. Scott, *Revolution in Statecraft: Informal Penetration* (New York: Random House 1965), 1-29.
73 Richard W. Cottam, *Competitive Interference and Twentieth Century Diplomacy* (Pittsburgh: University of Pittsburgh Press 1967), 36-43.
74 Bryant, *Japanese Private Economic Diplomacy*, 1-3.
75 Watson, *Diplomacy*, 126-7.
76 Stephen D. Kertesz, *The Quest for Peace Through Diplomacy* (Englewood Cliffs, NJ: Prentice-Hall 1967), 7-8.
77 Louis Kriesberg, 'Formal and Quasi-Mediators in International Disputes: An Exploratory Analysis,' *Journal of Peace Research* 28 (February 1991):23.
78 Berman and Johnson, 'The Growing Role of Unofficial Diplomacy,' 3-5.
79 Berman and Johnson, 'The Growing Role of Unofficial Diplomacy,' 5-6, 21, 28 and Berman and Johnson, eds., *Unofficial Diplomats*, 263.
80 Berman and Johnson, 'The Growing Role of Unofficial Diplomacy,' 7, 27, 31 and Berman and Johnson, eds., *Unofficial Diplomats*, 259-62.
81 Bharati Mukherjee, *Kautilya's Concept of Diplomacy: A New Interpretation* (Calcutta: Minerva Associates 1976); Adda B. Bozeman, *Politics and Culture in International History* (Princeton: Princeton University Press 1960); and Watson, *Diplomacy*, 15-17 and ch. 7.
82 Watson, *Diplomacy*, 17-18, 158-75. See also Adam Watson, 'From a European to a Global International System,' *Jerusalem Journal of International Relations*, vol. 11, no. 2 (1989):17-26. For discussions of the link between culture and diplomacy, see Michael Haas, *The Asian Way to Peace: A Story of Regional Cooperation* (New York: Praeger 1989); Raymond Cohen, *Negotiating Across Cultures: Communication Obstacles in International Diplomacy* (Washington: United States Institute of Peace Press 1991); Rosalie L. Tung, 'Handshakes Across the Sea: Cross-Cultural Negotiating for Business Success,' *Organizational Dynamics* 19 (Winter 1991):30-40; and Lawrence T. Woods, 'Diplomacy and Culture: Lessons from the Asian-Pacific Region,' *Asian Culture Quarterly* 19 (Autumn 1991):1-12.
83 Gareth Porter and Janet Welsh Brown, *Global Environmental Politics* (Boulder, CO: Westview 1991) and John E. Carroll, ed., *International Environmental Diplomacy* (Cambridge: Cambridge University Press 1990).
84 Catherine Tinker, 'Making UNCED Work: Building the Legal and Institu-

tional Framework for Sustainable Development at the Earth Summit and Beyond,' *UNA-USA Occasional Papers*, no. 4 (March 1992).

85 Elise Boulding, 'The Old and New Transnationalism: An Evolutionary Perspective,' *Human Relations* 44 (August 1991):789-806; James N. Rosenau, *Turbulence in World Politics: A Theory of Change and Continuity* (Princeton: Princeton University Press 1990); James N. Rosenau and Ernst-Otto Czempiel, eds., *Governance Without Government: Order and Change in World Politics* (Cambridge: Cambridge University Press 1992); and Paul Ekins, *A New World Order: Grassroots Movements for Global Change* (London: Routledge 1992).

86 Ernst B. Haas, *When Knowledge is Power: Three Models of Change in International Organizations* (Berkeley: University of California Press 1990).

87 David Skidmore and Valerie M. Hudson, eds., *The Limits of State Autonomy: Societal Groups and Foreign Policy Formulation* (Boulder, CO: Westview 1992).

88 Marvin S. Soroos, *Beyond Sovereignty: The Challenge of Global Policy* (Columbia: University of South Carolina Press 1986).

89 Peter M. Haas, 'Introduction: Epistemic Communities and International Policy Coordination,' *International Organization* 46 (Winter 1992):1-35.

90 Ronnie D. Lipschutz, 'Bargaining Among Nations: Culture, History, and Perception in Regime Formation,' *Evaluation Review* 15 (February 1991):47-60.

91 Susan Strange, 'States, Firms and Diplomacy,' *International Affairs* 68 (January 1992):1-15.

Chapter 3: The Institute of Pacific Relations

1 See Christopher Thorne, *The Limits of Foreign Policy: The West, the League and the Far Eastern Crisis of 1931-33* (New York: Capricorn 1973).

2 George S. Kanahele and Michael Haas, 'Prospects for a Pacific Community,' *Pacific Community*, no. 6 (1974):87.

3 IPR, ed., *Institute of Pacific Relations: Honolulu Session, June 30-July 14 1925* (Honolulu: IPR 1925), 7-40 (hereafter cited as *Honolulu Session*).

4 J.B. Condliffe, ed., *Problems of the Pacific, 1929: Proceedings of the Third Conference of the Institute of Pacific Relations, Nara and Kyoto, Japan, 23 October-9 November 1929* (Chicago: University of Chicago Press 1930), 660.

5 *Honolulu Session*, 46-52, 136-8.

6 Institute of Pacific Relations (IPR), *War and Peace in the Pacific: A Preliminary Report of the Eighth Conference of the Institute of Pacific Relations on Wartime and Post-war Co-operation of the United Nations in the Pacific and the Far East, Mont Tremblant, Quebec, December 4-14 1942* (London: Royal Institute of International Affairs 1943), 164.

7 John N. Thomas, *The Institute of Pacific Relations: Asian Scholars and American Politics* (Seattle: University of Washington Press 1974), 4. See also Christopher Thorne, 'Chatham House, Whitehall, and Far Eastern Issues: 1941-45,' *International Affairs* 54 (January 1978):13-29 and Chalmers Johnson, *An Instance of Treason: Ozaki Hotsumi and the Sorge Spy Ring* (Tokyo: Charles E. Tuttle 1977), 111-13.

8 Condliffe, *Problems of the Pacific, 1929*, 212-13.

9 See, for example, *Honolulu Session*, 35-40; Condliffe, *Problems of the Pacific, 1929*, 623-30; W.L. Holland and Kate L. Mitchell, eds., *Problems of the Pacific, 1936: Aims and Results of Social and Economic Policies in Pacific Countries – Proceedings of the Sixth Conference of the Institute of Pacific Relations, Yosemite National Park, California, 15-29 August 1936* (Chicago: University of Chicago Press 1937), 435-42; and IPR, *War and Peace in the Pacific*, 154-62.

10 IPR, *War and Peace in the Pacific*, vi-vii.

11 IPR, *War and Peace in the Pacific*, vii. See also Paul Hasluck, *Diplomatic Witness: Australian Foreign Affairs 1941-1947* (Melbourne: Melbourne University Press 1980), 68.

12 Holland and Mitchell, *Problems of the Pacific, 1936*, vii-viii and Quincy Wright, 'Diplomatic Machinery in the Pacific Area,' paper prepared for the Sixth Conference of the Institute of Pacific Relations, Yosemite Park, California, 15-29 August 1936, *Secretariat Papers*, 2A, IPR, New York, 1936, 7-8.

13 'The Origin and Present Activity of the Institute of Pacific Relations,' undated (about October 1931), 3-4, quoted in White, *The Structure of Private International Organizations* (Philadelphia: George S. Ferguson 1933), 143.

14 Paul F. Hooper, 'The Institute of Pacific Relations and the Origins of Asian and Pacific Studies,' *Pacific Affairs* 61 (Spring 1988):98-121; William L. Holland, 'Source Materials on the Institute of Pacific Relations: Bibliographical Note,' *Pacific Affairs* 58 (Spring 1985):91-7; and IPR, International Secretariat, *The Study of International Affairs in the Pacific Area: A Review of Nine Years' Work in the International Research Program of the Institute of Pacific Relations* (New York: IPR 1936).

15 Hasluck, *Diplomatic Witness*, 68, 71.

16 Johnson, *An Instance of Treason*, 111-13.

17 Thorne, 'Chatham House,' 15-29.

18 Thorne, 'Chatham House,' 13-20; Thomas, *The Institute of Pacific Relations*, 96-9; United States, *Institute of Pacific Relations: Hearings Before the Subcommittee to Investigate the Administration of the Internal Security Act and Other Internal Security Laws of the Committee on the Judiciary, United States Senate, Eighty-Second Congress* (Washington: United States Government Printing Office 1951-3), parts 1-15 (hereafter cited as *IPR: Hearings*); Ralph de Toledano, *Spies, Dupes and Diplomats* (New York: Duell, Sloan and Pearce 1952); and Field, *From Right to Left: An Autobiography* (Westport, CT: Lawrence Hill 1983), 117, 126, 132-3. I am indebted to Alexander Craig for bringing Frederick Field's commentary to my attention.

19 See Condliffe, *Problems of the Pacific, 1929*, 217-18, 658 and IPR, *War and Peace in the Pacific*, 20-8, 84.

20 Thorne, 'Chatham House,' 16.

21 Wright, 'Diplomatic Machinery in the Pacific Area,' foreword.

22 Wright, 'Diplomatic Machinery in the Pacific Area,' 12-33.

23 Wright, 'Diplomatic Machinery in the Pacific Area,' 5-7. See also Wright, 'Diplomatic Machinery in the Pacific Area,' 8-12, 33-7.

24 Condliffe, *Problems of the Pacific, 1929*, 234-7. See also Wright, 'Diplomatic Machinery in the Pacific Area,' 34, 40-1.

25 Condliffe, *Problems of the Pacific, 1929*, 237-8.

26 See IPR, *War and Peace in the Pacific*, 13-15, 78-84, 102-3; Hasluck, *Diplomatic Witness*, 80-2; and Royal Institute of International Affairs, *The Pattern of Pacific Security: A Report by a Chatham House Study Group* (London 1946), 29-48.

27 J.G. Crawford, 'Australia as a Pacific Power,' in W.G.K. Duncan, ed., *Australia's Foreign Policy* (Sydney: Angus and Robertson 1938), 69-121. See also Peter Drysdale, 'The Relationship with Japan: Despite the Vicissitudes,' in L.T. Evans and J.D.B. Miller, eds., *Policy and Practice: Essays in Honour of Sir John Crawford* (Sydney: Australian National University Press 1987), 67-71.

28 'Pacific Rim,' *Japan Quarterly* 15 (April/June 1980):151-2.

29 F.C. Jones, *Japan's New Order in East Asia: Its Rise and Fall 1937-45* (London: Oxford University Press 1954).

30 Soesastro, 'Institutional Aspects of Pacific Economic Cooperation,' in Hadi Soesastro and Han Sung-Joo, eds., *Pacific Economic Cooperation: The Next Phase* (Jakarta: Centre for Strategic and International Studies 1983), 14.

31 Saburo Okita, *Japan's Challenging Years: Reflections On My Life* (Sydney: Allen and Unwin 1983), 14-16.

32 Bernard K. Gordon, 'Japan and the Pacific Basin Proposal,' *Korea and World Affairs* 5 (Summer 1981):270.

33 Tessa Morris-Suzuki, 'Japan and the Pacific Basin Community,' *World Today* 37 (December 1981):455.

34 Thomas, *The Institute of Pacific Relations*, 100-19.

35 Morris-Suzuki, 'Japan and the Pacific Basin,' 455.

36 Saburo Okita, 'Pacific Regional Co-operation,' in L.T. Evans and J.D.B. Miller, eds., *Policy and Practice*, 123-4.

37 See, for example, 'The Sydney Report: Free Enterprise and Pacific Development – A Report on the Pacific Industrial Conference,' *SRI-International* 1 (1967):1.

38 Soesastro, 'Institutional Aspects,' 3-52.

Chapter 4: The Pacific Trade and Development Conference

1 B. Jaye Miller, 'Educational Strategies in Pacific Basin Studies,' paper prepared for presentation at Pan-Pacific Conference II, Seoul, Korea, 13-15 May 1985, 5.

2 At PAFTAD 12 in Vancouver in 1981, confusion arose when the conference organizers introduced the acronym PACTAD. The acronyms PACTAD and PAFTAD were used interchangeably for a few years, until the International Steering Committee agreed to use PAFTAD in future documentation in order to avoid confusion. (The acronyms PACTRAD and PTDC can also be found in the literature.) However, the acronym PAFTAD is sometimes still mistaken for Kiyoshi Kojima's Pacific Free Trade Area (PAFTA) proposal (the proposal which led to the holding of the first PAFTAD in 1968) or the concept of an Organization for Pacific Trade and Development (OPTAD) (put forward by Kojima and Peter Drysdale at PAFTAD 1). See Correspondence, 2 July 1984, Files of the PAFTAD Secretariat held at the Australia-Japan Research Centre, Research School of Pacific Studies, Australian National University, Canberra (hereafter cited as AJRC Files); Minutes of the PAFTAD International Steering Committee Meeting, Singapore, 18-21

June 1984, 4-5, AJRC Files; and Miller, 'Educational Strategies in Pacific Basin Studies,' 28, n. 3.

3 Correspondence, 25 November 1981, AJRC Files.

4 Peter Drysdale, 'The Pacific Trade and Development Conference Series: A Brief History,' *Pacific Economic Papers*, no. 112, Australia-Japan Research Centre, Research School of Pacific Studies, Australian National University, June 1984, vi. Short overviews of PAFTAD are also provided in PAFTAD, *The Pacific Trade and Development Conference: The First Twenty Years* (Canberra: PAFTAD International Secretariat, April 1989); H.E. English, 'PAFTAD – A Quiet Success,' *PAFTAD Newsletter*, no. 7 (July 1992):4-6; and Palmer, *The New Regionalism in Asia and the Pacific* (Lexington, MA: Lexington 1991), 133-7. Drysdale's observation about the relationship between scholarly research, policy-making, and diplomacy allows one to situate the PAFTAD example within the emerging body of literature on 'epistemic communities' or 'networks of knowledge-based experts.' See Peter M. Haas, 'Introduction: Epistemic Communities and International Policy Coordination,' *International Organization* 46 (Winter 1992). On the policy relevance of academics in the East Asian context in particular, see Sylvia Ostry, ed., *Authority and Academic Scribblers: The Role of Research in East Asian Policy Reform* (San Francisco: ICS Press 1991).

5 Bela Balassa et al., *Studies in Trade Liberalization: Problems and Prospects* (Baltimore: Johns Hopkins Press 1967); Confidential interview, Tokyo, 10 November 1986.

6 Kiyoshi Kojima and Hiroshi Kurimoto, 'A Pacific Economic Community and Asian Developing Countries,' in *Measures for Trade Expansion of Developing Countries* (Tokyo: Japan Economic Research Centre 1966), 93-134; Kiyoshi Kojima, *Japan and a Pacific Free Trade Area* (London: Macmillan 1971), chs. 3 and 7; Kiyoshi Kojima, *Economic Cooperation in a Pacific Community* (Tokyo: Japan Institute of International Affairs 1980), 4-7; and Soesastro, 'Institutional Aspects of Pacific Economic Cooperation,' in Hadi Soesastro and Han Sung-Joo, eds., *Pacific Economic Cooperation: The Next Phase* (Jakarta: Centre for Strategic and International Studies 1983), 17-18.

7 Confidential interview, Tokyo, 8 November 1986, and Okita, 'Pacific Regional Co-operation,' in Evans and Miller, eds., *Policy and Practice*, 123. Okita is listed as the contributor of a 1951 article in *Far Eastern Survey*, published by the American Council of the IPR. See *IPR: Hearings*, Part 14 (2 May/20 July 1952), 5,584-5.

8 'Kiyoshi Kojima: Contribution to PAFTAD,' *Pacific Trade and Development Conference Newsletter* (hereafter cited as *PAFTAD Newsletter*), no. 2 (March 1986):1-2.

9 Confidential interview, Tokyo, 10 November 1986, and 'Kiyoshi Kojima,' 2.

10 Okita was an economic policy advisor to Prime Minister Sato at the time of Miki's statement and, later, served Miki in the same capacity when the latter became prime minister. Okita and Kojima had been approached by Foreign Minister Miki for a clarification of the as yet vague notion of Pacific cooperation, and Okita suspects his thinking may have influenced Miki's policy announcement. Toshio Shishido and Ryuzo Sato, eds., *Economic Policy and*

Development: New Perspectives (Essays in Honor of Dr. Saburo Okita) (Dover, MA: Auburn House 1985), xiii.

11 Confidential interview, Canberra, 29 June 1988, and John Curtis Perry, 'Private Philanthropy and Foreign Affairs: The Case of John D. Rockefeller and Japan,' *Asian Perspective* 8 (Fall/Winter 1984):268-84.

12 Okita's career and involvement in PAFTAD are chronicled in 'Saburo Okita: Contribution to PAFTAD,' *PAFTAD Newsletter*, no. 4 (May 1988):1-2.

13 Drysdale included the word 'Aid' in the title of the organization he proposed – an organization which was to be aimed at facilitating greater contact between business leaders and public servants, overcoming protectionism, and enhancing regional trade and investment links. See Kiyoshi Kojima, 'Japan's Interest in Pacific Trade Expansion' and Peter Drysdale, 'Pacific Economic Integration: An Australian View,' in Kiyoshi Kojima, ed., *Pacific Trade and Development, I* (Tokyo: Japan Economic Research Centre 1968), 153-93 and 194-223, respectively, and Kojima, *Economic Cooperation in a Pacific Community*, 12-13.

14 Drysdale, 'The Pacific Trade,' 1-2.

15 Confidential interview, Canberra, 29 June 1988. The late Arthur Paul, senior advisor to the San Francisco-based Asia Foundation, was an important figure in PAFTAD's formative years. See 'Arthur Paul (1898-1976): Contribution to PAFTAD,' *PAFTAD Newsletter*, no. 3 (July 1987):1.

16 Drysdale, 'The Pacific Trade,' 4; Kiyoshi Kojima and Miguel S. Wionczek, eds., *Technology Transfer in Pacific Economic Development* (Tokyo: Japan Economic Research Centre 1975); Lawrence B. Krause and Hugh Patrick, eds., *Mineral Resources in the Pacific Area* (San Francisco: Federal Reserve Bank of San Francisco 1978), 4; Minutes of the PAFTAD-ISC Meeting, Tokyo, 28-9 August 1985, 6, AJRC Files; Hugh Patrick, 'Report to the Executive Committee on the PAFTAD-ISC Meeting, Manila, 24 January 1983,' 6-7, AJRC Files; and confidential interviews, Ottawa and Toronto, 1 and 4 December 1986.

17 Drysdale, 'The Pacific Trade,' v-5; Minutes, PAFTAD-ISC, 28-9 August 1985, 1-4; Patrick, 'Report,' 5; and *PAFTAD Newsletter*, no. 3 (July 1987):3.

18 Drysdale, 'The Pacific Trade,' 7; Confidential interview, Tokyo, 10 November 1986.

19 The Asia Foundation had contributed U.S.$120,000 to eleven PAFTAD conferences as of 1984. It is also a major source of funds for the U.S. National Committee for Pacific Economic Cooperation. Correspondence, 12 January 1984 and 27 June 1985, AJRC Files.

20 Drysdale, 'The Pacific Trade,' 5-7; Peter Drysdale, 'Report to NIRA on Pacific Economy Research Programs,' 5 September 1983, 58, AJRC Files; Patrick, 'Report,' 2; Earle and Trigg, 'Pacific Economic Cooperation and an Overview of the Canberra Process,' *PBEC Papers, 1985*, 7.

21 Patrick, 'Report,' 4-6; Correspondence, 5 April 1983 and 2 July 1984, AJRC Files.

22 Correspondence, 21 March 1984, AJRC Files.

23 Confidential interview, Wellington, 28 January 1987; 'Formulating Beyond CER Strategy,' *Trans-Tasman* (Trans-Tasman News Services Ltd., Wellington)

86/623 (26 March 1986):2; Minutes, PAFTAD-ISC Meeting, 28-29 August 1985, 5; and *PAFTAD Newsletter*, no. 3 (July 1987):2-4.

24 Kojima, 'Economic Cooperation in a Pacific Community,' in Paul F. Hooper, ed., *Building a Pacific Community* (Honolulu: East-West Center 1982), 37.

25 Drysdale, 'The Pacific Trade,' v-vi.

26 M.K. Samuel, 'Board Information Paper,' first draft, Asian Development Bank, Manila, 8 February 1984, 3-4, AJRC Files; Drysdale, 'The Pacific Trade,' 4-5; and Drysdale, 'Report,' 59.

27 Correspondence, 25 November 1981, AJRC Files.

28 Drysdale, 'The Pacific Trade,' 4. On the origins, activities, and funding of AJRC, see John Crawford and Saburo Okita, *Australia, Japan and the Western Pacific Economic Relations: A Report to the Governments of Australia and Japan* (Canberra: Australian Government Publishing Service 1976); John Crawford and Saburo Okita, eds., *Raw Materials and Pacific Economic Integration* (Canberra: Australian National University Press 1978); and 'Australia-Japan Research Centre: Review,' Research School of Pacific Studies, Australian National University, January 1988, 4-6, 12-13.

29 Patrick, 'Report,' 3-4; Samuel, 'Board Information Paper,' 3-4; Drysdale, 'Report,' 20-3, 60-1; Correspondence, 21 October 1983, AJRC Files; and Minutes, PAFTAD-ISC Meeting, 18-21 June 1984, 4.

30 Drysdale, 'The Pacific Trade,' 7.

31 Patrick, 'Report,' 3; Correspondence, 5 April 1983, AJRC Files.

32 Drysdale, 'Report,' 60-1. Initial contributions to the funding consortium were as follows: the Asia Foundation U.S.$23,000 in 1984 and grants of $20-30,000/year over the next two years for a total commitment of $70,000 over three years; the Ford Foundation, $40,000 in 1984 and 1985 and $30,000 in 1986 ($110,000 over three years); the Rockefeller Brothers Fund, $10,000/year for three years; NIRA, $30,000/year or $150,000 over three years; and the Australian government, through the Department of Foreign Affairs and via the ANU, $30,000/year or $70,000 over three years. An additional $50,000/year was to be raised from other funding agencies and local assistance. Funding from the ADB is given in support of participants from Asian countries other than Japan and is more readily obtainable when conferences are held in ADB members' nations, which are large borrowers. These funding arrangements are discussed in correspondence, 5 April 1983 to 27 June 1985, AJRC Files; Drysdale, 'The Pacific Trade,' vi; Patrick, 'Report,' 2; and Minutes, PAFTAD-ISC Meeting, 28-9 August 1985, 4.

33 Drysdale, 'Report to NIRA on Pacific Economy Research Programs, 61; *PAFTAD Newsletter*, no. 1 (August 1985):1-4. The PAFTAD Secretariat can be contacted c/o Research School of Pacific Studies, Australian National University, GPO Box 4, Canberra, ACT, Australia 2601 (Tel: 61-62-493-780, 493-781; Fax: 61-62-490-169).

34 *PAFTAD Newsletter*, no. 3 (July 1987):4; *PAFTAD Newsletter*, no. 4 (May 1988):3-4; *PAFTAD Newsletter*, no. 5 (December 1989):4; *PAFTAD Newsletter*, no. 6 (March 1991):4; and *PAFTAD Newsletter*, no. 7 (July 1992):6.

35 Confidential interview, Canberra, 29 June 1988.

36 Correspondence, 2 July 1985, 19 September 1985, and 25 September 1985, AJRC Files; Minutes, PAFTAD-ISC Meeting, 28-29 August 1985, 2; and confidential interview, Tokyo, 8 November 1986.

37 Confidential interview, Tokyo, 5 November 1986; Lawrence T. Woods, 'Meeting Mikhail: Attitudes towards Soviet Involvement in Pacific Cooperation,' *Pacific Review* 3 (1990):214-21.

38 Minutes, PAFTAD-ISC Meeting, August 1985, 3; Correspondence, 2 July 1982, AJRC Files.

39 *PAFTAD Newsletter*, no. 3 (July 1987):4.

40 Guocang Huan, 'China's Open Door Policy, 1978-1984,' *Journal of International Affairs* 39 (Winter 1986):1-18; Lowell Dittmer, 'China's Opening to the Outside World: The Cultural Dimension,' *Journal of Northeast Asian Studies* 6 (Summer 1987):3-23; and Michael Oksenberg, 'China's Confident Nationalism,' *Foreign Affairs* 65 (1987):501-23.

41 Confidential interview, Canberra, 21 January 1986; Drysdale, 'The Pacific Trade,' 5; and *PAFTAD Newsletter*, no. 3 (July 1987):3.

42 See PAFTAD, *The Pacific Trade and Development Conference* and PAFTAD, Secretariat, 'Pacific Trade and Development Conference Series: List of Participants (1968-84),' AJRC, Research School of Pacific Studies, ANU, Canberra, 1985.

43 Drysdale, 'The Pacific Trade,' 1.

44 Patrick, 'Report,' 2; Minutes, PAFTAD-ISC Meeting, 18-21 June 1984, 2-3.

45 Confidential interviews, Ottawa and Toronto, 1 and 4 December 1986.

46 Participants in the former category include Okita (as a senior official in Japan's EPA, 1954-63), Crawford (as secretary of the Australian Department of Trade, 1956-60), and Hisao Kanamori (a senior member of Japan's EPA before taking over from Okita as president of JERC). In the latter category, one notes the 1969 attendance of Subroto, who later went from the University of Indonesia to become the Indonesian energy minister; Cesar Virata (1970), who participated as finance secretary of the Philippines and later became prime minister under former president Marcos; Harald B. Malmgren (1971), who participated while employed by the U.S. Overseas Development Council and later became a special trade representative under President Nixon; English, who participated in 1974 while on secondment to the Canadian government as acting assistant deputy minister (policy analysis) in the Department of Consumer and Corporate Affairs and who has frequently acted as an advisor on Canada-U.S. and Canada-Pacific trade issues; Ross Garnaut (1975), who became senior economic advisor to Prime Minister Hawke of Australia in 1984 and ambassador to China in 1986; Okita, who returned to public office in 1979 as foreign minister under Prime Minister Ohira; and Ippei Yamazawa, who, like Okita, participates as an advisor on several study groups established within the Japanese ministries of foreign affairs, international trade and industry, and finance. See Shishido and Sato, *Economic Policy and Development*, xii-xiii; L.T. Evans and J.D.B. Miller, eds., *Policy and Practice: Essays in Honour of Sir John Crawford* (Sydney: Australian National University Press 1987), 204; and confidential interviews, Tokyo, 5-6 November 1986.

47 Confidential interview, Toronto, 4 December 1986.
48 Confidential interviews, Canberra, 15 October 1986; Tokyo, 5 November 1986; and Ottawa, 1 December 1986.
49 Drysdale, 'Report,' 58; PAFTAD, *The Pacific Trade and Development Conference*, 7-34.
50 Earle and Trigg, 'Pacific Economic Cooperation,' 4.
51 Drysdale, 'The Pacific Trade,' 6-7.
52 Drysdale, 'Report,' 58.
53 Correspondence, 15 October 1985 and 17 September 1985, AJRC Files; Confidential interview, Ottawa, 1 December 1986.
54 Minutes, PAFTAD-ISC Meeting, 28-9 August 1985.
55 Drysdale, 'The Pacific Trade,' 3.
56 Drysdale, 'The Pacific Trade,' 1.
57 L.V. Castle, 'Alternative Policies in Trade Cooperation of the Advanced Pacific Countries in the Next Five Years' and Peter D. Drysdale, 'Japan, Australia, New Zealand: The Prospect for Western Pacific Economic Integration,' in Kiyoshi Kojima, ed., *Pacific Trade and Development, II* (Tokyo: Japan Economic Research Centre 1969), 159-78 and 204-7, respectively.
58 Peter Drysdale, ed., *Direct Foreign Investment in Asia and the Pacific* (Canberra: Australian National University Press 1972).
59 H. Edward English, 'Ocean of Opportunity,' Centre of Canadian Studies, School of Advanced International Studies, Johns Hopkins University, Washington, mimeo, n.d., 3 and H.E. English and Keith A.J. Hay, eds., *Obstacles to Trade in the Pacific Area* (Ottawa: School of International Affairs, Carleton University 1972), iv-vi.
60 Hugh T. Patrick, 'Summary,' in Kiyoshi Kojima, ed., *Structural Adjustments in Asian-Pacific Trade* (Tokyo: Japan Economic Research Centre 1973), 470.
61 V. Yakobovsky, 'Emergence of the Pacific Economic Complex and Some Aspects of the Economic Relations Between the Soviet Union and the Pacific Countries' and I.A. Lebedev, 'Integration Tendencies in Pacific Asia and External Economic Relations of the USSR,' in Kojima and Wionczek, eds., *Technology Transfer in Pacific Economic Development*, 24-9 and 30-5, respectively.
62 Heinz W. Arndt, 'The Role of Technology Transfer in Pacific Economic Development,' in Kojima and Wionczek, eds., *Technology Transfer in the Pacific Economic Development*, 232.
63 Leslie V. Castle and Frank Holmes, eds., *Cooperation and Development in the Asia-Pacific Region – Relations Between Large and Small Countries* (Tokyo: Japan Economic Research Centre 1976), v-vi; Grant L. Reuber, 'Problems of Development Assistance and Economic Cooperation Among Large and Small States in the Pacific Region,' in Castle and Holmes, eds., *Cooperation and Development in the Asia-Pacific Region*, 9-37; and Saburo Okita, 'Japan's Role in Pacific Basin Cooperation – Present and Future,' *Euro-Asia Business Review* 4 (February 1985):38.
64 Narongchai Akrasanee, Seiji Naya, and Vinyu Vichit-Vadakan, eds., *Trade and Employment in Asia and the Pacific* (Honolulu: University of Hawaii Press 1977).

65 Lawrence B. Krause, 'Introduction,' in Krause and Patrick, eds., *Mineral Resources in the Pacific Area*, 22-8.
66 Peter Drysdale, 'An Organization for Pacific Trade, Aid and Development: Regional Arrangements and the Resource Trade,' in Krause and Patrick, eds., *Mineral Resources in the Pacific Area*, 621.
67 Drysdale, 'An Organization,' 621-2.
68 See Makoto Ikema, 'Japan's Economic Relations with ASEAN,' in Ross Garnaut, ed., *ASEAN in a Changing Pacific and World Economy* (Canberra: Australian National University Press 1980), 473-4 and 474, n. 7.
69 David B. Yoffie and Robert O. Keohane, 'Responding to the New Protectionism: Strategies for the Advanced Developing Countries in the Pacific Basin,' in Wontack Hong and Lawrence B. Krause, eds., *Trade and Growth of Advanced Developing Countries in the Pacific Basin* (Seoul: Korea Development Institute 1981), 584.
70 Hong and Krause, eds., *Trade and Growth of the Advanced Developing Countries in the Pacific Basin*, 590-4 and Lawrence B. Krause, 'Summary,' in Hong and Krause, eds., *Trade and Growth of the Advanced Developing Countries in the Pacific Basin*, 609.
71 Gordon R. Munro, 'Cooperative Fisheries Arrangements Between Coastal States and Distant-Water Nations,' in H.E. English and Anthony Scott, eds., *Renewable Resources in the Pacific* (Ottawa: International Development Research Centre 1982), 247-55.
72 Richard N. Cooper, 'Inter-Regional and Intra-Regional Energy Cooperation in the Pacific Basin,' in Romeo Bautista and Seiji Naya, eds., *Energy and Structural Change in the Asia-Pacific Region* (Manila: Philippine Institute for Development Studies/Asian Development Bank 1984), 497-509.
73 Augustine H.H. Tan and Basant Kapur, eds., *Pacific Growth and Financial Interdependence* (Sydney: Allen and Unwin 1986); Hiromichi Mutoh et al., eds., *Industrial Policies for Pacific Economic Growth* (Sydney: Allen and Unwin 1986); Leslie V. Castle and Christopher Findlay, eds., *Pacific Trade in Services* (Sydney: Allen and Unwin 1988); Hadi Soesastro and Mari Pangestu, eds., *Technological Challenge in the Pacific* (Sydney: Allen and Unwin 1990); Mohamed Ariff, ed., *The Pacific Economy: Growth and External Stability* (Sydney: Allen and Unwin 1991); *PAFTAD Newsletter*, no. 6 (March 1991):1-2; *PAFTAD Newsletter*, no. 7 (July 1992):1-2; and *Australia-Japan Research Centre Newsletter*, no. 8 (July 1992):7.
74 These sentiments were expressed at PAFTAD 16 during Session 9, 28 January 1987 and Session 11, 29 January 1987, attended by the author.
75 *PAFTAD Newsletter*, no. 5 (December 1989):1-2 and *PAFTAD Newsletter*, no. 6 (March 1991):3-4.
76 United States, Congressional Research Service, Library of Congress, 'An Asian-Pacific Regional Economic Organization: An Exploratory Concept Paper,' prepared for the Committee on Foreign Relations, United States Senate, U.S. Government Printing Service, Washington, July 1979.
77 Pacific Basin Co-operation Study Group, 'Report on the Pacific Basin Co-operation Concept,' in John Crawford and Greg Seow, eds., *Pacific Economic*

Co-operation: Suggestions for Action (Selangor: Heinemann Educational 1981), 183-204.

78 Hooper, *Building a Pacific Community*, 9-11.

79 John Grenfell Crawford, 'Pacific Community: Dream or Reality?' in Hooper, *Building a Pacific Community*, 63-75.

80 Soesastro, 'Institutional Aspects,' 23.

81 'PAFTAD-ISC Report: PAFTAD and the Pacific Community Seminar,' September 1980, AJRC Files. See also Pacific Trade and Development Conference (PADTAD), International Steering Committee, 'The Pacific Trade and Development Conference Series,' in John Crawford and Greg Seow, eds., *Pacific Economic Co-operation*, 26.

82 *PAFTAD Newsletter*, no. 1 (August 1985):4.

83 Patrick, 'Report,' 4.

84 *PAFTAD Newsletter*, no. 1 (August 1985):4.

85 Earle and Trigg, 'Pacific Economic Cooperation,' 2.

86 Confidential interviews, Canberra, 21 January 1986 and Tokyo, 10 November 1986; 'PECC Standing Committee Meets in Tokyo, Preparations for Osaka Under Way,' *Pacific Cooperation Newsletter* (Japan National Committee for Pacific Economic Cooperation), no. 9 (Spring 1987):1-2; *PAFTAD Newsletter*, no. 3 (July 1987):4; *PAFTAD Newsletter*, no. 5 (December 1989):1; *PAFTAD Newsletter*, no. 6 (March 1991):4; and *PECC Report VII*, 144-7.

87 Confidential interview, Tokyo, 8 November 1986. For a more positive outlook on the relationships between PAFTAD, PECC, and APEC, see *PAFTAD Newsletter*, no. 5 (December 1989):1-2 and *PAFTAD Newsletter*, no. 6 (March 1991):3-4.

88 English, 'The Emerging Pacific Community,' in Hadi Soesastro and Han Sung-Joo, eds., *Pacific Economic Cooperation: The Next Phase*, 96-7.

89 Earle and Trigg, 'Pacific Economic Cooperation,' 7-8.

90 Crough and Wheelwright, *Australia: A Client State* (Harmondsworth, UK: Penguin 1982), 62.

91 Peter D. Bell, 'The Ford Foundation as a Transnational Actor,' in Robert O. Keohane and Joseph S. Nye, eds., *Transnational Relations and World Politics* (Cambridge, MA: Harvard University Press 1973), 115-28 and Perry, 'Private Philanthropy and Foreign Affairs,' 268-84.

Chapter 5: The Pacific Basin Economic Council

1 PBEC was originally known as the Pacific Basin Economic Cooperation Committee. In 1969, the word *Committee* was replaced by *Council*. The word *Cooperation* was dropped in 1971. See Bryant, *Japanese Private Economic Diplomacy: An Analysis of Business-Government Linkages* (New York: Praeger 1975), 71.

2 Bryant, *Japanese Private Economic Diplomacy*, 72; R.W.C. Anderson, *Pacific Initiative – Concept to Reality: International Business Cooperation Committees: The First Decade* (Canberra: AJBCC/PBEC 1971), 1-2, papers of R.W.C. Anderson, Director-General of the Associated Chambers of Manufacturers of Australia, MS 4872, National Library of Australia (NLA), Canberra (hereafter cited as Anderson Papers), box 4; Opening address by the leader of the Australian delegation to the inaugural meeting of the Australia/Japan Coop-

eration Committee, Tokyo, May 1963, 1-5, Australia-Japan Business Cooperation Committee Papers, NLA, Canberra (hereafter cited as AJBCC Papers).

3 Shigeo Nagano, 'The Establishment of the Pacific Basin Economic Cooperation Committee,' *Japan/Australia Agenda Papers*, Pacific Economic Cooperation Committee, Japan/Australia Business Cooperation Committee, Fifth Joint Meeting, Tokyo, 24-7 April 1967, 1, SRI Files; 'Minutes of the First Day of the Second Joint Meeting of the Australia-Japan Business Cooperation Committee,' Canberra, 2 September 1964, 5-13, AJBCC Papers.

4 R.W.C. Anderson and I.H. Seppelt, 'Formation of a Pacific Basin Organization for Economic Cooperation and Development,' paper presented on behalf of the Australian Committee of the AJBCC to the Second Joint Meeting, Canberra, 2-3 September 1964, 1-6, AJBCC Papers; Shigeo Nagano, 'Formation of a Pacific Basin Organization for Economic Cooperation and Development,' paper presented on behalf of the Japanese Committee of the AJBCC to the Second Joint Meeting, Australia/Japan Agenda Papers, Canberra, 2-3 September 1964, AJBCC Papers.

5 'Minutes of the Third Joint Meeting of the Australia and Japan Business Cooperation Committees,' provisional draft, Tokyo, 6 May 1965, AJBCC Papers; 'Pacific Basin Organisation for Economic Cooperation and Development,' Australia-Japan Agenda Papers, Third Joint Meeting, Tokyo, 6-8 May 1965, 5-6, AJBCC Papers; and H. Roy Crabtree, 'Report on 1966 Australia-Japan Businessmen's Conference,' 1966, 1-2, SRI Files.

6 Pacific Basin Organization for Economic Cooperation and Development, Australia-Japan Agenda Papers, Fourth Joint Meeting, Canberra, April 1966, 1-7, AJBCC Papers.

7 Bryant, *Japanese Private Economic Diplomacy*, 75. See also Crabtree, 'Report on 1966 Australia-Japan Businessmen's Conference,' 6 and *Canberra Letter* (Associated Chambers of Manufacturers of Australia) 937 (26 April 1965):3.

8 'International Conferences in Japan,' *Japan Commerce and Industry* 11 (1970):75 and U. Alexis Johnson, 'The Pacific Basin,' *Pacific Community* 1 (October 1969):11, n. 1.

9 See Nagano, 'The Establishment,' 2-5 and Pacific Basin Economic Cooperation Committee, Japan/Australia Agenda Papers, Pacific Basin Economic Cooperation Committee, Japan/Australia Business Cooperation Committee, Fifth Joint Meeting, Tokyo, 24-7 April 1967, 2-4, SRI Files.

10 Bryant, *Japanese Private Economic Diplomacy*, 71-5; E.J. Donath, 'Closer Ties,' *Far Eastern Economic Review*, 23 May 1968, 404; and 'Sydney Meeting, Pacific Basin Committee: A Report on the First General Meeting, 9-10 May 1968,' *SRI-International* 6 (July 1968):i-3.

11 PBEC, Memorandum to International Officers, 28 September 1984, SRI Files; PBEC – San Francisco Meeting, 18-21 May 1987: General Information, SRI Files.

12 PBEC, Report of Steering Committee Meetings, Honolulu, 29-30 October 1973, 1-2, Anderson Papers, box 4.

13 PBEC, Minutes of Seventh General Meeting, Washington, 12-15 May 1974, Appendix C1, Anderson Papers, box 4; PBEC, Report of the PBEC Steering Committee Meetings, Honolulu, 29-30 October 1973, 1-2, Anderson Papers,

box 4; 'Sydney Meeting,' 7; 'The Sydney Report – Free Enterprise and Pacific Development: A Report on the Pacific Industrial Conference, 12-15 April 1967, Sydney, Australia,' *SRI-International* 1 (June 1967):i-2, 28-32; 'The Djakarta Report: A Summary of the Pacific-Indonesia Business Association Meeting, Djakarta, Indonesia, 2-5 August 1967,' *SRI-International* 3 (September 1967):36-7; and confidential interviews, Menlo Park, 12 and 20 January 1987.

14 *PBEC Executive Summary: San Francisco Meeting, 1987*, 3; *Australian* (25 May 1987):7; *PBEC Report* (Canadian Committee) 8 (Winter 1990):1, 10; and *Vancouver Sun*, 26 May 1992, D3. The PBEC Secretariat can be contacted c/o Pauahi Tower, 1001 Bishop Street, Suite 1150, Honolulu, Hawaii, USA 96813 (Tel: 808-523-2429; Fax: 808-599-8690).

15 Bryant, *Japanese Private Economic Diplomacy*, 71-4.

16 PBEC-Japan, 'Committee Activities Report: 1985,' SRI Files; Lawrence T. Woods, 'The Business of Canada's Pacific Relations,' *Canadian Journal of Administrative Sciences* 4 (December 1987):413-14; and *PBEC Bulletin* (U.S. National Committee), November 1978 and January 1983.

17 Palmer, *The New Regionalism in Asia and the Pacific* (Lexington, MA: Lexington 1991), 139; *PAFTAD Newsletter*, no. 5 (December 1989):1; Confidential interview, Ottawa, 14 June 1989; and *New Pacific*, no. 5 (Summer 1992):36.

18 Record of the First General Meeting of the Pacific Basin Economic Cooperation Committee, Sydney, 8-10 May 1968, Japan National Committee of the Pacific Basin Economic Cooperation Committee, July 1968, 16, SRI Files.

19 Opening speech by the chairperson of the Australian National Committee, the Honourable Sir Edward Warren, May 1969, 2-3, SRI Files; Report of the Pacific Basin Economic Cooperation Council, Second General Meeting, 14-17 May 1969, 16, SRI Files.

20 A.N. Parbo, Managing Director, Western Mining Corporation, Letter to Sir James Vernon, Australian National Committee of PBEC, 14 July 1972, Anderson Papers, box 3.

21 C.W. Robinson, Pacific Basin Economic Council, Report of Steering Committee, Oahu, Hawaii, 30-1 October 1972, SRI Files; PBEC, Minutes of Sixth General Meeting, Sydney, Australia, May 1973, 49, Anderson Papers, box 6; PBEC, Report of the PBEC Steering Committee Meetings, Honolulu, 29-30 October 1973, 2-3, Anderson Papers, box 4; and Australian National Committee of PBEC, Agenda Papers, Eighth General Meeting, Kyoto, Japan, May 1975, Anderson Papers, box 5.

22 Richard G. Landis, 'Organization of the Regional Member Committee,' *PBEC Report: Santiago Meeting – 1983*, 65; Bruce Roscoe, 'The No-Frontiers Men,' *Far Eastern Economic Review*, 12 June 1986, 75; Statement of the Latin American Group, PBEC Plenary Meeting, Auckland, 12-16 May 1985, 3-4, SRI Files; M. Mark Earle, Jr., Memorandum to International Officers, 4 November 1985, SRI Files; and *Vancouver Sun*, 26 May 1992, D3.

23 PBEC, Memorandum to International Officers, 1 April 1985, SRI Files and 'The Quest for Talent,' *Far Eastern Economic Review*, 23 May 1985, 91.

24 'PBEC: The Age of the Pacific,' *Fortune* (September 1972):55; PBEC, Minutes of Fifth General Meeting, 12-13; and PBEC, Minutes of Sixth General Meeting, 12-13.

25 Weldon B. Gibson, Memorandum No. 13 to PBEC Officers, 15 April 1975, SRI Files; Japan Member Committee, PBEC, Memorandum Concerning Concept of the Pacific Economic Community, 1984, 12, SRI Files; 'PBEC: The Pacific Economic Community Concept Symposium Opens,' *Japan Commerce and Industry* 26 (1985):15; *Far Eastern Economic Review*, 4 August 1988, 4; *PBEC Report* 8 (Summer 1989):1; Lawrence T. Woods, 'Meeting Mikhail: Attitudes towards Soviet Involvement in Pacific Cooperation,' *Pacific Review* 3 (1990):214-21; Palmer, *The New Regionalism in Asia and the Pacific*, 139; and PBEC, Twenty-Fourth International General Meeting, Mexico, Guadalajara, 4-8 May 1991 (Mexico City: PBEC Mexico Member Committee 1991), 11-12.

26 Bryant, *Japanese Private Economic Diplomacy*, 75 and 83, n. 5; Roscoe, 'The No-Frontiers Men,' 75.

27 Bryant, *Japanese Private Economic Diplomacy*, 81-2 and 83, n. 5.

28 Bryant, *Japanese Private Economic Diplomacy*, 70-4 and *Canberra Letter* 976 (4 August 1970):4. On nondecision-making, see Peter Bachrach and Morton S. Baratz, *Power and Poverty: Theory and Practice* (New York: Oxford University Press), 43-4.

29 Ransom M. Cook, 'Private Sector Initiatives in Pacific Basin Area Development,' 1969, 2, SRI Files.

30 The keynote address by Shigeo Nagano, President, at the opening session of the Third General Meeting of the Pacific Basin Economic Council, Kyoto, 21 May 1970, 1, Anderson Papers, box 1.

31 Ransom M. Cook, 'A Perspective from the United States,' remarks at the opening session, Second General Meeting, Pacific Basin Economic Cooperation Committee, San Francisco, 14 May 1969, 3-4, SRI Files.

32 Bryant, *Japanese Private Economic Diplomacy*, 73.

33 Arnold F.C. Hean, 'Report of Human Resources Development Committee,' Kyoto, 23 May 1970; Charles S. Dennison, 'A Proposal to Encourage Private Philanthropy in Asia,' paper presented to PBEC 3, prepared 10 April 1970, Anderson Papers, box 1; and Steering Committee of PBEC, Vancouver, 14 May 1971, Anderson Papers, box 4.

34 'PBEC: The Age of the Pacific,' 44.

35 Steering Committee Minutes, Honolulu, 28-9 October 1973, Anderson Papers, box 4 and PBEC International Director-General, Memorandum No. 2 to PBEC Officers, 22 August 1974, Anderson Papers, box 5.

36 Canadian Committee, PBEC, notes on the meeting between PBEC Canadian Committee and senior government officials, 24 September 1986, 1-6, Canadian Chamber of Commerce Files (hereafter cited as CCC files). For a positive assessment, see Chalmers Johnson, 'Pacific Regional Development: Myth and Reality,' *Asian Pacific Review*, no. 7 (Summer 1987):2.

37 *Canberra Letter* 968 (14 February 1969):5 and Woods, 'The Business of Canada's Pacific Relations,' 410-25. I am also grateful to Frank Langdon for bringing this theme to my attention.

38 M. Mark Earle, Jr., and Eric A. Trigg, 'Pacific Economic Cooperation and an Overview of the Canberra Process,' *PBEC Papers, 1985*, 4-5.

39 'Santiago Resolution,' *PBEC Report: Santiago Meeting – 1983*, 62; J.H. Stevens, Report of the PBEC Ad Hoc Committee on New Initiatives (draft), 25

November 1982, 5-10, SRI Files; M. Mark Earle, Jr., Memoranda to International Officers, 1 September 1983, 4 November 1985 and 30 June 1986, SRI Files.

40 Frederick B. Whittemore, 'PBEC's President's Address,' *PBEC Report: Auckland Meeting – 1985*, 5-6.

41 Peter Drysdale and Hugh Patrick, 'An Asian-Pacific Regional Economic Organization: An Exploratory Concept Paper,' in John Crawford and Greg Seow, eds., *Pacific Economic Co-operation: Suggestions for Action* (Selangor: Heinemann Educational 1981), 75 and H. Edward English, 'The Emerging Pacific Community,' in Hadi Soesastro and Han Sung-Joo, eds., *Pacific Economic Cooperation: The Next Phase* (Jakarta: Centre for Strategic and International Studies 1983), 96. See also Soesastro, 'Institutional Aspects of Pacific Economic Cooperation,' in Soesastro and Sung-Joo, eds., *Pacific Economic Cooperation: The Next Phase*, 3-52.

42 *Canberra Letter* 960 (16 May 1968):3-5.

43 PBEC, U.S. National Committee, Memorandum: Steering Committee Meeting, Honolulu, 1-2 November 1971, 6, Anderson Papers, box 4; Steering Committee of PBEC, Minutes, 11 May 1971, Anderson Papers, box 4.

44 R.W.C. Anderson, Director-General, AJBCC/PBEC, Letter to Sir James Vernon, Director, CSR Ltd., 2 August 1973, 3-4, Anderson Papers, box 3.

45 Noboru Gotoh, 'An Economic Community,' *PBEC Report: Los Angeles Meeting, 1979*, 2-3 and PBEC-Japan National Committee, 'Approaches Toward a Pacific Economic Community,' *PBEC Report: Sydney Meeting, 1980*, 27.

46 PBEC, Canadian Committee, 'A Canadian Perception of the Pacific Community,' April 1980, 8-9, SRI Files; PBEC, U.S. National Committee, 'Pacific Economic Community Concept,' January 1980, SRI Files; and 'Policy Position on the Pacific Economic Community,' *PBEC Report: Sydney Meeting, 1980*, 27.

47 Quoted in Crawford and Seow, *Pacific Economic Co-operation*, 20.

48 Crawford and Seow, *Pacific Economic Co-operation*, 241-3.

49 James Vernon, 'Toward a Pacific Economic Community,' *PBEC Report: Hong Kong Meeting, 1981*, 4-5 and James Vernon, 'The Pacific Economic Community Concept: Resolution,' revised draft, October 1981, SRI Files.

50 J.H. Stevens, 'Report of the Special Committee on the PEC,' *PBEC Report: Nagoya Meeting, 1982*, 34.

51 J.H. Stevens, 'The Pacific Economic Community: A Framework for Discussion and Study,' *PBEC Papers: Nagoya Meeting, 1982*, 4-6.

52 Noboru Gotoh, 'Summary Report,' *PBEC Report: Nagoya Meeting, 1982*, 3.

53 *PBEC Report: Santiago Meeting, 1983*, ii.

54 Eric A. Trigg, 'PBEC and the PEC Task Forces,' *PBEC Report: Santiago Meeting, 1983*, 23.

55 Eric A. Trigg, 'Pacific Cooperation: Status of the Canberra Process' and 'PBEC Chairmen's Views,' *PBEC Report: Vancouver Meeting, 1984*, 13, 31.

56 Trigg, 'Pacific Cooperation,' 14.

57 M. Mark Earle, Jr., 'PBEC: The Changing Scene,' 20 October 1982, 3-4, SRI Files.

58 'PBEC: The Pacific Economic Community Concept Symposium Opens,' 15.

59 M. Mark Earle, Jr., Memorandum to International Officers, 15 August 1985, 2-3, SRI Files; *PBEC Executive Summary: Seoul Meeting, 1986*, 27.
60 *PBEC Executive Summary: San Francisco Meeting, 1987*, 22-3.
61 Palmer, *The New Regionalism in Asia and the Pacific*, 139.
62 *PECC VII Report*, 141-7.
63 Donald J. Puchala, 'The Integration Theorists and the Study of International Relations,' in Charles W. Kegley, Jr. and Eugene R. Wittkopf, eds., *The Global Agenda: Issues and Perspectives*, 2nd edition (New York: Random House 1988), 198-215.
64 *PBEC Report* 8 (Summer 1989):1-2; *PBEC Report* 8 (Winter 1990):1; Palmer, *The New Regionalism in Asia and the Pacific*, 140; PBEC, Twenty-Fourth International General Meeting, 1; and *Vancouver Sun*, 26 May 1992, D3.
65 *PECC Newsletter*, vol. 2, no. 1 (January 1992):1.
66 Michael Taylor, 'Business Knows Best,' *Far Eastern Economic Review*, 8 March 1990, 41 and *Far Eastern Economic Review*, 19 April 1990, 7.
67 The fund was established with gifts of U.S.$1 million from the outgoing international president, Chen-Fu Koo, $300,000 from the incoming president, Pyong-Hwoi Koo, and $1 million from the Japanese member committee. Perhaps predictably, the Council's future has also been coloured environmental green (*Vancouver Sun*, 26 May 1992, D3). For PBEC's view of itself in 1992, see *New Pacific*, no. 5 (Summer 1992):36-9.

Chapter 6: The Pacific Economic Cooperation Council

1 Carl J. Green, 'Towards Pacific Economic Integration: Making Haste Slowly,' and Takeshi Watanabe, 'Pan-Pacific Solidarity Without Domination,' in *The Pacific Community Concept: Views from Eight Nations* (Tokyo: Japan Center for International Exchange 1980), 103-7 and 101-2, respectively, and 'ASEAN and Pacific Economic Cooperation,' *Indonesian Quarterly* 10 (July 1982):74. On the Trilateral Commission, see Stephen Gill, 'From Atlanticism to Trilateralism: The Case of the Trilateral Commission,' in Steve Smith, ed., *International Relations: British and American Perspectives* (Oxford: Basil Blackwell/British International Studies Association 1985), 185-212. The Anderson/Seppelt design for a tripartite regional organization was inspired by the International Labor Organization (ILO). It is likely that the ILO format was also considered in the formative stages of the PECC process, especially by those such as Gough Whitlam, who noted the need for trade unions to be involved. See Whitlam, *A Pacific Community* (Cambridge, MA: Harvard University Press 1981), 44-51. Ernst Haas has documented the experience of tripartism in the ILO, highlighting the 'patterns of consensus' amongst workers, employers, and governments. See Ernst Haas, *Beyond the Nation State: Functionalism and International Organization* (Stanford, CA: Stanford University Press 1964), 194-244.
2 Charles E. Morrison and Anne F. Miyashiro, 'Issues in Pan-Pacific Cooperation,' in *The Pacific Community Concept: Views from Eight Nations*, 13-14.
3 'Pacific Rim,' *Japan Quarterly* 15 (April/June 1980):149; Okita, 'Pacific Regional Co-operation,' in Evans and Miller, eds., *Policy and Practice*, 125;

Yasushi Hara, 'How to Make a Concept Real – The Idea of Pacific Basin Cooperation,' *Japan Quarterly* 27 (October/December 1980):471-2; and Davies, 'Exploiting the Pacific Tide,' 47.

4 *Backgrounder* (Department of Foreign Affairs, Australia) (14 November 1979) vi, and Gerardo P. Sicat, 'ASEAN and the Pacific Region,' in John Crawford and Greg Seow, eds., *Pacific Economic Co-operation: Suggestions for Action* (Selengor: Heinemann Educational 1981), 220.

5 Australia, Department of Foreign Affairs, 'Pacific Community Seminar – ANU Seminar,' *Backgrounder* (3 September 1980):1 and Mitsuro Donawaki, 'The Pacific Basin Community – A Japanese Overview,' *Asia Pacific Community*, no. 15 (Winter 1982):16-17.

6 Confidential interview, Canberra, 22 September 1986 and Shishido and Sato, *Economic Policy and Development: New Perspectives (Essays in Honor of Dr. Saburo Okita)* (Dover, MA: Auburn House 1985), xi.

7 Malcolm Fraser, 'Pacific Community: Further Steps,' in Robert L. Downen and Bruce J. Dickson, eds., *The Emerging Pacific Community: A Regional Perspective* (Boulder, CO: Westview 1984), 5 and Alan Renouf, *Malcolm Fraser and Australian Foreign Policy* (Sydney: Australian Professional Publications 1986), 48.

8 John Crawford, 'The Pacific Basin Cooperative Concept,' in *Business Cooperation Between Asia-Pacific and Japan in the Eighties* (Tokyo: Export-Import Bank of Japan 1980), 36.

9 Crawford, 'Pacific Community: Dream or Reality?' 64.

10 The proceedings and recommendations of the Canberra Seminar are reviewed in Crawford and Seow, *Pacific Economic Co-operation*, 1-32. This volume also contains the papers issued in advance to seminar participants.

11 Soesastro, 'Institutional Aspects of Pacific Economic Cooperation,' in Hadi Soesastro and Han Sung-Joo, eds., *Pacific Economic Cooperation: The Next Phase* (Jakarta: Centre for Strategic and International Studies 1983), 32-44 and Hadi Soesastro, 'ASEAN and the Political Economy of Pacific Cooperation,' *Asian Survey* 23 (December 1983):1,262-9. For the text of the PBCSG report, see Pacific Basin Co-operation Study Group, 'A Japanese Perspective: Reports of the Pacific Basin Co-operation Study Group,' in *The Pacific Community Concept: Views from Eight Nations* (Tokyo: Japan Center for International Exchange 1980), 17-31 and The Pacific Basin Co-operation Study Group (Japan), 'Report on the Pacific Basin Co-operation Concept,' in Crawford and Seow, eds., *Pacific Economic Co-operation*, 183-204.

12 Earle and Trigg, 'Pacific Economic Cooperation and an Overview of the Canberra Process,' *PBEC Papers, 1985*, 11.

13 This list draws upon the seminar summary and recommendations presented in Crawford and Seow, *Pacific Economic Co-operation*, 27-32. For other summaries, see Crawford, 'Pacific Community: Dream or Reality?' 63-75; Peter Drysdale, 'Australia's Interest in Pacific Economic Cooperation,' *ASEAN Economic Bulletin* 2 (November 1985):104-5; Peter Drysdale, 'Building the Foundations of a Pacific Economic Community,' in Shishido and Sato, eds., *Economic Policy and Development: New Perspectives*, 56-7; PECC, *Pacific Economic Cooperation Conference IV: Announcement, Seoul, Korea, 29 April-1 May*

1985 (Seoul: Korea Development Institute 1985), 8-9, 19-25 (hereafter cited as *PECC IV Announcement*); and *PECC V Report*, 159-63.

14 Crawford, 'Pacific Community: Dream or Reality?' 72.

15 *PECC IV Announcement*, 9. Following the Canberra Seminar, Crawford undertook extensive consultations with ASEAN governments in order to clarify the cooperation concept. Drysdale, 'Building the Foundations,' 57.

16 Hiroshi Kitamura, 'Asian-Pacific Economic Cooperation: The Role of Governments,' *Asia Pacific Community*, no. 18 (Fall 1982):17-19.

17 George R. Ariyoshi, 'Hawaii's Role in the Pacific Community,' in Paul F. Hooper, ed., *Building a Pacific Community* (Honolulu: East-West Center 1982), 83-4 and Soesastro, 'Institutional Aspects,' 25-7.

18 Ali Moertopo, 'Pacific Economic Cooperation: The Practice of Meaningful Consultation,' in Soesastro and Sung-Joo, eds., *Pacific Economic Cooperation: The Next Phase*, 206.

19 Moertopo, 'Pacific Economic Cooperation,' 207.

20 Confidential interview, Wellington, 28 January 1987; Earle and Trigg, 'Pacific Economic Cooperation,' 11; and Stevens, 'The Pacific Economic Community,' *PBEC Papers: Nagoya Meeting – 1982*, 3.

21 Saburo Okita, 'Japan's Role in Pacific Basin Cooperation – Present and Future,' *Euro-Asia Business Review* 4 (February 1985):38; *PECC IV Announcement*, 9, 26-7; and 'ASEAN and Pacific Economic Cooperation,' 67.

22 *PECC IV Announcement*, 9. See also Jusuf Wanandi, 'Pacific Economic Cooperation: An Indonesian View,' *Asian Survey* 23 (December 1983):1,272-3 and Mark Borthwick, 'ASEAN and Pacific Economic Cooperation: The Bangkok Conference in June,' *Pacific Basin Quarterly* 7 (Spring/Summer 1982): 18-20.

23 Stevens, 'The Pacific Economic Community,' 3. The ASEAN reservations towards the recommendations emanating from PECC I included a perceived lack of urgency; uncertainty about the gains and costs of participation; dissatisfaction with the vague objectives of regional cooperation; and a sensitivity to overriding political considerations such as leadership and membership. See Jusuf Wanandi, 'ASEAN and Pacific Basin Economic Cooperation,' in Hiroshi Matsumoto and Noordin Sopiee, eds., *Into the Pacific Era: Southeast Asia and Its Place in the Pacific* (Kuala Lumpur/Tokyo: Institute of Strategic and International Studies/Association of Promotion of International Cooperation 1986), 27-31.

24 *PECC IV Announcement*, 9-10, 27.

25 'ASEAN and Pacific Economic Cooperation,' 67-8.

26 Nam Duck-Woo, 'Changing Pattern of Trade and Trends in Trade Policy in the Asia-Pacific Region,' in Hooper, ed., *Building a Pacific Community*, 119; 'ASEAN and Pacific Economic Cooperation,' 67-8; and English, 'The Emerging Pacific Community,' in Soesastro and Sung-Joo, eds., *Pacific Economic Cooperation: The Next Phase*, 98-9.

27 'ASEAN and Pacific Economic Cooperation,' 67-8; Landis, 'Pacific Cooperation: Recent Developments,' 11; Stevens, 'The Pacific Economic Community,' 3; and *PECC IV Announcement*, 9-11, 26-7.

28 English, 'The Emerging Pacific Community,' 98.

29 *PECC IV Announcement*, 11-16, 28-9 and Okita, 'Japan's Role in Pacific Basin Cooperation,' 38.

30 *Pacific Cooperation Newsletter* (Japan National Committee for Pacific Economic Cooperation, hereafter cited as *PCN*), no. 7 (April 1985):1-2 and *PECC IV Announcement*, 13.

31 Dick Wilson, 'The Pacific Basin is Coming Together,' *Asia Pacific Community*, no. 30 (Fall 1985):5; Eric A. Trigg, Minutes of the PECC Standing Committee Meetings, Seoul, Korea (26 April and 1 May 1985), 4 September 1985 (hereafter cited as Seoul Minutes); and Derek Davies, 'Pacific's Flying Geese,' *Far Eastern Economic Review*, 23 May 1985, 88, 91.

32 The 'flying geese' analogy was used in the 1930s by the Japanese economist Kaname Akamatsu as an alternative to the traditional vertical (i.e., imperialist) and horizontal (i.e., European, a group of industrialized countries trading amongst themselves) patterns in the international division of labour. See Davies, 'Pacific's Flying Geese,' 91 and Saburo Okita, 'Pacific Development and Its Implications for the World Economy,' in James W. Morley, ed., *The Pacific Basin: New Challenges for the United States* (New York: Academy of Political Science 1986), 26-8.

33 Davies, 'Pacific's Flying Geeese,' 88, 91. In his comments to the PECC-ISC following his post-PECC III conversation with Prime Minister Nakasone, Okita had reported this to be the position of the Japanese government. See Eric A. Trigg, Memorandum on Meeting of Standing Committee of the PECC, Bangkok, 3 March 1984, 2 (hereafter cited as Bangkok Memorandum).

34 Correspondence, 9 September 1986, in the papers of the PECC Secretariat held at the Canadian Chamber of Commerce, Ottawa; Heather Gibb, Canadian National Committee on Pacific Economic Cooperation, Minutes of the Meeting of the PECC Standing Committee, San Francisco, 22-3 August 1986, draft, 8 September 1986, 2 (hereafter cited as San Francisco Minutes), CCC Files; *PCN* 9 (Spring 1987):1; and *Pacific Economic Cooperation* (United States National Committee for Pacific Economic Cooperation) 3 (Fall 1987):1.

35 Confidential interviews, Tokyo, 10 November 1986, and Ottawa, 25 November 1986; Correspondence, 9 September 1986, CCC Files; and *PECC V Report*, 13.

36 *PECC VI Report*, 19-20.

37 *PECC VI Report*, 9-21.

38 *PECC VII Report*, 1-4.

39 Australia, Department of Foreign Affairs and Trade, 'APEC Comes of Age,' *Backgrounder* 2 (6 December 1991):6-7.

40 PECC, Minutes of the Standing Committee of the Pacific Economic Cooperation Conference, Singapore, 4 May 1990, draft, mimeo, 4 and *PECC Newsletter* (PECC Secretariat, Singapore), vol. 1, no. 3 (July 1991):2-3.

41 *PECC Newsletter*, vol. 2, no. 2 (April 1992):8.

42 *PECC Newsletter*, vol. 2, no. 2 (April 1992):1 and vol. 2, no. 4 (October 1992):1, 8.

43 *PECC IV Announcement*, 13-14 and Wilson, 'The Pacific Basin is Coming Together,' 4.

44 *PECC IV Announcement*, 14-15; Trigg, Seoul Minutes, 3; Trigg, Bangkok Memorandum, 4-5; and Gibb, San Francisco Minutes.

45 Confidential interviews, Canberra, 8 April 1986, Tokyo, 6 and 10 November 1986, and Ottawa, 25 November 1986; Drysdale, 'Australia's Interest,' 105; and R. Sean Randolph, 'Pacific Overtures,' *Foreign Policy*, no. 57 (Winter 1984-5):140.

46 PECC, 'Report of the Ad Hoc Task Force on Institutional Development,' mimeo, May 1990. The PECC Secretariat can be contacted c/o 4 Nassim Road, Singapore 1025 (Tel: 65-737-9823; Fax: 65-737-9824).

47 Confidential interviews, Tokyo, 6 November 1986, and Ottawa, 25 November 1986; National Pacific Cooperation Committee of Australia, *Australia and Pacific Economic Cooperation: Report by the National Pacific Cooperation Committee to the Australian Government* (Canberra: Australian National University 1985), 27 (hereafter cited as *NPCCA 1985 Report*); Canada, Department of External Affairs, 'Secretary of State Addresses the First Meeting of the National Committee on Pacific Economic Cooperation,' *Communiqué*, no. 144 (4 October 1985); and 'Formulating Beyond CER Strategy,' 2.

48 Eric Trigg, 'PECC's Progress: An Insider's View,' *Asia Pacific Business* 2 (Fall 1986):38.

49 *PCN 7* (April 1985):2 and *PECC IV Announcement*, 2.

50 *PECC IV Announcement*, 15-16; *PCN 7* (April 1985):2; and Randolph, 'Pacific Overtures,' 125-7. A Soviet national PECC committee was established in March 1988. See Sophie Quinn-Judge, 'Moscow Looks East,' *Far Eastern Economic Review*, 2 June 1988, 59.

51 *NPCCA 1985 Report*, 27; Canada, Department of External Affairs, 'Secretary of State Addresses'; Correspondence between the author and a member of the Canadian National Committee on Pacific Economic Cooperation, 15 May 1987; and correspondence between the author and a member of the Asia and Pacific Branch, Department of External Affairs, Canada, 29 July 1987.

52 Confidential interviews, Canberra, 13 and 20 October 1986, and Tokyo, 10 November 1986.

53 Crawford and Seow, *Pacific Economic Co-operation*, 12.

54 Confidential interview, Canberra, 13 October 1986.

55 For a list of participants and observers at PECC I, see Crawford and Seow, *Pacific Economic Co-operation*, 241-3. In spite of requests from Chile, Mexico, and Peru, the conveners decided not to invite Latin American delegates or observers. See Solidum, 'The Pacific Community in Search of a Form,' *Asian Perspective* 9 (Fall/Winter 1985):208. A request for observer status made by Russel Madigan on behalf of the AJBCC was also refused (confidential interview, Canberra, 30 April 1987).

56 Crawford, 'Pacific Community: Dream or Reality?' 64-6. Crawford also noted that 'the only rejection ... was regrettably by the Prime Minister of Fiji, Ratu Sir Kamisese Mara, who felt that it was improper for the South Pacific Island states to be represented by a single delegation and who saw the seminar as an overly ambitious project which might have a negative impact upon the more limited aspirations of South Pacific regionalism.' On South

Pacific reluctance, see also C.C. Aikman, 'Regional Cooperation Among Asian-Pacific Nations: A View from the South Pacific,' in Soesastro and Sung-Joo, eds., *Pacific Economic Cooperation: The Next Phase*, 216-19 and Ratu Kamisese K.T. Mara, 'Building a Pacific Community,' in Hooper, ed., *Building a Pacific Community*, 47.

57 Hiroshi Kitamura, 'The Case for Asia-Pacific Regionalism: Regional and Sub-Regional Approaches to Multilateralism,' in *Prospects for Closer Economic Cooperation in the Asia-Pacific Area*, Occasional Paper A-5, the Asian Society, February 1981, 1 and Okita, 'Japan's Role in Pacific Basin Cooperation,' 38.

58 Crawford, 'Pacific Community: Dream or Reality?' 65-6.

59 Randolph, 'Pacific Overtures,' 135-6.

60 Osborne and Fourt, *Pacific Basin Economic Cooperation* (Paris: Development Centre, Organization for Economic Cooperation and Development 1983), 88-92.

61 See *PECC III Report*, 26-9 and *PECC IV Announcement*, 11-12, 28-9.

62 *PECC IV Report*, 2, 39-46 and Davies, 'Pacific's Flying Geese,' 88.

63 *PECC V Report*, 35-44; Rod Nutt, 'Soviets Get Observer Role at Conference,' *Vancouver Sun*, 14 November 1986, H10; *PECC VI Report*, 33-66; *PECC VII Report*, 112-40; and *Dialogue* (Asia Pacific Foundation of Canada) 6 (November 1992):8.

64 Trigg, Seoul Minutes, 2; Correspondence, 18 August 1986, CCC Files; *PECC V Report*, 50-2; Nigel Holloway, 'A Window on the Pacific,' *Far Eastern Economic Review*, 2 June 1988, 59; and confidential interviews, Ottawa, 25 November and 1 December 1986.

65 English, *Tomorrow the Pacific* (Toronto: C.D. Howe Institute 1991), 11-13 and *PECC Newsletter*, vol. 1, no. 1 (July 1991):1.

66 *Australia-Japan Research Centre Newsletter*, no. 8 (July 1992):7.

67 Randolph, 'Pacific Overtures,' 129-30.

68 The report of the American delegation was followed by the appointment of Ambassador Richard Fairbanks as the national committee representative of Secretary of State Shultz (Trigg, Bangkok Memorandum, 1-2).

69 Dick Wilson, 'The Pacific Basin is Coming Together,' 5.

70 Correspondence, 21 January 1986, CCC Files.

71 *PECC III Report*, 28; *NPCCA 1985 Report*, 34-5; National Pacific Cooperation Committee of Australia, *Australia and Pacific Economic Cooperation: Second Report by the National Pacific Cooperation Committee to the Australian Government* (Canberra: Australian National University 1987), 31 (hereafter cited as *NPCCA 1987 Report*); *PCN* 8 (Spring 1986):1; List of Indonesian Committee Members, October 1986, mimeo, supplied to the author by CSIS, Jakarta; Confidential interview, Jakarta, 24 October 1986; and *PECC Newsletter*, vol. 2, no. 4 (October 1992):1. A call for the inclusion of labour was made during the closing session of the Canberra Seminar (PECC I) in 1980 by former Australian prime minister Gough Whitlam, who noted the need to counter the Australian union movement's tendency to support protectionist policies. Helen Ester, 'Slow Start in the Pacific' and Gough Whitlam, 'A View from Australia,' *Far Eastern Economic Review*, 26 September 1980, 90-1 and 91-3, respectively, and Whitlam, *A Pacific Community*, 44-51.

72 Drysdale, 'Australia's Interest,' 105.
73 Confidential interview, Tokyo, 11 November 1986.
74 Seizaburo Sato, 'Transcending Diversity,' *Look Japan* 34 (June 1988):12-13.
75 Drysdale, 'Building the Foundations,' 57-8; Okita, 'Pacific Regional Co-operation,' 126, 130; Wilson, 'The Pacific Basin is Coming Together,' 5-6; Randolph, 'Pacific Overtures,' 138-9; Kiyoshi Kojima, 'Economic Coopera-tion in a Pacific Community,' *Asia Pacific Community*, no. 12 (Spring 1981):1-10; and Soesastro, 'Institutional Aspects,' 37-40.
76 Confidential interview, Jakarta, 31 October 1986.
77 Wilson, 'The Pacific Basin is Coming Together,' 4-5.
78 Davies, 'Pacific's Flying Geese,' 88, 91. The term *musjawarat* or *musjawarah* refers to a traditional Indonesian consensus-building and decision-making process, which is characterized by extensive deliberations among elders or consultations with, and negotiations between, all interested parties. See Bruce Grant, *Indonesia* (Harmondsworth, UK: Penguin 1967), 40, 117, 122.
79 Wanandi, 'ASEAN and Pacific Basin Economic Co-operation' and Zakaria Haji Ahmad, 'Obstacles to Greater Pan-Pacific Co-operation: A View from ASEAN,' in Matsumoto and Sopiee, eds., *Into the Pacific Era*, 28 and 39-41, respectively. Randolph suggests that this oblique approach reflects a prefer-ence for 'structural ambiguity.' See Randolph, 'Scenarios and Pathways Towards Greater Pan-Pacific Co-operation,' in Matsumoto and Sopiee, eds., *Into the Pacific Era*, 46. Ahn observes that preference for a consensual approach is the result of the ardent economic nationalism underscoring Asian regional cooperation efforts. See Ahn Chung-Si, 'Forces of National-ism and Economics in Asian Regional Cooperation,' *Asia Pacific Community*, no. 7 (Winter 1980):106-18. Consensus decision-making is also a trait found amongst the peoples of the South Pacific Island nations. See Sione Tupouniua, Ron Crocombe, and Claire Slatter, *The Pacific Way: Social Issues In National Development* (Suva: South Pacific Social Sciences Association 1975).
80 On the dynamics of consensus decision-making, see El-Hakim, 'The Struc-ture and Dynamics of Consensus Decision-Making,' *Man* 13 (March 1978):55-71.
81 'Materials on Pacific Summit Conference,' *Korea and World Affairs* 7 (Sum-mer 1983):304-28.
82 Kiyoshi Kojima, 'Economic Cooperation in a Pacific Community,' *Asia Pacific Community*, no. 12 (Spring 1981):1-10; *NPCCA 1985 Report*, 6-7; and James Clad, 'Rising Sense of Drift,' *Far Eastern Economic Review*, 10 July 1986, 15.
83 *Pacific Economic Cooperation* (United States National Committee for Pacific Economic Cooperation) 4 (Summer 1988):2-3 and Jusuf Wanandi, 'The Role of PECC in the 1990's and Pacific Institutions,' in PECC, *Report of the Seventh Pacific Economic Cooperation Conference, Auckland, November 12-15, 1989* (Wellington: New Zealand Committee for Pacific Economic Cooperation 1990), 22-3.
84 Australia, Department of the Prime Minister and Cabinet, 'Regional Co-operation: Challenges for Korea and Australia,' Speech by the prime

minister to luncheon of Korean Business Associations, Seoul, Korea, 31 January 1989.

85 See articles in *Far Eastern Economic Review*, 16 November 1989, 10-19 and (8 June 1989):51-90.

86 'Unspecific Pacific,' *Far Eastern Economic Review*, 11 May 1989, 20; Aznam Suhaini, 'Pacific Possibilities,' *Far Eastern Economic Review*, 20 July 1989, 10-11; and Cotton, 'APEC: Australia Hosts Another Pacific Acronym,' *Pacific Review* 3 (1990):171.

87 Elek, 'The Evolution of Asia Pacific Economic Cooperation,' *Backgrounder* (Department of Foreign Affairs and Trade, Australia) 1 (15 June 1990):4-8. See also the series of articles in *Far Eastern Economic Review*, 16 November 1989, 10-19.

88 Crone, 'The Politics of Emerging Pacific Cooperation,' *Pacific Affairs* 65 (Spring 1992):70-83; Michael Vatikiotis, 'Faltering First Steps,' *Far Eastern Economic Review*, 9 August 1990, 9-10; Jacqueline Rees, 'First Step Taken,' *Far Eastern Economic Review*, 16 November 1989, 10-11; 'Unspecific Pacific,' 20; Elek, 'The Evolution of Asia Pacific Economic Cooperation,' 7-8; and Cotton, 'APEC: Australia Hosts Another Pacific Acronym,' 171. ASEAN's concerns and the possibility of an expanded APD fulfilling the role suggested for APEC are also explored in Wanandi, 'The Role of PECC,' 24-6 and Jusuf Wanandi, 'Building on ASEAN,' *Far Eastern Economic Review*, 17 August 1989, 24-5.

89 Nigel Holloway et al., 'An Insurance Policy,' *Far Eastern Economic Review*, 25 July 1991, 52-6.

90 Crone, 'The Politics of Emerging Pacific Cooperation,' 82-3; Peter Drysdale, 'Growing Pains,' *Far Eastern Economic Review*, 16 November 1989, 14, 19; H. Edward English, 'An OECD of the Pacific?: A Canadian Perspective,' Working Paper No. 1, Asian Pacific Research and Resource Centre, Carleton University, 1990, 15-17; *PECC VII Report*, 14; and Elek, 'The Evolution of Asia Pacific Economic Cooperation,' 6.

91 Grant Battersby, 'APEC Moves Another Step,' *Insight* (Department of Foreign Affairs and Trade, Australia) 1 (24 July 1992):4-5 and Australia, Department of Foreign Affairs and Trade, 'APEC Ministers Meet in Bangkok,' *Insight* 1 (21 September 1992):3

92 *Globe and Mail*, 8 September 1992, B4 and 11 September 1992, B4.

93 Australia, Department of Foreign Affairs and Trade, 'APEC Comes of Age,' 4.

94 Paul Keating, 'Australia and Asia: Knowing Who We Are,' *Backgrounder* (Department of Foreign Affairs and Trade, Australia) 3 (24 April 1992):2-16.

95 Persons who participated in the Canberra Seminar and remained active in the PECC process through PECC VII in 1989 included Peter Drysdale and Stuart Harris (Australia); Eric Trigg and H.E. English (Canada); Hadi Soesastro (Indonesia); Saburo Okita and Seizaburo Sato (Japan); Lim Chong-Yah (Singapore); Thanat Khoman (Thailand); and Lawrence Krause (U.S.). Kiyoshi Kojima (PAFTAD) participated through PECC VI.

Chapter 7: The PECC Process in Action

1 Reports of all task force activities between conferences are presented to each conference and issued as part of the conference proceedings. For a review of

Trade Policy Task Force reports, see *PECC III Report*, 63-72; *PECC IV Report*, 61-73; and *PECC V Report*, 67-77. The latter task force report has also been issued as PECC, *Pacific Trade Policy Cooperation: Goals and Initiatives* (Seoul: Korea Development Institute 1986). This volume includes the papers presented to PECC's first trade policy forum.

2 *PECC III Report*, 63-71. The call for a 'Pacific coalition' in the GATT and other multilateral negotiating fora was voiced by Drysdale at PAFTAD 11 in 1980 and stressed by him once again in a 1985 article. See Hong and Krause, *Trade and Growth of the Advanced Developing Countries in the Pacific Basin* (Seoul: Korea Development Institute 1981), 511 and Drysdale, 'Building the Foundations of a Pacific Economic Community,' in Toshio Shishido and Ryuzo Sato, eds., *Economic Policy and Development: New Perspectives* (Dover, MA: Auburn House 1985), 55.

3 *PECC III Report*, 1-2.

4 *PECC IV Report*, 62, 69-70.

5 *PECC IV Report*, 61-2.

6 New Zealand, Department of Foreign Affairs, 'Agreement on Uruguay Round,' *New Zealand Foreign Affairs Review* 36 (July-September 1986):4-5.

7 *NPCCA 1987 Report*, 10. The text of Hawke's 'Bangkok Initiative' is presented in Australia, Department of Foreign Affairs, 'Speech by the Prime Minister, Mr. Bob Hawke, M.P., to the Australian-Thai Chamber of Commerce, Bangkok, on 22 November 1983,' *Australian Foreign Affairs Record* 54 (November 1983):688-94.

8 Founded at a meeting held in Cairns, Australia, in response to an Australian government initiative, the original members of the Cairns Group were Argentina, Australia, Brazil, Canada, Chile, Colombia, Fiji, Hungary, Indonesia, Malaysia, the Philippines, New Zealand, Thailand, and Uruguay. Representatives from Japan, the U.S., and the EEC have been allowed to attend as observers. See Australia, Department of Foreign Affairs, 'Ministerial Meeting of Fair Traders in Agriculture,' *Backgrounder* 540 (4 September 1986):7-8; New Zealand, 'Cairns Declaration,' *New Zealand Foreign Affairs Review* 36 (July/September 1986):5-6; *NPCCA 1987 Report*, 10; and Peter W. Gallagher, 'Setting the Agenda for Trade Negotiations: Australia and the Cairns Group,' *Australian Outlook* 44 (April 1988):3-8.

9 *NPCCA 1987 Report*, 11.

10 Confidential interviews, Canberra, 8 April 1986, and 17 and 20 October 1986; Jakarta, 3 November 1986; Tokyo, 10 November 1986; and Ottawa, 26 November and 1 December 1986; and *PECC V Report*, 12. On 'specific issue coalitions,' see Canada, Department of External Affairs, 'Changes in World Trade and Investment,' Speech by Sylvia Ostry, Ambassador for Multilateral Trade Negotiations, to the Twenty-Fifth Anniversary Conference of the Atlantic Institute of International Affairs, Brussels, Belgium, 20 November 1986, *Statements and Speeches* (Canadian Foreign Policy Series) and Gallagher, 'Setting the Agenda for Trade Negotiations,' 5.

11 Confidential interviews, Canberra, 8 April and 20 October 1986 and Ottawa, 1 December 1986; and Gallagher, 'Setting the Agenda for Trade Negotiations,' 3-6. Recent studies have found Australian foreign policy elites to be

solidly in support of pursuing regional cooperation as a way of resolving international problems, whereas Japanese leaders, for example, place more emphasis on international diplomatic activities. See Trevor Matthews and John Ravenhill, 'Bipartisanship in the Australian Foreign Policy Elite,' *Australian Outlook* 42 (April 1988):15 and Neville Meaney, Trevor Matthews, and Sol Encel, *The Japanese Connection: A Survey of Australian Leaders' Attitudes Towards Japan and the Australia-Japan Relationship* (Melbourne: Longman Cheshire 1988), 38-40, 53-60, 80, 84.

12 *PECC V Report*, 70-2. The rationale behind these PECC trade initiatives is reviewed in H. Edward English, 'Canada and Pacific Cooperation,' *Research Paper Series I*, Pacific Basin Project No. 2, Centre for Japan-U.S. Relations, International University of Japan, 1986, 71-6.

13 *PECC V Report*, 17, 73.

14 *PECC VI Report*, 27-8, 101-14; *PECC VII Report*, 5-6, 69-79; English, *Tomorrow the Pacific* (Toronto: C.D. Howe Institute 1991), 22-55; and H.E. English, ed., *Pacific Initiatives in Global Trade* (Halifax: Institute for Research on Public Policy 1990).

15 Confidential interviews, Canberra, 13 October 1986.

16 *PCN* 7 (April 1985):2 and Gibb, San Francisco Minutes, 2, CCC Files.

17 See Robert F. Dernberger, 'Economic Cooperation in the Asia-Pacific Region and the Role of the P.R.C.,' *Journal of Northeast Asian Studies* 7 (Spring 1988):3-21.

18 Dick Wilson, 'The Pacific Basin is Coming Together,' *Asia Pacific Community*, no. 30 (Fall 1985):7.

19 Wilson, 'The Pacific Basin is Coming Together,' 7.

20 Stephen Uhalley, Jr., 'China and the Pacific Basin: Questions and Apprehensions,' *Contemporary Southeast Asia* 8 (March 1987):304 and Akira Chiba, 'Pacific Co-operation and China,' *Pacific Review* 2 (1989):46-55.

21 Wilson, 'The Pacific Basin is Coming Together,' 9-10.

22 Correspondence, 12 November 1985, CCC Files. The examples Trigg garnered included the following titles: Chinese Taipei Olympic Committee (International Olympic Committee); Chinese Taipei Amateur Hockey Association (Federation of International Hockey); and Chinese Taipei Tennis Association (International Tennis Federation). It is noted that Taiwan is a member of PBEC but that China is not, largely because of the organization's private sector emphasis. Chinese and Taiwanese scholars have participated in PAFTAD. See also Gerald Chan, *China and International Organizations: Participation in Non-Governmental Organizations Since 1971* (Hong Kong: Oxford University Press 1989).

23 See Gerald Chan, 'The Two-Chinas Problem and the Olympic Formula,' *Pacific Affairs* 58 (Fall 1985):473-90. Confidential interviews, Ottawa, 25 November and 3 December 1986.

24 Trigg and Koo had been active in PBEC since 1978 and 1970, respectively. SRI Files.

25 Correspondence, 19 November 1985, CCC Files.

26 Correspondence, 22 November 1985, CCC Files.

27 Correspondence, 11 December 1985 and 7 July 1986, CCC Files.

28 Correspondence, 18 August 1986, CCC Files.
29 Correspondence, 23 September 1986, CCC Files.
30 Correspondence, 7 and 10 October 1986, CCC Files.
31 Erratum, Conference Papers, Fifth Pacific Economic Cooperation Conference, Vancouver, Canada, November 16-19, 1986.
32 Stuart Harris, 'Regional Economic Cooperation, Trading Blocs and Australian Interests,' *Australian Outlook* 43 (August 1989):16-24.
33 S. Bilveer, 'The Pacific Community Concept: The View from Moscow,' *World Today* 41 (January 1985):19-21.
34 Bilveer Singh, 'Gorbachev and a Pacific Community,' *Pacific Review* 1 (1989):227-35.
35 Wilson, 'The Pacific Basin is Coming Together,' 10-11.
36 See, for example, Lesek Buszynski, 'International Linkages and Regional Interests in Soviet Asia-Pacific Policy,' *Pacific Affairs* 61 (Summer 1988):213-21.
37 Gibb, San Francisco Minutes, 1, CCC Files.
38 Correspondence, 4 September 1986, CCC Files.
39 Correspondence, 27 August-25 September 1986, CCC Files.
40 Confidential interviews, Tokyo, 11-12 November 1986; Susumu Awanohara, 'Will Nakasone Rush In Where Some Fear to Tread?' *Far Eastern Economic Review*, 13 November 1986, 34-6; and Charles Smith, 'Snubbed by Gorbachev,' *Far Eastern Economic Review*, 18 December 1986, 28.
41 Correspondence, 19 September 1986, CCC Files.
42 Correspondence, 19 September 1986, CCC Files.
43 See Stuart Harris, 'Vladivostok and Australian Foreign Policy,' in Ramesh Thakur and Carlyle A. Thayer, eds., *The Soviet Union as an Asian Pacific Power: Implications of Gorbachev's 1986 Vladivostok Initiative* (Boulder, CO: Westview 1987), 126-8.
44 Correspondence, 9, 14, and 17 October 1986, CCC Files.
45 See Donald E. Weatherbee, 'Indonesia in 1985: Chills and Thaws,' *Asian Survey* 26 (February 1986):141-9 and Donald K. Emmerson, 'ASEAN as an International Regime,' *Journal of International Affairs* 41 (Summer/Fall 1987):12-16.
46 Correspondence, 18 August and 14 October 1986, CCC Files.
47 Correspondence, 18-28 October 1986, CCC Files.
48 *PECC V Report*, 13, 28-31, 57.
49 Soviet membership aspirations continued to run afoul of the Northern Territories dispute with Japan. The PECC-ISC has also agreed that the unanimous consent of the membership will now be required for the admission of new members and the extension of invitations to non-member guests for general meetings. Non-members may attend task force sessions at the invitation of the host national committee. See Sophie Quinn-Judge, 'Bleak Prospects,' *Far Eastern Economic Review*, 20 July 1989, 30-2; Vladimir Ivanov, 'Perestroika in the Pacific,' *Far Eastern Economic Review*, 22 February 1990, 24-5; and *PECC VI Report*, 19-20.
50 *Pacific Economic Cooperation* (United States National Committee for Pacific Economic Cooperation) 3 (Fall 1987):1 and Charles Smith, 'Seeking a New Role,' *Far Eastern Economic Review*, 8 June 1989, 51-5.

51 *PECC Newsletter*, vol. 2, no. 1 (January 1992):8 and vol. 2, no. 2 (April 1992):8.

52 Trigg, Bangkok Memorandum, 6 and Trigg, 'PECC's Progress,' 38.

53 *PCN 7* (April 1985):3.

54 Wilson, 'The Pacific Basin is Coming Together,' 5; Trigg, Seoul Minutes, 2; and 'Statement on the PECC Process,' draft of statement referred to national committees for comment, 1985, AJRC Files.

55 The Vancouver Statement was signed at PECC V by PECC-ISC members from Australia, Canada, China, Chinese Taipei, Indonesia, Japan, Malaysia, New Zealand, PBEC, the Philippines, Singapore, South Korea, Thailand, and the United States. *PECC V Report*, 28-31; *Vancouver Sun*, 21 November 1986, D8; *Globe and Mail*, 20 November 1986, A5; and Trigg, 'PECC's Progress,' 38.

56 The exchange between Harris and Trigg is reviewed in *PECC V Report*, 55-8.

57 Soesastro, Choo, and Armstrong, *Pacific Economic Development Report 1992-1993* (Singapore: PECC Secretariat 1992), 122-7.

58 Kaneko, 'A New Pacific Initiative: Strengthening the PECC Process,' *Japan Review of International Affairs* 2 (Spring/Summer 1988):85; Okita, 'Pacific Development and Its Implications,' 33; Anthony Rowley, 'OECD Looks East,' *Far Eastern Economic Review*, 31 March 1988, 48-9; Anthony Rowley, 'Joining the Rich Man's Club,' *Far Eastern Economic Review*, 2 June 1988, 60-3 and Crone, 'The Politics of Emerging Pacific Cooperation,' *Pacific Affairs* 65 (Spring 1992):68-71. Similarly, moving beyond the range of subjects stipulated at PECC I, recent discussions of Asia-Pacific regionalism have also considered the possibility of forming a military security organization modelled after the Conference on Security and Cooperation in Europe. See David B. Dewitt and Paul M. Evans, 'The Changing Dynamics of Asia-Pacific Security: A Canadian Perspective,' Working Paper No. 3, North Pacific Cooperative Security Dialogue Research Programme, York University, January 1992 and Paul M. Evans, 'The Emergence of Eastern Asia and Its Implications for Canada,' *International Journal* 47 (Summer 1992):504-28.

59 Harris, 'Regional Economic Cooperation,' 16-24.

60 Doran, 'U.S. and Canadian Pacific Perspectives,' in Gavin Boyd, ed., *Region Building in the Pacific* (New York: Harper and Row 1981), 177-8.

61 Chalmers Johnson, 'Pacific Regional Development: Myth and Reality,' *Asian Pacific Review*, no. 7 (Summer 1987): 9.

62 Nigel Holloway, 'Pacific Boosterism,' *Far Eastern Economic Review*, 9 June 1988, 34; *PECC VII Report*, 20-1, 67-8; and Pacific Economic Cooperation Council (PECC), *Pacific Economic Outlook 1992-1993* (San Francisco: U.S. National Committee for Pacific Economic Cooperation 1992).

63 David Sycip, 'Is Regional Economic Cooperation PECC's Goal?' *Euro-Asia Business Review* 5 (January 1986):37-8. Sycip, who expressed similar misgivings at PECC I, II, and III as well as in various PECC-ISC meetings, argues that ASEAN member nations should not support PECC until there is more evidence of regional economic cooperation. He suggests a regional plan similar to President Reagan's Caribbean Basin Initiative, in which, with special provisions, industrialized countries of the Pacific Basin would freely admit all products from developing countries of the region. See also David

Sycip, 'Why Not a Pacific Economic Community Initiative?' *Asia Pacific Community*, no. 17 (Summer 1982):71-3; *PECC III Report*, 131-3; H. Edward English, 'Pacific Economic Community: A Consensual Region,' *International Journal* 38 (Spring 1983):347; and English, 'The Emerging Pacific Community,' in Hadi Soesastro and Han Sung-Joo, eds., *Pacific Economic Cooperation: The Next Phase* (Jakarta: Centre for Strategic and International Studies 1983), 100-1. The misgivings voiced by Sycip provided much of the impetus for the drafting of the Vancouver Statement. Correspondence, 21 January 1986, CCC Files.

64 *PECC Newsletter*, vol. 2, no. 4 (October 1992):1.

Appendixes

1 From *PAFTAD Newsletter*, no. 3 (July 1987):3.

2 From *PBEC Report: Seoul Meeting, 1986*, 54 (revised 13 May 1983).

3 From PECC, *Report of the Fifth Pacific Economic Cooperation Conference*, Vancouver, 16-19 November 1986 (Ottawa: Canadian Chamber of Commerce 1987), 28-31. The Vancouver Statement was endorsed 16 November 1986 by PECC-ISC representatives from Australia, Canada, China, Chinese Taipei, Indonesia, Japan, Malaysia, New Zealand, PBEC, the Philippines, Singapore, South Korea, Thailand, and the United States; it was unanimously approved 18 November 1986 by plenary session of PECC V. In 1991, it was incorporated as part of a new PECC charter. In 1992, the name of the organization was changed from Pacific Economic Cooperation Conference to Pacific Economic Cooperation Council.

Bibliography

Books and Articles

Abdulgani, Roeslau. 'Political Development and Regional Cooperation in the Asian-Pacific Region.' *Asian Culture Quarterly* 14 (Autumn 1986):1-14

Ahmad, Zakaria Haji. 'ASEAN and Pan-Pacific Cooperation: The Long Way Ahead.' *Asia Pacific Community*, no. 30 (Fall 1985):13-29

– 'Obstacles to Greater Pan-Pacific Co-operation.' In Hiroshi Matsumoto and Noordin Sopiee, eds., *Into the Pacific Era: Southeast Asia and Its Place in the Pacific*. Kuala Lumpur/Tokyo: Institute of Strategic and International Studies/Association of Promotion of International Cooperation 1986, 33-42

Ahn Chung-Si. 'Forces of Nationalism and Economics in Asian Regional Cooperation.' *Asia Pacific Community*, no. 7 (Winter 1980):106-18

Aichi, Kiichi. 'ASPAC Still Young and Fluid.' *Pacific Community* 1 (October 1969):4-10

Aikman, C.C. 'Regional Cooperation among Asian-Pacific Nations: A View from the South Pacific.' In Hadi Soesastro and Han Sung-Joo, eds., *Pacific Economic Cooperation: The Next Phase*. Jakarta: Centre for Strategic and International Studies 1983, 214-21

Aikman, David. *Pacific Rim: Area of Change, Area of Opportunity*. Toronto: Little, Brown 1986

Albinski, Henry S. *Canadian and Australian Politics in Comparative Perspective*. New York: Oxford University Press 1973

Alley, Roderic, Bruce Wallace, and Terence Wesley-Smith, eds. *Linking the Pacific: A Report of an International Seminar on New Zealand and the Pacific Basin Concept, April 1980*. Wellington: New Zealand Institute of International Affairs 1980

Almond, Gabriel. 'The Elites and Foreign Policy.' In James N. Rosenau, ed., *International Politics and Foreign Policy: A Reader in Research and Theory*. New York: Free Press 1961, 268-72

Anderson, Kym, et al. 'Pacific Economic Growth and the Prospects for Australian Trade.' *Pacific Economic Papers*, no. 122, Australian Japan Research Centre, Research School of Pacific Studies, Australian National University, May 1985

Anderson, R.W.C. 'Australia-Japan Economic Relations.' *Pacific Community* 1 (January 1970):303-17

– *Pacific Initiative – Concept to Reality: International Business Co-operation Committees: The First Decade.* Canberra: Australia/Japan Business Cooperation Committee and the Pacific Basin Economic Council 1971

Angell, Robert Cooley. *Peace on the March: Transnational Participation.* New York: Van Nostrand Reinhold 1969

Angus, H.F. *Canada and the Far East 1940-1953.* Toronto: University of Toronto Press 1953

Arase, David. 'Pacific Economic Cooperation: Problems and Prospects.' *Pacific Review* 1 (1988):128-44

Ariff, Mohamed, ed. *The Pacific Economy: Growth and External Stability.* Sydney: Allen and Unwin 1991

Ariyoshi, George R. 'Hawaii's Role in the Pacific Community.' In Paul F. Hooper, ed., *Building a Pacific Community.* Honolulu: East-West Center 1982, 76-84

Arndt, H.W. *A Course Through Life: Memoirs of an Australian Economist.* Canberra: National Centre for Development Studies, Australian National University 1985

– *Economic Development: The History of an Idea.* Chicago: University of Chicago Press 1987

– 'The Role of Technology Transfer in Pacific Economic Development: A Summing-Up.' In Kiyoshi Kojima and Miguel S. Wionczek, eds., *Technology Transfer in Pacific Economic Development.* Tokyo: Japan Economic Research Center 1975, 225-32

– 'Sir John Crawford.' *Pacific Economic Papers*, no. 128, Australia-Japan Research Centre, Research School of Pacific Studies, Australian National University, November 1985

Arnove, Robert F., ed. *Philanthropy and Cultural Imperialism: The Foundations at Home and Abroad.* Boston: G.K. Hall 1980

'ASEAN and Pacific Economic Cooperation.' *Indonesian Quarterly* 10 (July 1982):67-109

Ashiya Einosuke. 'A Pacific Bank for Investment and Settlement: Its Conception.' In Kiyoshi Kojima, ed., *Pacific Trade and Development, I.* Tokyo: Japan Economic Research Center 1968, 307-24

Ashworth, Georgina. 'The United Nations Women's Conference and International Linkages in the Women's Movement.' In Peter Willetts, ed., *Pressure Groups in the Global System: The Transnational Relations of Issue-Orientated Non-Governmental Organizations.* London: Frances Pinter 1982, 125-47

Asia-Pacific in the 1980s: Toward Greater Symmetry in Economic Interdependence. Jakarta: Centre for Strategic and International Studies 1980

Aslund, Anders. 'The New Soviet Policy Towards International Economic Organisations.' *World Today* 44 (February 1988):27-30

Atarashi Kinju. 'Japan's Economic Cooperation Policy Towards the ASEAN Countries.' *International Affairs* 61 (Winter 1984-5):109-27

Australia-New Zealand Businessmen's Council Limited/IMG Consultants. *The Role of Australia and New Zealand in the Asian and Pacific Region.* Sydney: IMG Consultants, May 1985

Axelrod, Robert and Robert O. Keohane. 'Achieving Cooperation under Anarchy: Strategies and Institutions.' *World Politics* 38 (October 1985):226-54

Axline, W. Andrew. *Caribbean Integration: The Politics of Regionalism*. London: Frances Pinter 1979

– 'South Pacific Region Cooperation in Comparative Perspective: An Analytical Framework.' *Political Science* 37 (July 1985):40-9

Bachrach, Peter, ed. *Political Elites in a Democracy*. New York: Atherton 1971

Bachrach, Peter and Morton S. Baratz. *Power and Poverty: Theory and Practice*. New York: Oxford University Press 1970

Baker, Richard. 'Asian-Pacific Regionalism: New Structures, Old Impulses.' Occasional Paper, East-West Center, Honolulu, 1985

Balassa, Bela, et al. *Studies in Trade Liberalization: Problems and Prospects*. Baltimore: Johns Hopkins Press 1967

Baldwin, David A. *Economic Statecraft*. Princeton, NJ: Princeton University Press 1985

Bandura, Y. 'The Pacific Community: A Brainchild of Imperialist Diplomacy.' *International Affairs* (Moscow), no. 6 (June 1980):63-70

Barraclough, Geoffrey. *An Introduction to Contemporary History*. Harmondsworth: Penguin 1977

Barzun, Jacques. *The House of Intellect*. New York: Harper's 1961

Battersby, Grant. 'APEC Moves Another Step,' *Insight* (Department of Foreign Affairs and Trade, Australia) 1 (24 July 1992):4-5

Bautista, Romeo M. 'Structural Change in the Philippines.' In Lawrence B. Krause and Sueo Sekiguchi, eds., *Economic Interaction in the Pacific Basin*. Washington: Brookings Institution 1980, 147-80

Bautista, Romeo M. and Seiji Naya, eds. *Energy and Structural Change in the Asia-Pacific Region*. Manila: Philippine Institute for Development Studies and Asian Development Bank 1984

Bedeski, Robert E. 'Reorienting the Orient.' *International Perpsectives* 17 (March/April 1988):8-10

Bedeski, Robert E. and Christopher MacLean. 'Canada, Korea and the Pacific Community.' *Asian Perspective* 8 (Spring/Summer 1984):1-12

Beitz, Charles R. *Political Theory and International Relations*. Princeton, NJ: Princeton University Press 1979

Bell, J. Bowyer. 'Contemporary Revolutionary Organizations.' In Robert O. Keohane and Joseph S. Nye, Jr., eds., *Transnational Relations and World Politics*. Cambridge, MA: Harvard University Press 1973, 153-68

Bell, Peter D. 'The Ford Foundation as a Transnational Actor.' In Robert O. Keohane and Joseph S. Nye, Jr., eds., *Transnational Relations and World Politics*. Cambridge, MA: Harvard University Press 1973, 115-28

Benjamin, Roger and Robert T. Kudrle, eds. *The Industrial Future of the Pacific Basin*. Boulder, CO: Westview 1984

Berman, Maureen R. and Joseph E. Johnson. 'The Growing Role of Unofficial Diplomacy.' In Maureen R. Berman and Joseph E. Johnson, eds., *Unofficial Diplomats*. New York: Columbia University Press 1977, 1-33

Berman, Maureen R. and Joseph E. Johnson, eds. *Unofficial Diplomats*. New York: Columbia University Press 1977

Bettignies, Henri-Claude de. 'Can Europe Survive the Pacific Century?' *Euro-Asia Business Review* 1 (October 1982):10-14

Biermeier, Jens D. 'America's Shifting Emphasis to the Pacific.' *Intereconomics* 20 (September/October 1985):245-50

Bilveer, S. 'The Pacific Community Concept: The View from Moscow.' *World Today* 41 (January 1985):19-21

Bobrow, David B. and Steve Chan. 'Assets, Liabilities, and Strategic Conduct: Status Management by Japan, Taiwan, and South Korea.' *Pacific Focus* 1 (Spring 1986):23-56

Bogomolov, Aleksandr. 'Evolution of Pacific Cooperation Ideas.' *Far Eastern Affairs* (Moscow), no. 1 (1987):57-69

– 'Problems of Cooperation in the Pacific Region.' *International Affairs* (Moscow) 1 (January 1987):38-44

Bollard, Allan and David Mayes. 'Regionalism and the Pacific Rim.' *Journal of Common Market Studies* 30 (June 1992):195-209

Borthwick, Mark. 'ASEAN and Pacific Economic Cooperation: The Bangkok Conference in June.' *Pacific Basin Quarterly* 7 (Spring/Summer 1982): 18-20

– 'U.S. Governmental Responses to the Pacific Community Idea.' In Hadi Soesastro and Han Sung-Joo, eds., *Pacific Economic Cooperation: The Next Phase.* Jakarta: Centre for Strategic and International Studies 1983, 278-89

Boulding, Elise. 'Nongovernmental Organizations.' *Bulletin of the Atomic Scientists*, August 1985, 94-6

– 'The Old and New Transnationalism: An Evolutionary Perspective.' *Human Relations* 44 (August 1991):789-806

Boyd, Gavin. 'Foreign Economic and Security Policies.' In Gavin Boyd, ed., *Regionalism and Global Security.* Lexington, MA: D.C. Heath 1984, 1-23

– 'Pacific Community Building.' In Gavin Boyd, ed., *Regionalism and Global Security.* Lexington, MA: D.C. Heath 1984, 83-117

– 'A Pacific Regional Economic Order.' In Hadi Soesastro and Han Sung-Joo, eds., *Pacific Economic Cooperation: The Next Phase.* Jakarta: Centre for Strategic and International Studies 1983, 143-57

– 'Political Designing for Pacific Cooperation.' In Robert L. Downen and Bruce J. Dickson, eds., *The Emerging Pacific Community: A Regional Perspective.* Boulder, CO: Westview 1984, 57-65

– 'Regional Designing.' In Gavin Boyd, ed., *Regionalism and Global Security.* Lexington, MA: D.C. Heath and Company 1984, 175-91

– 'Strategic Aspects of Pacific Cooperation Proposals.' Operational Research and Analysis Establishment Extra-Mural Paper No. 25, Department of National Defence (Canada), Ottawa, August 1983

Boyd, Gavin, ed. *Region Building in the Pacific.* New York: Pergamon 1982

– *Regionalism and Global Security.* Lexington, MA: D.C. Heath 1984

Bozeman, Adda B. *Politics and Culture in International History.* Princeton, NJ: Princeton University Press 1960

Bresnan, John. 'Strengthening Human Ties.' In James W. Morley, ed., *The Pacific Basin: New Challenges for the United States.* New York: Academy of Political Science 1986, 88-100

Brown, Bruce. 'New Zealand's Approach to Asia and the Pacific.' *Pacific Community* 2 (April 1971):549-63

Bryant, William E. *Japanese Private Economic Diplomacy: An Analysis of Business-Government Linkages.* New York: Praeger 1975

Bull, Hedley, ed. *Asia and the Western Pacific: Towards a New International Order.* Sydney: Thomas Nelson and Sons/Australian Institute of International Affairs 1975

– 'Introduction: Towards a New International Order in Asia and the Western Pacific?' In Hedley Bull, ed., *Asia and the Western Pacific: Towards a New International Order.* Sydney: Thomas Nelson and Sons/Australian Institute of International Affairs 1975, xi-xxviii

– 'The New Course of Australian Policy.' In Hedley Bull, ed., *Asia and the Western Pacific: Towards a New International Order.* Sydney: Thomas Nelson and Sons/Australian Institute of International Affairs 1975, 357-71

Bundy, William P. 'The Nixon Policies in Asia and the Pacific.' *Pacific Community* 2 (October 1970):77-86

Burke, Tom. 'Friends of the Earth and the Conservation of Resources.' In Peter Willetts, ed., *Pressure Groups in the Global System: The Transnational Relations of Issue-Orientated Non-Governmental Organizations.* London: Frances Pinter 1982, 105-24

Burlington, Thomas. 'Summary: Barriers to Trade in the Pacific Region.' In H.E. English and Keith A.J. Hay, eds., *Obstacles to Trade in the Pacific Area.* Ottawa: School of International Affairs, Carleton University 1972, 3-12

Business Cooperation Between Asia-Pacific and Japan in the Eighties. Tokyo: Export-Import Bank of Japan 1980

Buszynski, Leszek. 'International Linkages and Regional Interests in Soviet Asia-Pacific Policy.' *Pacific Affairs* 61 (Summer 1988):213-34

Butterfield, Herbert. 'The New Diplomacy and Historical Diplomacy.' In Herbert Butterfield and Martin Wight, eds., *Diplomatic Investigations: Essays in the Theory of International Politics.* London: Allen and Unwin 1966, 181-92

Butterfield, Herbert and Martin Wight, eds. *Diplomatic Investigations: Essays in the Theory of International Politics.* London: Allen and Unwin 1966

Carlson, Sevinc. 'Energy Interdependence in the Pacific Basin.' In Bruce J. Dickson, ed., *The Emerging Pacific Community Concept: A Staff Report on the CSIS Pacific Basin Congressional Study Group.* Washington: Center for Strategic and International Studies, Georgetown University 1983, 33-9

Carr, E.H. *The Twenty Years' Crisis, 1919-1939: An Introduction to the Study of International Relations.* 2nd edition. London: Macmillan 1983

Carroll, John E., ed. *International Environmental Diplomacy.* Cambridge Cambridge University Press 1990

Castle, L.V. 'Alternative Policies in Trade Cooperation of the Advanced Pacific Countries in the Next Five Years.' In Kiyoshi Kojima, ed., *Pacific Trade and Development, II.* Tokyo: Japan Economic Research Center 1969, 159-78

Castle, Leslie V. and Christopher Findlay, eds. *Pacific Trade in Services.* Sydney: Allen and Unwin 1988

Castle, Leslie V. and Frank Holmes, eds. *Cooperation and Development in the Asia/Pacific Region: Relations Between Large and Small Countries.* Tokyo: Japan Economic Research Center 1976

Castro, Amado A. 'The Outlook for Cooperation: An ASEAN View.' In Robert L.

Downen and Bruce J. Dickson, eds., *The Emerging Pacific Community: A Regional Perspective*. Boulder, CO: Westview 1984, 161-5

Caves, Richard E. 'Industrial Policy and Trade Policy: A Framework.' In Hiromichi Mutoh et al., eds., *Industrial Policies for Pacific Economic Growth*. Sydney: Allen and Unwin 1986, 42-55

Chan, Gerald. 'The Two-Chinas Problem and the Olympic Formula.' *Pacific Affairs* 58 (Fall 1985):473-90

– *China and International Organizations: Participation in Non-Governmental Organizations since 1971*. Hong Kong: Oxford University Press 1989

Chan, Steve. *East Asian Dynamism: Growth, Order, and Security in the Pacific Region*. Boulder, CO: Westview 1991

Chang King-Yuh. 'Building the Pacific Community: An Incrementalist Approach.' *Korea and World Affairs* 7 (Summer 1983):218-26

Chekhutov, Andrei I. 'USSR: Economic Cooperation with the Developing Nations of Asia and the Pacific Area.' In Leslie V. Castle and Frank Holmes, eds., *Cooperation and Development in the Asia/Pacific Region*. Tokyo: Japan Economic Research Center 1976, 192-7

Chia Siow Yue. 'ASEAN and the Pacific Economic Community.' In Hadi Soesastro and Han Sung-Joo, eds., *Pacific Economic Cooperation: The Next Phase*. Jakarta: Centre for Strategic and International Studies 1983, 167-88

Chiba Akira. 'Pacific Co-operation and China.' *Pacific Review* 2 (1989):46-55

Chipman, John. *Survey of International Relations Institutes in the Developing World*. London: International Institute for Strategic Studies 1987

Chufrin, Gennady. 'USSR and the Asia-Pacific Region.' *Indonesian Quarterly* 15 (April 1987):238-42

Clark, Cal and Steve Chan, eds. *The Evolving Pacific Basin in the Global Political Economy: Domestic and International Linkages*. Boulder, CO: Lynne Rienner 1992

Clarke, Michael. 'Transnationalism.' In Steve Smith, ed., *International Relations: British and American Perspectives*. Oxford: Basil Blackwell/British International Studies Association 1985, 146-70

Cohen, Benjamin J. 'Balance-of-Payments Financing: Evolution of Regime Change.' *International Organization* 36 (Spring 1982):457-78

Cohen, Raymond. *Negotiating Across Cultures: Communication Obstacles in International Diplomacy*. Washington: United States Institute of Peace Press 1991

Coker, Christopher. 'The Myth or Reality of the Pacific Century.' *Washington Quarterly* 11 (Summer 1988):5-16

Colbert, Evelyn. 'Regional Cooperation and the Tilt to the West.' In James W. Morley, ed., *The Pacific Basin: New Challenges for the United States*. New York: Academy of Political Science 1986, 46-56

Collins, Hugh. 'Theme Paper.' In A.C. Milner and Trevor Wilson, eds., *Australian Diplomacy: Challenges for the Department of Foreign Affairs*. Occasional Paper No. 5, Australian Institute of International Affairs, August 1986, 1-17

Condliffe, J.B., ed. *Problems of the Pacific, 1929: Proceedings of the Third Conference of the Institute of Pacific Relations, Nara and Kyoto, Japan, 23 October-9 November 1929*. Chicago: University of Chicago Press 1930

Cooper, Richard N. 'Financial Aspects of Economic Cooperation Around the

Pacific.' In Kiyoshi Kojima, ed., *Pacific Trade and Development, I*. Tokyo: Japan Economic Research Center 1968, 283-306
- 'Inter-Regional and Intra-Regional Energy Cooperation in the Pacific Basin.' In Romeo M. Bautista and Seiji Naya, eds., *Energy and Structural Change in the Asia-Pacific Region*. Manila: Philippine Institute for Development Studies and Asian Development Bank 1984, 497-509
Cottam, Richard W. *Competitive Interference and Twentieth Century Diplomacy*. Pittsburgh: University of Pittsburgh Press 1967
Cotton, James. 'APEC: Australia Hosts Another Pacific Acronym.' *Pacific Review* 3 (1990):171-3
Couloumbis, Theodore A. and James H. Wolfe. *Introduction to International Relations*. Englewood Cliffs, NJ: Prentice-Hall 1986
Cox, Robert W. 'ILO: Limited Monarchy.' In Robert W. Cox and Harold K. Jacobson, eds., *The Anatomy of Influence: Decision Making in International Organization*. London: Yale University Press 1974, 102-38
- 'Labor and Transnational Relations.' In Robert O. Keohane and Joseph S. Nye, Jr., eds., *Transnational Relations and World Politics*. Cambridge, MA: Harvard University Press 1973, 204-34
Cox, Robert W. and Harold K. Jacobson, eds. *The Anatomy of Influence: Decision Making in International Organization*. London: Yale University Press 1974
Craig, Gordon A. 'On the Nature of Diplomatic History: The Relevance of Some Old Books.' In Paul Gordon Lauren, ed., *Diplomacy: New Approaches in History, Theory, and Policy*. New York: Free Press 1979, 21-42
Craig, Gordon A. and Alexander L. George. *Force and Statecraft: Diplomatic Problems of Our Time*. New York: Oxford University Press 1983
Crane, Diana. 'Transnational Networks in Basic Science.' In Robert O. Keohane and Joseph S. Nye, Jr., eds., *Transnational Relations and World Politics*. Cambridge, MA: Harvard University Press 1973, 235-51
Crawford, J.G. 'Australia as a Pacific Power.' In W.G.K. Duncan, ed., *Australia's Foreign Policy*. Sydney: Angus and Robertson 1938, 69-121
- 'Pacific Community: Dream or Reality?' In Paul F. Hooper, ed., *Building a Pacific Community*. Honolulu: East-West Center 1982, 63-75
Crawford, J.G. and G.H. Board. 'Japan's Trade Policy and Trade in Temperate Zone Agricultural Products.' In H.E. English and Keith A.J. Hay, eds., *Obstacles to Trade in the Pacific Area*. Ottawa: School of International Affairs, Carleton University 1972, 15-65
Crawford, John. 'The Pacific Basin Cooperative Concept.' In *Business Cooperation Between Asia-Pacific and Japan in the Eighties*. Tokyo: Export-Import Bank of Japan 1980, 35-49
- 'The Pacific Basin Co-operative Concept.' In John Crawford and Greg Seow, eds., *Pacific Economic Co-operation: Suggestions for Action*. Selangor: Heinemann Educational 1981, 35-40
- 'The Pacific Basin Cooperative Concept.' Research Paper No. 70, Australia-Japan Economic Relations Research Project, Australia-Japan Research Centre, Research School of Pacific Studies, Australian National University, August 1980
Crawford, John and Saburo Okita. *Australia, Japan and the Western Pacific Eco-*

nomic Relations: A Report to the Governments of Australia and Japan. Canberra: Australian Government Publishing Service 1976

Crawford, John and Saburo Okita, eds. *Raw Materials and Pacific Economic Integration.* Canberra: Australian National University Press 1978

Crawford, John and Greg Seow, eds. *Pacific Economic Co-operation: Suggestions for Action.* Selangor: Heinemann Educational 1981

Crone, Donald K. *The ASEAN States: Coping with Dependence.* New York: Praeger 1983

– 'The Politics of Emerging Pacific Cooperation.' *Pacific Affairs* 65 (Spring 1992):68-83

Crough, Greg and Ted Wheelwright. *Australia: A Client State.* Ringwood, Vic.: Penguin 1982

Dahlen, Olle. 'A Governmental Response to Pressure Groups: The Case of Sweden.' In Peter Willetts, ed., *Pressure Groups in the Global System: The Transnational Relations of Issue-Orientated Non-Governmental Organizations.* London: Frances Pinter 1982, 148-70

Dalrymple, F. Rawdon. 'The Pacific Basin Community Concept.' *Indonesian Quarterly* 9 (October 1981):43-7

Dean, Arthur L. 'The Approach to Pacific Relations.' In Institute of Pacific Relations, ed., *Institute of Pacific Relations: Honolulu Session, June 30-July 14, 1925.* Honolulu: IPR 1925, 46-52

Dernberger, Robert F. 'Economic Cooperation in the Asia-Pacific Region and the Role of the P.R.C.' *Journal of Northeast Asian Studies* 7 (Spring 1988):3-21

Dewitt, David B. and Paul M. Evans. 'The Changing Dynamics of Asia-Pacific Security: A Canadian Perspective.' Working Paper No. 3, North Pacific Cooperative Security Dialogue Research Programme, York University, January 1992

Dibb, Paul. 'The Soviet Union as a Pacific Power.' *International Journal* 38 (Spring 1983):234-50

Dickson, Bruce J., ed. *The Emerging Pacific Community Concept: A Staff Report on the CSIS Pacific Basin Congressional Study Group.* Washington: Center for Strategic and International Studies, Georgetown University 1983

Dittmer, Lowell. 'China's Opening to the Outside World: The Cultural Dimension.' *Journal of Northeast Asian Studies* 6 (Summer 1987):3-23

Djiwandono, J. Soedjati. 'Current Events: The Pacific Region.' *Indonesian Quarterly* 12 (October 1984):400-1

– 'Indonesia and the Asia-Pacific Region in the 1990s: Prospects for Regional Cooperation.' *Indonesian Quarterly* 15 (April 1987):243-50

Dobell, Peter C. *Canada in World Affairs: Volume XVII, 1971-1973.* Toronto: Canadian Institute of International Affairs 1985

Donnelly, Michael W. and Victor C. Falkenheim. 'Canada and the Pacific Community.' Working Paper No. 4, Canada and the Pacific: Agenda for the Eighties, Joint Centre on Modern East Asia, University of Toronto-York University, May 1981

Donowaki Mitsuro. 'The Pacific Basin Community: A Japanese Overview.' *Asia Pacific Community,* no. 15 (Winter 1982):15-29

Doran, Charles. 'U.S. and Canadian Pacific Perspectives.' In Gavin Boyd, ed., *Region Building in the Pacific.* New York: Pergamon 1982, 162-83

Dougherty, James E. and Robert L. Pfaltzgraff, Jr. *Contending Theories of International Relations: A Comprehensive Survey.* 2nd edition. New York: Harper and Row 1981

Downen, Robert L. 'America's Stake in a Western Pacific Collective Security System.' In Bruce J. Dickson, ed., *The Emerging Pacific Community Concept: An American Perspective.* Washington: Center for Strategic and International Studies, Georgetown University 1983, 49-55

Downen, Robert L. and Bruce J. Dickson, eds. *The Emerging Pacific Community: A Regional Perspective.* Boulder, CO: Westview 1984

Downton, Eric. *Pacific Challenge: Canada's Future in the New Asia.* Toronto: Stoddart 1986

Drifte, Reinhold. *Japan's Foreign Policy.* New York: Council on Foreign Relations Press 1990

Drysdale, Peter. 'Australia and Japan in the Pacific and World Economy.' In Peter Drysdale and Hironobu Kitaoji, eds., *Japan and Australia: Two Societies and Their Interaction.* Canberra: Australian National University Press 1981, 419-38

– 'Australia and the Pacific Economic Community.' In John Crawford and Greg Seow, eds., *Pacific Economic Co-operation: Suggestions for Action.* Selangor: . Heinemann Educational 1981, 83-7

– 'Australia's Interest in Pacific Economic Cooperation.' *ASEAN Economic Bulletin* 2 (November 1985):101-6

– 'Building the Foundations of a Pacific Economic Community.' In Toshio Shishido and Ryuzo Sato, eds., *Economic Policy and Development: New Perspectives (Essays in Honor of Dr. Saburo Okita).* Dover, MA: Auburn House 1985, 46-58

Drysdale, Peter, ed. *Direct Foreign Investment in Asia and the Pacific.* Canberra: Australian National University Press 1972

– *International Economic Pluralism: Economic Policy in East Asia and the Pacific.* New York: Columbia University Press 1988

– 'Japan, Australia, New Zealand: The Prospect for WesternPacific Economic Integration.' In Kiyoshi Kojima, ed., *Pacific Trade and Development, II.* Tokyo: Japan Economic Research Center 1969, 183-209

– 'An Organisation for Pacific Trade, Aid and Development: Regional Arrangements and the Resource Trade.' Research Paper No. 49, Australia-Japan Economic Relations Research Project, Australia-Japan Research Centre, Research School of Pacific Studies, Australian National University, Canberra, May 1978

– 'An Organization for Pacific Trade, Aid and Development: Regional Arrangements and the Resource Trade.' In Lawrence B. Krause and Hugh Patrick, eds., *Mineral Resources in the Pacific Area.* San Francisco: Federal Reserve Bank of San Francisco 1978, 611-48

– 'The Pacific Basin and Its Economic Vitality.' In James W. Morley, ed., *The Pacific Basin: New Challenges for the United States.* New York: Academy of Political Science 1986, 11-22

– 'Pacific Economic Integration: An Australian View.' In Kiyoshi Kojima, ed., *Pacific Trade and Development, I.* Tokyo: Japan Economic Research Center 1968, 194-223

– 'The Pacific Trade and Development Conference: A Brief History.' *Pacific*

Economic Papers, no. 112, Australia-Japan Research Centre, Research School of Pacific Studies, Australian National University, Canberra, Australia, June 1984

– 'Pacific Trade Diplomacy.' *Look Japan* 10 (February 1986):7

– 'The Proposal for an Organisation for Pacific Trade and Development Revisited.' *Asian Survey* 23 (December 1983):1,293-304

– 'Prospects for Economic Cooperation Among Pacific Basin Countries.' In Hadi Soesastro and Han Sung-Joo, eds., *Pacific Economic Cooperation: The Next Phase.* Jakarta: Centre for Strategic and International Studies 1983, 84-90

– 'The Relationship with Japan: Despite the Vicissitudes.' In L.T. Evans and J.D.B. Miller, eds., *Policy and Practice: Essays in Honour of Sir John Crawford.* Sydney: Australian National University Press 1987, 66-81

Drysdale, Peter and Hugh Patrick. 'An Asian-Pacific Regional Economic Organisation: An Exploratory Concept Paper.' In John Crawford and Greg Seow, eds., *Pacific Economic Co-operation: Suggestions for Action.* Selangor: Heinemann Educational 1981, 63-82

Duncan, W.G.K., ed. *Australia's Foreign Policy.* Sydney: Angus and Robertson 1938

Dunn, Frederick Sherwood. *The Practice and Procedure of International Conferences.* Baltimore: Johns Hopkins Press 1929

Dunn, Lydia. 'Scope for Asian-Pacific Action on Protectionism.' *Asia-Pacific Community*, no. 22 (Fall 1983):7-19

Ekins, Paul. *A New World Order: Grassroots Movements for Global Change.* London: Routledge 1992

Elek, Andrew. 'The Challenge of Asia-Pacific Economic Cooperation.' *Pacific Review* 4 (1991):322-32

– 'The Evolution of Asia Pacific Economic Cooperation.' *Backgrounder* (Department of Foreign Affairs and Trade, Australia) 1 (15 June 1990):4-8

El-Hakim, Sherif. 'The Structure and Dynamics of Consensus Decision-Making.' *Man* 13 (March 1978):55-71

Emmerson, Donald K. 'ASEAN as an International Regime.' *Journal of International Affairs* 41 (Summer/Fall 1987):1-16

English, H. Edward. 'Canada and Pacific Cooperation.' *Research Paper Series I*, Pacific Basin Project No. 2, Center for Japan-U.S. Relations, International University of Japan, 1986

– 'Canada and Pacific Trade Policy.' In Kiyoshi Kojima, ed., *Pacific Trade and Development, I.* Tokyo: Japan Economic Research Center 1968, 3-29

– 'Economic Prospects for the Asia-Pacific Region in the 1980s.' In John Crawford and Greg Seow, eds., *Pacific Economic Co-operation: Suggestions for Action.* Selangor: Heinemann Educational 1981, 50-6

– 'The Emerging Pacific Community.' In Hadi Soesastro and Han Sung-Joo, eds., *Pacific Economic Cooperation: The Next Phase.* Jakarta: Centre for Strategic and International Studies 1983, 91-103

– 'An OECD of the Pacific?: A Canadian Perspective.' Working Paper No. 1, Asian Pacific Research and Resource Centre, Carleton University 1990

– 'Pacific Economic Community: A Consensual Region.' *International Journal* 38 (Spring 1983):330-53

– 'Pacific Trade and Development in the 1970s.' *Pacific Community* 2 (January 1971):272-82

– *Tomorrow the Pacific*. Toronto: C.D. Howe Institute 1991

English, H. Edward, ed. *Pacific Initiatives in Global Trade*. Halifax: Institute for Research on Public Policy 1990

English, H.E. and Keith A.J. Hay, eds. *Obstacles to Trade in the Pacific Area*. Ottawa: School of International Affairs, Carleton University 1972

English, H.E. and Anthony Scott, eds. *Renewable Resources in the Pacific*. Ottawa: International Development Research Centre 1982

Ennals, Martin. 'Amnesty International and Human Rights.' In Peter Willetts, ed., *Pressure Groups in the Global System: The Transnational Relations of Issue-Orientated Non-Governmental Organizations*. London: Frances Pinter 1982, 63-83

Eulau, Heinz and Moshe M. Czudnowski, eds. *Elite Recruitment in Democartic Polities: Comparative Studies Across Nations*. New York: Sage 1976

Europe Unites: The Hague Congress and After. London: Hollis and Carter 1949

Evans, L.T. and J.D.B. Miller, eds. *Policy and Practice: Essays in Honour of Sir John Crawford*. Sydney: Australian National University Press 1987

Evans, Paul M. 'The Emergence of Eastern Asia and Its Implications for Canada.' *International Journal* 47 (Summer 1992):504-28

Evans, Peter B. 'National Autonomy and Economic Development: Critical Perspectives on Multinational Corporations in Poor Countries.' In Robert O. Keohane and Joseph S. Nye, Jr., eds., *Transnational Relations and World Politics*. Cambridge, MA: Harvard University Press 1973, 325-42

Fairbanks, Richard M. III. 'Networking in the Pacific: Private Actions with a Public Purpose.' *Speaking of Japan* 7 (November 1986):27-32

Farran, Andrew. 'Energy, Politics and Pacific Basin Development.' *Asia Pacific Community*, no. 15 (Winter 1982):82-95

Feld, Werner J. 'Nongovernmental Entities and the International System: A Preliminary Quantitative Overview.' *Orbis* 15 (Fall 1971):879-922

– *Nongovernmental Forces in World Politics: A Study of Business, Labor, and Political Groups*. New York: Praeger 1972

Feltham, R.G. *Diplomatic Handbook*. London: Longman Group 1970

Field, Frederick Vanderbilt. *From Right to Left: An Autobiography*. Westport, CT: Lawrence Hill 1983

Field, James A., Jr. 'Transnationalism and the New Tribe.' In Robert O. Keohane and Joseph S. Nye, Jr., eds., *Transnational Relations and World Politics*. Cambridge, MA: Harvard University Press 1973, 3-22

Fifield, Russel H. 'ASEAN and the Pacific Community.' In Hadi Soesastro and Han Sung-Joo, eds., *Pacific Economic Cooperation: The Next Phase*. Jakarta: Centre for Strategic and International Studies 1983, 189-97

Foster, Leonie. *High Hopes: The Men and Motives of the Australian Round Table*. Carleton, Vic.: Melbourne University Press 1986

Fraser, Malcolm. 'Australia and the Pacific Community Concept.' In John Crawford and Greg Seow, eds., *Pacific Economic Co-operation: Suggestions for Action*. Selangor: Heinemann Educational 1981, 88-90

– 'Pacific Community: Further Steps.' In Robert L. Downen and Bruce J. Dickson, eds., *The Emerging Pacific Community: A Regional Perspective.* Boulder, CO: Westview 1984, 3-11

Frost, Michael S. 'Security Models and the Concept of an Asia-Pacific Community.' *Asia Pacific Community,* no. 26 (Fall 1984):1-15

Fry, Gerald W. 'The Pacific Challenge: A Transnational Future.' *Pacific Community,* no. 21 (Summer 1983):36-44

Fry, Gregory E. 'Regionalism and International Politics of the South Pacific.' *Pacific Affairs* 54 (Fall 1981):455-84

Gallagher, Peter W. 'Setting the Agenda for Trade Negotiations: Australia and the Cairns Group.' *Australian Outlook* 44 (April 1988):3-8

Gardner, Matthew M., Jr. 'The Pacific Basin Invitation and American Interests.' In Bruce J. Dickson, ed., *The Emerging Pacific Community Concept: An American Perspective.* Washington: Center for Strategic and International Studies, Georgetown University 1983, 44-8

Garnaut, Ross, ed. *ASEAN in a Changing Pacific and World Economy.* Canberra: Australian National University Press 1980

– 'Australia in the Western Pacific Economy.' In John Crawford and Greg Seow, eds., *Pacific Economic Co-operation: Suggestions for Action.* Selangor: Heinemann Educational 1981, 91-5

– 'Australia's Shrinking Markets.' In Lawrence B. Krause and Sueo Sekiguchi, eds., *Economic Interaction in the Pacific Basin.* Washington: Brookings Institution 1980, 79-116

Gaselee, Stephen. *The Language of Diplomacy.* Cambridge: Bowes and Bowes 1939

Gill, Stephen. 'From Atlanticism to Trilateralism: The Case of the Trilateral Commission.' In Steve Smith, ed., *International Relations: British and American Perspectives.* Oxford: Basil Blackwell/British International Studies Association 1985, 185-212

Gilmour, David. 'The Creation and Evolution of the Palestine Liberation Organization.' In Peter Willetts, ed., *Pressure Groups in the Global System: The Transnational Relations of Issue-Orientated Non-Governmental Organizations.* London: Frances Pinter 1982, 46-62

Gilpin, Robert. 'The Politics of Transnational Economic Relations.' In Robert O. Keohane and Joseph S. Nye, Jr., eds., *Transnational Relations and World Politics.* Cambridge, MA: Harvard University Press 1973, 48-69

Goh Chok Tong. 'The Role of National Governments in Strengthening Economic Interdependence in the Asia-Pacific Region.' In John Crawford and Greg Seow, eds., *Pacific Economic Co-operation: Suggestions for Action.* Selangor: Heinemann Educational 1981, 59

Goldmann, Kjell and Gunnar Sjstedt, eds. *Power, Capabilities, Interdependence: Problems in the Study of International Influence.* London: Sage 1979

Gorbachev, Mikhail. *Perestroika: New Thinking for Our Country and the World.* New York: Harper and Row 1987

– 'Speech by Mikhail Gorbachev at a Ceremonial Meeting Devoted to the Presentation of the Order of Lenin to the City of Vladivostock. July 28, 1986.' *Far Eastern Affairs* (Moscow), no. 1 (1987):3-21

Gordon, Bernard K. 'Japan and the Pacific Basin Proposal.' *Korea and World Affairs* 5 (Summer 1981):268-88

Gordon, Bernard K. and Kenneth J. Rothwell, eds. *The New Political Economy of the Pacific.* Cambridge, MA: Ballinger 1975

Gotoh Noboru. 'Prospects for a Pacific Economic Community.' *Journal of Japanese Trade and Industry,* no. 2 (March/April 1985):51-2

Grant, Bruce. *Indonesia.* Ringwood, Vic.: Penguin 1967

Green, Carl J. 'Towards Pacific Economic Integration: Making Haste Slowly.' In *The Pacific Community Concept: Views from Eight Nations.* Tokyo: Japan Center for International Exchange 1980, 103-8

Gregory, R.G. 'Overview.' In Hiromichi Mutoh et al., eds., *Industrial Policies for Pacific Economic Growth.* Sydney: Allen and Unwin 1986, 1-19

Grieg, D.W. *International Law.* London: Butterworth's 1970

Guocang Huan. 'China's Open Door Policy, 1978-1984.' *Journal of International Affairs* 39 (Winter 1986):1-18

Haas, Ernst B. *Beyond the Nation State: Functionalism and International Organization.* Stanford, CA: Stanford University Press 1964

– *The Obsolescence of Regional Integration Theory.* Berkeley: Institute of International Studies, University of California 1975

– *The Uniting of Europe: Political, Social and Economic Forces 1950-57.* London: Stevens and Sons 1958

– 'Words Can Hurt You; Or, Who Said What to Whom About Regimes.' *International Organization* 36 (Spring 1982):207-43

– *When Knowledge Is Power: Three Models of Change in International Organizations.* Berkeley: University of California Press 1990

Haas, Michael. *The Asian Way to Peace: A Story of Regional Cooperation.* New York: Praeger 1989

– 'Sick Man of the Pacific.' *Asia Pacific Community,* no. 21 (Summer 1981):45-63

Haas, Peter M. 'Introduction: Epistemic Communities and International Policy Coordination.' *International Organization* 46 (Winter 1992):1-35

Haggard, Stephan. 'The International Politics of East Asian Industrialization.' *Pacific Focus* 1 (Spring 1986):97-124

Hahn, Walter F. and Robert L. Pfaltzgraff, Jr. *Atlantic Community in Crisis: A Redefinition of the Transatlantic Relationship.* New York: Pergamon 1979

Haines, C. Grove, ed. *European Integration.* London: Oxford University Press 1957

Hall, H. Duncan. 'Political and Legal Cooperation.' In Institute of Pacific Relations, eds., *Institute of Pacific Relations: Honolulu Session, June 30-July 14, 1925.* Honolulu: IPR 1925, 136-8

Han Sung-Joo. 'The Pacific Cooperation Concept: Scope and Limitations.' *Korea and World Affairs* 7 (Summer 1983):181-90

– 'The Politics of Pacific Cooperation.' *Asian Survey* 23 (December 1983):1,281-92

Hankey, The Rt. Hon. Lord. *Diplomacy by Conference: Studies in Public Affairs, 1920-1946.* London: Ernest Benn 1946

Hara Yasushi. 'How to Make a Concept Real: The Idea of Pacific Basin Cooperation.' *Japan Quarterly* 27 (October/December 1980):471-8

Harris, Stuart. 'Linking of Politics and Economics in Foreign Policy.' *Australian Foreign Affairs Record* 56 (August 1985):690-8

– 'Regional Economic Cooperation, Trading Blocs and Australian Interests.' *Australian Outlook* 43 (August 1989):16-24
– 'Varieties of Pacific Economic Cooperation.' *Pacific Review* 4 (1991):301-11
– 'Vladivostok and Australian Foreign Policy.' In Ramesh Thakur and Carlyle A. Thayer, eds., *The Soviet Union as an Asian Pacific Power: Implications of Gorbachev's 1986 Vladivostok Initiative*. Boulder, CO: Westview 1987, 113-28

Harrison, Reginald J. *Europe in Question: Theories of Regional International Integration*. London: Allen and Unwin 1974

Hasluck, Paul. *Diplomatic Witness: Australian Foreign Affairs 1941-47*. Melbourne: Melbourne University Press 1980

Hassan, Fuad. 'Indonesia's Foreign Policy.' *Indonesian Quarterly* 13 (January 1985):39-46

Hay, Keith A.J. and Peter Price. *Canada, Japan and the Pacific Community*. Ottawa: Canada-Japan Trade Council 1981

Hazama Otohiko. *Nagano Shigeo Ron*. Tokyo: Life Sha 1977

Head, Ivan L. 'Introduction.' In H. E. English and Anthony Scott, eds., *Renewable Resources in the Pacific*. Ottawa: International Development Research Centre 1982, 7-9

Heatley, D.P. *Diplomacy and the Study of International Relations*. Oxford: Clarendon 1919

Hernadi, Andras. 'Pacific Region as a Growth Sub-Center and Japan's Role.' *Asia-Pacific Community*, no. 5 (Summer 1979):109-28

Hervouet, Gérard, ed. *Asie-Pacifique: Les Nouveaux Espaces de Coopération et de Conflits*. Sainte-Foy: Les Presses de l'Université Laval 1991

Higgins, Ean. 'Options and Constraints for U.S. Far Eastern Policy.' *Asia Pacific Community*, no. 20 (Spring 1983):124-56

Higgott, Richard A., Andrew Fenton Cooper,and Jenelle Bonnor. 'Asia-Pacific Economic Cooperation: An Evolving Case-Study in Leadership and Co-operation Building.' *International Journal* 45 (Autumn 1990):823-66

Hinsley, F.H. *Power and the Pursuit of Peace: Theory and Practice in the History of Relations between States*. Cambridge: Cambridge University Press 1982

Hirata Masami. 'Economics in a Global Perspective: Interview with Dr. Saburo Okita.' *Journal of Japanese Trade and Industry*, no. 1 (January/February 1984):36-9

Hirono Ryokichi. 'Towards Increased Intra-ASEAN Economic Cooperation.' *Asia Pacific Community*, no. 3 (Winter 1978- 9):92-118

Hoffman, Stanley. 'International Organization and the International System.' *International Organization* 24 (Summer 1970):389-413

Holbraad, Carsten. *The Concert of Europe: A Study in German and British International Theory 1815-1914*. London: Longman 1970

Holland, William L. 'Source Materials on the Institute of Pacific Relations: Bibliographical Note.' *Pacific Affairs* 58 (Spring 1985):91-7

Holland, W.L. and Kate L. Mitchell, eds. *Problems of the Pacific, 1936: Aims and Results of Social and Economic Policies in Pacific Countries. Proceedings of the Sixth Conference of the Institute of Pacific Relations, Yosemite National Park, California, 15-29 August 1936*. Chicago: University of Chicago Press 1937

Holsti, K.J. *The Dividing Discipline: Hegemony and Diversity in International Theory*. Boston: Allen and Unwin 1985

– 'The Horsemen of the Apocalypse: At the Gate, Detoured or Retreating?' *International Studies Quarterly* 30 (December 1986):355-72

– *International Politics: A Framework for Analysis*. 3rd edition. Englewood Cliffs, N.J.: Prentice-Hall 1977

Hong, Wontack and Lawrence B. Krause, eds. *Trade and Growth of the Advanced Developing Countries in the Pacific Basin*. Seoul: Korea Development Institute 1981

Hooper. Paul F. 'The Institute of Pacific Relations and the Origins of Asian and Pacific Studies.' *Pacific Affairs* 61 (Spring 1988):98-121

– 'Pacific Regional Organizations.' In Paul F. Hooper, ed., *Building a Pacific Community*. Honolulu: East-West Center 1982, 139-54

Hooper, Paul F., ed. *Building a Pacific Community*. Honolulu: East-West Center 1982

Huntington, Samuel P. 'Transnational Organizations in World Politics.' *World Politics* 25 (April 1973):333-68

Hyde, Jim. *Australia: The Asia Connection*. Melbourne: Kibble 1978

Ikema Makoto. 'Japan's Economic Relations with ASEAN.' In Ross Garnaut, ed., *ASEAN in a Changing Pacific and World Economy*. Canberra: Australian National University Press 1980, 453-86

Institute of Pacific Relations (IPR). *IPR, Honolulu Session, 30 June-14 July 1925, History, Organization, Proceedings, Discussions and Addresses*. Honolulu: IPR 1925

– *War and Peace in the Pacific: A Preliminary Report of the Eighth Conference of the Institute of Pacific Relations on Wartime and Post-war Co-operation of the United Nations in the Pacific and the Far East, Mont Tremblant, Quebec, 4-14 December 1942*. London: Royal Institute of International Affairs 1943

– International Secretariat. *IPR Publications on the Pacific 1925-1952*. New York: IPR 1953

– International Secretariat. *The Study of International Affairs in the Pacific Area: A Review of Nine Years' Work in the International Research Program of the Institute of Pacific Relations*. New York: IPR 1936

Iwasa Yoshizane. 'Japan-U.S. Economic Cooperation with Asia in the Seventies.' *Pacific Community* 1 (January 1970):382-94

Iwasaki Teruyuki, ed. *Economic Interdependence in the Western Pacific Basin in Perspective*. Tokyo: Institute for Developing Economics 1984

Jacobson, Harold K. *Networks of Interdependence: International Organizations and the Global Political System*. New York: Alfred A. Knopf 1979

Jaeger, Gilbert. 'Participation of Non-Governmental Organizations in the Activities of the United Nations High Commissioner for Refugees.' In Peter Willetts, ed., *Pressure Groups in the Global System: The Transnational Relations of Issue-Orientated Non-Governmental Organizations*. London: Frances Pinter 1982, 171-8

Jervis, Robert. 'Security Regimes.' *International Organization* 36 (Spring 1982):357-78

Johansson, J.K. and Robert K. Spich. 'Trade Interdependencies in the Pacific Rim Basin and the EC: A Comparative Analysis.' *Journal of Common Market Studies* 20 (September 1981):41-59

Johnson, Chalmers. *An Instance of Treason: Ozaki Hotsumi and the Sorge Spy Ring.* Tokyo: Charles E. Tuttle 1977

– 'Pacific Regional Development: Reality and Myth.' *Asian Pacific Review,* no. 7 (Summer 1987):2-10

Johnson, Harry G. 'A New World Trade Policy in the Post Kennedy Round Era: A Survey of Alternatives, with Special Reference to the Position of the Pacific and Asian Regions.' In Kiyoshi Kojima, ed., *Pacific Trade and Development, I.* Tokyo: Japan Economic Research Center 1968, 234-50

– 'Summary.' In Peter Drysdale, ed., *Direct Foreign Investment in Asia and the Pacific.* Canberra: Australian National University Press 1972, 344-52

– 'Survey of Issues.' In Peter Drysdale, ed., *Direct Foreign Investment in Asia and the Pacific.* Canberra: Australian National University Press 1972, 1-18

Johnson, Harry G. and Hugh Corbet. 'Pacific Trade in an Open World.' *Pacific Community* 1 (April 1970):521-35

Johnson, U. Alexis. 'The Pacific Basin.' *Pacific Community* 1 (October 1969): 11-19

Jones, F.C. *Japan's New Order in East Asia: Its Rise and Fall 1937-45.* London: Oxford University Press 1954

Kaiser, Karl. 'Transnational Politics: Toward a Theory of Multinational Politics.' *International Organization* 25 (Autumn 1971):790-817

– 'Transnational Relations as a Threat to the Democratic Process.' In Robert O. Keohane and Joseph S. Nye, Jr., eds., *Transnational Relations and World Politics.* Cambridge, MA: Harvard University Press 1973, 356-70

Kajima Morinosuke. *A Brief Diplomatic History of Modern Japan.* Tokyo: Charles E. Tuttle 1965

– *Memories and Recollections of Dr. Morinosuke Kajima: A Dialogue.* Tokyo: Japan Times 1967

– *The Road to Pan-Asia.* Tokyo: Japan Times 1973

Kanahele, George S. and Michael Haas. 'Prospects for a Pacific Community.' *Pacific Community* 6 (October 1974):83-93

Kanamori Hisao. 'Will Gorbachev's Economic Reforms Be Successful?' *Journal of Japanese Trade and Industry,* no. 6 (November/December 1985):47-50

Kaneko Kumao. 'A New Pacific Initiative: Strengthening the PECC Process.' *Japan Review of International Affairs* 2 (Spring/Summer 1988):67-90

Kattenburg, Paul M. 'Commentary.' In Smith Simpson, ed., *Instruction in Diplomacy: The Liberal Arts Approach.* Philadelphia: American Academy of Political and Social Science 1972, 40-4

Kaufmann, Johan. *Conference Diplomacy: An Introductory Analysis.* Leyden: A.W. Sijthoff 1968

Keating, Paul. 'Australia and Asia: Knowing Who We Are,' *Backgrounder* (Department of Foreign Affairs and Trade, Australia) 3 (24 April 1992):2-16

Kegley, Charles W., Jr. and Eugene R. Wittkopf, eds. *The Global Agenda: Issues and Perspectives.* New York: Random House 1984

Keohane, Robert O. *After Hegemony: Cooperation and Discord in the World Political Economy.* Princeton, N.J.: Princeton University Press 1984

– 'The Demand for International Regimes.' *International Organization* 36 (Spring 1982):325-55

Keohane, Robert O. and Joseph S. Nye, Jr. 'Power and Interdependence Revisited.' *International Organization* 41 (Autumn 1987):725-53
– *Power and Interdependence: World Politics in Transition.* Toronto: Little, Brown 1977
– 'Two Cheers for Multilateralism.' *Foreign Policy*, no. 60 (Fall 1985):148-67
Keohane, Robert O. and Joseph S. Nye, Jr., eds. *Transnational Relations and World Politics.* Cambridge, MA: Harvard University Press 1973
Kertesz, Stephen D. 'Commentary.' In Smith Simpson, ed., *Instruction in Diplomacy: The Liberal Arts Approach.* Philadelphia: American Academy of Political and Social Science 1972, 26-39
– *The Quest for Peace Through Diplomacy.* Englewood Cliffs, N.J.: Prentice-Hall 1967
Kim Cae-One. 'Towards a New International Economic Policy of the Asia-Pacific Region.' *Korean Journal of International Studies* 16 (Summer 1985):253-70
Kim Hong N. 'Politics of Japan's Economic Aid to South Korea.' *Asia Pacific Community*, no. 20 (Spring 1983):80-102
Kim Kihwan. 'Economic Cooperation Among the Pacific Basin Countries: An Alliance for Free Trade.' In Hadi Soesastro and Han Sung-Joo, eds., *Pacific Economic Cooperation: The Next Phase.* Jakarta: Centre for Strategic and International Studies 1983, 269-72
Kim Kook-Chin. 'A Plea for the Asia-Pacific Regional Cooperation: Emphasis on the Evolving Developmental Partnership between Korea and the ASEAN.' *Korea and World Affairs* 7 (Summer 1983):208-17
Kim Seung Hwan. 'Korea's Role in the Pacific Evolution.' In Bruce J. Dickson, ed., *The Emerging Pacific Community Concept: An American Perspective.* Washington: Center for Strategic and International Studies, Georgetown University 1983, 40-3
Kissinger, Henry A. 'The Policymaker and the Intellectual.' In James N. Rosenau, ed., *International Politics and Foreign Policy: A Reader in Research and Theory.* New York: Free Press 1961, 273-8
Kitamura Hiroshi. 'Asian-Pacific Economic Cooperation: The Role of Governments.' *Asia Pacific Community*, no. 18 (Fall 1982):17-25
– 'The Case for Asia-Pacific Regionalism: Regional and Sub-Regional Approaches to Multilateralism.' In *Prospects for Closer Economic Cooperation in the Asia-Pacific Area.* Occasional Paper A-5, The Asian Club, February 1981, 1-29
Knott, James E., Jr. *Freedom of Association: A Study of the Role of International Non-Governmental Organizations in the Development Process of Emerging Countries.* Brussels: Union of International Associations 1962
Kohona, Palitha T.B. 'The Evolving Concept of a Pacific Basin Community.' *Asian Survey* 26 (April 1986):399-419
Kojima Kiyoshi. 'Asian Developing Countries and PAFTA: Development, Aid and Trade Preferences.' In Kiyoshi Kojima, ed., *Pacific Trade and Development, II.* Tokyo: Japan Economic Research Center 1969, 102-28
– 'Economic Cooperation in a Pacific Community.' *Asia Pacific Community*, no. 12 (Spring 1981):1-10
– 'Economic Cooperation in a Pacific Community.' In Paul F. Hooper, ed., *Building a Pacific Community.* Honolulu: East-West Center 1982, 22-37

– *Economic Cooperation in a Pacific Community*. Tokyo: Japan Institute of International Affairs 1980
– 'How to Strengthen Economic Cooperation in the Asia-Pacific Region?' In Hadi Soesastro and Han Sung-Joo, eds., *Pacific Economic Cooperation: The Next Phase*. Jakarta: Centre for Strategic and International Studies 1983, 116-26
– *Japan and a Pacific Free Trade Area*. London: Macmillan 1971
– 'Japan's Interest in the Pacific Trade Expansion.' In Kiyoshi Kojima, ed., *Pacific Trade and Development, I*. Tokyo: Japan Economic Research Center 1968, 153-93
Kojima Kiyoshi, ed. *Pacific Trade and Development, I*. Tokyo: Japan Economic Research Center 1968
– *Pacific Trade and Development, II*. Tokyo: Japan Economic Research Center 1969
– *Structural Adjustments in Asian-Pacific Trade, Volumes I-II*. Tokyo: Japan Economic Research Centre 1973
Kojima Kiyoshi and Hiroshi Kurimoto. 'A Pacific Economic Community and Asian Developing Countries.' In *Measures for Trade Expansion of Developing Countries*. Tokyo: Japan Economic Research Centre 1966, 93-134
Kojima Kiyoshi and Miguel S. Wionczek, eds. *Technology Transfer in Pacific Economic Development*. Tokyo: Japan Economic Research Center 1975
Kolde, Endel-Jacob. *The Pacific Quest: The Concept and Scope of an Oceanic Community*. Toronto: Lexington/D.C. Heath 1976
Komiza Ryutaro. 'Japan's Non-Tariff Barriers to Trade in Manufactured Products.' In H.E. English and Keith A.J. Hay, eds., *Obstacles to Trade in the Pacific Area*. Ottawa: School of International Affairs, Carleton University 1972, 221-39
Koo, Wellington, Jr. *Voting Procedures in International Political Organizations*. New York: Columbia University Press 1947
Krasner, Stephen D. 'Regimes and the Limits of Realism: Regimes as Autonomous Variables.' *International Organization* 36 (Spring 1982):497-510
– 'Structural Causes and Regime Consequences: Regimes as Intervening Variables.' *International Organization* 36 (Spring 1982):185-205
Krause, Lawrence B. 'Harry G. Johnson (1923-1977).' In Lawrence B. Krause and Hugh Patrick, eds., *Mineral Resources in the Pacific*. San Francisco: Federal Reserve Bank of San Francisco 1978, 1-3
– 'Introduction.' In Lawrence B. Krause and Hugh Patrick, eds., *Mineral Resources in the Pacific Area*. San Francisco: Federal Reserve Bank of San Francisco 1978, 18-28
– 'The Pacific Community Idea: Preparing for the Next Phase.' In Hadi Soesastro and Han Sung-Joo, eds., *Pacific Economic Cooperation: The Next Phase*. Jakarta: Centre for Strategic and International Studies 1983, 104-15
– 'Private International Finance.' In Robert O. Keohane and Joseph S. Nye, Jr., eds., *Transnational Relations and World Politics*. Cambridge, MA: Harvard University Press 1973, 173-90
– 'Summary.' In Wontack Hong and Lawrence B. Krause, eds., *Trade and Growth of the Advanced Developing Countries in the Pacific Basin*. Seoul: Korea Development Institute 1981, 597-611
Krause, Lawrence B. and Hugh Patrick, eds. *Mineral Resources in the Pacific Area*. San Francisco: Federal Reserve Bank of San Francisco 1978

Krause, Lawrence B. and Sueo Sekiguchi, eds. *Economic Interaction in the Pacific Basin*. Washington: Brookings Institution 1980

Kriesberg, Louis. 'Formal and Quasi-Mediators in International Disputes: An Exploratory Analysis.' *Journal of Peace Research* 28 (February 1991):19-27

Kubota Akira. 'Japan: Social Structure and Work Ethic.' *Asia Pacific Community*, no. 20 (Spring 1983):35-65

– 'Political Influence of Japanese Higher Civil Service.' *Asia Pacific Community*, no. 12 (Spring 1981):62-74

Kunimasa Tsunehiro. 'Japan's Economic Organizations: The Zaikai.' *Journal of Japanese Trade and Industry*, no. 3 (1985):10-13

Kuroda Makato. 'Japan's Policy on Economic Cooperation.' *Journal of Japanese Trade and Industry*, no. 2 (1985):10-13

Lador-Lederer, J.J. *International Non-Governmental Organizations and Economic Entities: A Study in Autonomous Organization and Ius Gentium*. Leyden: A.W. Sythoff 1963

Lande, Carl H., ed. *Rebuilding a Nation: Philippine Challenges and American Policy*. Washington, DC: Washington Institute Press 1987

Langdon, F.C. *Japan's Foreign Policy*. Vancouver: UBC Press 1973

– *The Politics of Canadian-Japanese Economic Relations, 1952-1983*. Vancouver: UBC Press 1983

Lapidus, Gail W. 'The USSR and Asia in 1986: Gorbachev's New Initiatives.' *Asian Survey* 27 (January 1987):1-9

Lasswell, Harold D., Daniel Lerner, and C. Easton Rothwell. 'The Elite Concept.' In Peter Bachrach, ed., *Political Elites in a Democracy*. New York: Atherton 1971, 13-26

Lauren, Paul Gordon. *Diplomats and Bureaucrats: The First Institutional Responses to Twentieth-Century Diplomacy in France and Germany*. Stanford, CA: Hoover Institution Press 1976

Lauren, Paul Gordon, ed. *Diplomacy: New Approaches in History, Theory, and Policy*. New York: Free Press 1979

Lebedev, S.A. 'Integration Tendencies in Pacific Asia and External Economic Relations of the USSR.' In Kiyoshi Kojima and Miguel S. Wionczek, eds., *Technology Transfer in Pacific Economic Development*. Tokyo: Japan Economic Research Center 1975, 30-6

Lee Poh Ping. 'Reflections on the Pacific Community Concept.' *Asia Pacific Community*, no. 8 (Spring 1980):35-43

Lim, Hank. 'Pacific Rim Economic Cooperation in a Changing Global Environment.' *Asia Horizon* (Canadian Asian Studies Association) 12 (November 1990):23-7

Lim, Robyn. 'Implications for Southeast Asia.' In Ramesh Thakur and Carlyle A. Thayer, eds., *The Soviet Union as an Asian Pacific Power: Implications of Gorbachev's 1986 Vladivostok Initiative*. Boulder, CO: Westview 1987, 81-92

Linder, Staffan Burenstam. *The Pacific Century: Economic and Political Consequences of Asian-Pacific Dynamism*. Stanford, CA: Stanford University Press 1986

Lipschutz, Ronnie D. 'Bargaining Among Nations: Culture, History, and Perception in Regime Formation.' *Evaluation Review* 15 (February 1991):47-60

Lipson, Charles. 'International Cooperation in Economic and Security Affairs.' *World Politics* 37 (October 1984):1-23

– 'The Transformation of Trade: The Sources and Effects of Regime Change.' *International Organization* 36 (Spring 1982):417-55

Liska, George F. *Nations in Alliance: The Limits of Interdependence*. Baltimore: Johns Hopkins Press 1962

Lockwood, William. 'Economic Cooperation within the Asia-Pacific Region: A Summary View.' In Kiyoshi Kojima, ed., *Pacific Trade and Development, II*. Tokyo: Japan Economic Research Center 1969, 397-405

Low, Linda. 'The East Asia Economic Grouping.' *Pacific Review* 4 (1991):375-82

Luard, Evan, ed. *The Evolution of International Organizations*. London: Thames and Hudson 1966

McCloskey, Jean. 'New Realities in the Pacific: The Political Perspective.' *Behind the Headlines* 46 (Winter 1988-9):1-13.

Mackenzie, W.J.M. *Politics and Social Science*. Harmondsworth, UK: Penguin 1967

McKinnon, Ronald I. 'Issues and Perspectives: An Overview of Banking Regulation and Monetary Control.' In Augustine H.H. Tan and Basant Kapur, eds., *Pacific Growth and Financial Interdependence*. Sydney: Allen and Unwin 1986, 319-36

McMahon, John. 'The International Labor Organization.' In Evan Luard, ed., *The Evolution of International Organizations*. London: Thames and Hudson 1966, 177-99

McMichael, Heath. 'Indonesian Foreign Policy: Towards a More Assertive Style.' *Australia-Asia Papers*, no. 40, Centre for the Study of Australian-Asian Relations, Griffith University, February 1987

McMillen, Donald Hugh. 'China in Asia's International Relations.' *International Journal* 38 (Spring 1983):209-33

Macedo, Jorge Braga de. 'Trade and Financial Interdependence under Flexible Exchange Rates: The Pacific Area.' In Augustine H.H. Tan and Basant Kapur, eds., *Pacific Growth and Financial Interdependence*. Sydney: Allen and Unwin 1986, 277-315

Madigan, Russel. *Of Business and Foreign Policy*. Canberra: Australian Institute of International Affairs 1985

Mahathir bin Mohamad. 'Tak Kenal Maka Tak Cinta.' In John Crawford and Greg Seow, eds., *Pacific Economic Co-operation: Suggestions for Action*. Selangor: Heinemann Educational 1981, 42-5

Malakhovsky, K.V. 'Problems of Security Strengthening and Development in the Pacific Area.' In Hedley Bull, ed., *Asia and the Western Pacific: Towards a New International Order*. Sydney: Thomas Nelson and Sons/Australian Institute of International Affairs 1975, 45-50

Malmgren, Harald B. 'Trade Liberalization and the Economic Development of the Pacific Basin: The Need for Cooperation.' In H.E. English and Keith A.J. Hay, eds., *Obstacles to Trade in the Pacific Area*. Ottawa: School of International Affairs, Carleton University 1972, 271-83

Malygin, Valery V. 'USSR Foreign Policy in the 1990s.' *Indonesian Quarterly* 15 (April 1987):250-8

Mansbach, Richard W., Yale H. Ferguson, and Donald E. Lampert. *The Web of*

World Politics: Non-State Actors in the Global System. Englewood Cliffs, N.J.: Prentice-Hall 1976

Mansfield, Michael. 'Prospects for a Pacific Community.' In Paul F. Hooper, ed., *Building a Pacific Community.* Honolulu: East-West Center 1982, 85-93

Mara, Ratu Kamisese K.T. 'Building a Pacific Community.' In Paul F. Hooper, ed., *Building a Pacific Community.* Honolulu: East-West Center 1982, 38-48

Marous, John C. 'The Abacus Economy in a Computer World: China's Emerging Role in Pacific Basin Trade.' In Bruce J. Dickson, ed., *The Emerging Pacific Community Concept: A Staff Report on the CSIS Pacific Basin Congressional Study Group.* Washington: Center for Strategic and International Studies, Georgetown University 1983, 25-32

Marx, Karl and Friedrich Engels. 'The Global Consequences of the Discovery of Gold in California.' In Karl Marx and Friedrich Engels, 'Revue,' *Neue Rheinische Zeitung. Politisch-Okonomische Revue,* 2nd Issue, January/February 1850. Reprinted in Saul K. Padover, ed., *On America and the Civil War: The Karl Marx Library, Volume II.* New York: McGraw-Hill 1972, 14-15

Masuda Hiroshi. 'The Roles of Semigovernmental Organizations in Japanese-American Relations.' *Journal of Northeast Asian Studies* 6 (Spring 1987):77-83

'Materials on Pacific Community Concept.' *Korea and World Affairs* 7 (Summer 1983):276-303

'Materials on Pacific Summit Conference.' *Korea and World Affairs* 7 (Summer 1983):304-28

Mates, Leo. 'The Nonaligned as a Pressure Group?' *Pacific Community* 2 (April 1971):512-22

Matsumoto Hiroshi and Noordin Sopiee, eds. *Into the Pacific Era: Southeast Asia and Its Place in the Pacific.* Kuala Lumpur/Tokyo: Institute of Strategic and International Studies/Association of Promotion of International Cooperation 1986.

Matthews, Trevor and John Ravenhill. 'Bipartisanship in the Australian Foreign Policy Elite.' *Australian Outlook* 42 (April 1988):9-20

Mattingly, Garrett. *Renaissance Diplomacy.* London: Jonathan Cape 1955

Maule, Christopher J. 'Foreign Investment in the Pacific Rim.' *International Perspectives,* Janauary/February 1987, 21-3

Maule, Christopher J. and Andrew Vanderwal. 'International Regulation of Foreign Investment.' *International Perspectives,* November/December 1985, 22-7

Meaney, Neville, Trevor Matthews, and Sol Encel. *The Japanese Connection: A Survey of Australian Leaders' Attitudes Towards Japan and the Australia-Japan Relationship.* Melbourne: Longman Cheshire 1988

Miles, Edward. 'Transnationalism in Space: Inner and Outer.' In Robert O. Keohane and Joseph S. Nye, Jr., eds., *Transnational Relations and World Politics.* Cambridge, MA: Harvard University Press 1973, 252-75

Miller, J.D.B. *The Nature of Politics.* Harmondsworth: Penguin 1962

– 'A Pacific Economic Community: Problems and Possibilities.' *Asia Pacific Community,* no. 9 (Summer 1980):10-20

– *The Shape of Diplomacy.* Canberra: Australian National University 1963

– 'Summing-Up of Discussion.' In Hedley Bull, ed., *Asia and the Western Pacific: Towards a New International Order.* Sydney: Thomas Nelson and Sons/The Australian Institute of International Affairs 1975, 372-81

– *The World of States: Connected Essays.* London: Croom Helm 1981

Milner, A.C. and Trevor Wilson, eds. *Australian Diplomacy: Challenges and Options for the Department of Foreign Affairs.* Occasional Paper No. 5, Australian Institute of International Affairs, August 1986

Mino Hokaji. 'High Economic Growth Forecast for Pacific Nations: Interview with Noboru Gotoh, President, The Japan Chamber of Commerce and Industry.' *Business Japan*, January 1985, 24-6

Minty, Abdul S. 'The Anti-Apartheid Movement and Racism in Southern Africa.' In Peter Willetts, ed., *Pressure Groups in the Global System: The Transnational Relations of Issue-Orientated Non-Governmental Organizations.* London: Frances Pinter 1982, 28-45

Mizoguchi Michio. 'Japan, the Pacific and the New Round.' In *Pacific Trade Policy Cooperation: Goals and Initiatives.* Seoul: Korea Development Institute 1986, 55-69

Moe, Terry M. *The Organization of Interests: Incentives and the Internal Dynamics of Political Interest Groups.* Chicago: University of Chicago Press 1980

Moertopo, Ali. *Indonesia in Regional and International Cooperation: Principles of Implementation and Construction.* Jakarta: Centre for Strategic and International Studies 1973

– 'Pacific Economic Cooperation: The Practice of Meaningful Consultation.' In Hadi Soesastro and Han Sung-Joo, eds., *Pacific Economic Cooperation: The Next Phase.* Jakarta: Centre for Strategic and International Studies 1983, 204-7

– 'A Reflection on Pacific Economic Cooperation.' In *Regional Dimensions of Indonesia-Australia Relations.* Jakarta: Centre for Strategic and International Studies 1984, 69-72

Moon, Chung-in. 'Conclusion: A Dissenting View on the Pacific Future.' In Stephen Haggard and Chung-in Moon, eds., *Pacific Dynamics: The International Politics of Industrial Change.* Boulder, CO: Westview 1989, 359-74

Morgenthau, Hans J. *Politics Among Nations: The Struggle for Power and Peace.* 4th edition, New York: Alfred A. Knopf 1967

Morita Akio. 'Business and Japan's New World Role: As Seen Through Personal Experience.' *Journal of International Affairs* 37 (Summer 1983):141-5

Morley, James W. 'The New World in the Pacific.' In James W. Morley, ed., *The Pacific Basin: New Challenges for the United States.* New York: Academy of Political Science 1986, 1-7

Morley, James W., ed. *The Pacific Basin: New Challenges for the United States.* New York: Academy of Political Science 1986

Morris-Suzuki, Tessa. 'Japan and the Pacific Basin Community.' *World Today* 37 (December 1981):454-61

– *Showa: An Inside History of Hirohito's Japan.* London: Athlone 1984

Morrison, Charles E. and Anne F. Miyashiro. 'Issues in Pan-Pacific Cooperation.' In *The Pacific Community Concept: Views from Eight Nations.* Tokyo: Japan Center for International Exchange, 3-14

Morse, Edward L. 'Transnational Economic Processes.' In Robert O. Keohane and Joseph S. Nye, Jr., eds., *Transnational Relations and World Politics.* Cambridge, MA: Harvard University Press 1973, 23-47

Mowat, R.B. *Diplomacy and Peace.* London: Williams and Norgate 1935

Mukherjee, Bharati. *Kautilya's Concept of Diplomacy: A New Interpretation.* Calcutta: Minerva 1976

Mundell, Robert A. *Man and Economics: The Science of Choice.* New York: McGraw-Hill 1968

Munro, Gordon R. 'Cooperative Fisheries Arrangements Between Pacific Coastal States and Distant-Water Nations.' In H.E. English and Anthony Scott, eds., *Renewable Resources in the Pacific.* Ottawa: International Development Research Centre 1982, 247-55

Mutoh Hiromichi, et al., eds. *Industrial Policies for Pacific Economic Growth.* Sydney: Allen and Unwin 1986

Naisbitt, John. *Megatrends: Ten New Directions Transforming Our Lives.* Sydney: Futura 1984

Nakajima Mineo. 'Pacific Basin Cooperation Concept and Japan's Options.' *Asia Pacific Community,* no. 9 (Summer 1980):1-9

Nam Duck-Woo. 'Asia-Pacific Cooperation: An Alliance for Progress.' In Hadi Soesastro and Han Sung-Joo, eds., *Pacific Economic Cooperation: The Next Phase.* Jakarta: Centre for Strategic and International Studies 1983, 273-7

– 'Changing Patterns of Trade and Trends in Trade Policy in the Asia-Pacific Region.' In Paul F. Hooper, ed., *Building a Pacific Community.* Honolulu: East-West Center 1982, 119-38

Namiki Nobuyoshi. 'An Eye to the Pacific: Interview with Noboru Goto, President of the Japan Chamber of Commerce and Industry.' *Journal of Japanese Trade and Industry,* no. 4 (July/August 1984):35-7

Narongchai Akrasanee. 'Issues in ASEAN Economic Regionalism.' *Indonesian Quarterly* 11 (July 1983):27-47

Narongchai Akrasanee, Seiji Naya, and Vinyu Vichit-Vadakan, eds. *Trade and Employment in Asia and the Pacific.* Honolulu: University of Hawaii Press 1977

National Pacific Cooperation Committee of Australia (NPCCA). *Australia and Pacific Economic Cooperation: Report by the National Pacific Cooperation Committee to the Australian Government.* Canberra: Australian National University 1985

– *Australia and Pacific Economic Cooperation: Second Report by the National Pacific Cooperation Committee to the Australian Government.* Canberra: Australian National University 1987

Ness, Gayl D. and Steven R. Brechin. 'Bridging the Gap: International Organizations as Organizations.' *International Organization* 42 (Spring 1988):245-73

Nicholas, Rhondda M. 'ASEAN and the Pacific Community Debate: Much Ado About Something?' *Asian Survey* 21 (December 1981):1,197-210

Nicolson, Harold. *Diplomacy.* 3rd edition. London: Oxford University Press 1963

Nossal, Kim Richard. 'Analyzing the Domestic Sources of Canadian Foreign Policy.' *International Journal* 39 (Winter 1983-4):1-22

Nye, Joseph S., Jr. and Robert O. Keohane. 'Transnational Relations and World Politics: A Conclusion.' In Robert O. Keohane and Joseph S. Nye, Jr., eds., *Transnational Relations and World Politics.* Cambridge, MA: Harvard University Press 1973, 371-98

– 'Transnational Relations and World Politics: An Introduction.' In Robert O. Keohane and Joseph S. Nye, Jr., eds., *Transnational Relations and World Politics.* Cambridge, MA: Harvard University Press 1973, ix-xxix

Okita Saburo. 'Japan and the Pacific Basin.' *Journal of International Affairs* 37 (Summer 1983):13-20
– *Japan's Challenging Years: Reflections on My Lifetime.* Sydney: Allen and Unwin/ Australia-Japan Research Centre 1983
– 'Japan's Role in Pacific Basin Cooperation: Present and Future.' *Euro-Asia Business Review* 4 (February 1985):37-8
– 'The Outlook for Pacific Cooperation and the Role of Japan.' *Indonesian Quarterly* 15 (July 1987):494-505
– 'Pacific Development and Its Implications for the World Economy.' In James W. Morley, ed., *The Pacific Basin: New Challenges for the United States.* New York: Academy of Political Science 1986, 23-34
– 'Pacific Regional Co-operation.' In L.T. Evans and J.D.B. Miller, eds., *Policy and Practice: Essays in Honour of Sir John Crawford.* Sydney: Australian National University Press 1987, 122-32
– 'A View of the Pacific Basin Cooperation Concept.' In Hadi Soesastro and Han Sung-Joo, eds., *Pacific Economic Cooperation: The Next Phase.* Jakarta: Centre for Strategic and International Studies 1983, 254-59
Okita Saburo and Akira Ohnishi. 'Japan's Role in Asian Economic Development.' In Kiyoshi Kojima, ed., *Pacific Trade and Development, I.* Tokyo: Japan Economic Research Center 1968, 359-80
Oksenberg, Michael. 'China's Confident Nationalism.' *Foreign Affairs* 65 (1987):501-23
Okuno Masahiro and Kotaro Suzumura. 'The Economic Analysis of Industrial Policy: A Conceptual Framework Through the Japanese Experience.' In Hiromichi Mutoh et al., eds., *Industrial Policies for Pacific Economic Growth.* Sydney: Allen and Unwin 1986, 23-41
Olson, Mancur. 'Increasing the Incentives for International Cooperation.' *International Organization* 25 (Autumn 1971):866-74
– *The Logic of Collective Action: Political Goods and the Theory of Groups.* Cambridge, MA: Harvard University Press 1965
Ong Leng Chuan. 'A New Co-Prosperity Sphere.' *Asia Pacific Community*, no. 5 (Summer 1979):65-9
Osbaldeston, Gordon. 'Models for the Future: Canada.' In A.C. Milner and Trevor Wilson, eds., *Australian Diplomacy: Challenges for the Department of Foreign Affairs.* Occasional Paper No. 5, Australian Institute of International Affairs, August 1986, 18-25
Osborne, Michael West and Nicolas Fourt. *Pacific Basin Economic Cooperation.* Paris: Development Centre of the Organization for Economic Cooperation and Development 1983
Osborne, Milton. *Southeast Asia: An Illustrated Introductory History.* Sydney: Allen and Unwin 1985
Ostry, Sylvia, ed. *Authority and Academic Scribblers: The Role of Research in East Asian Policy Reform.* San Francisco: ICS Press 1991
Overholt, William. 'The Rise of the Pacific Basin.' *Pacific Community* 5 (July 1974):516-33
Oye, Kenneth A. 'Explaining Cooperation Under Anarchy: Hypotheses and Strategies.' *World Politics* 38 (October 1985):1-24

Pacific Basin Co-operation Study Group. 'A Japanese Perspective: Reports of the Pacific Basin Cooperation Study Group.' In *The Pacific Community Concept: Views from Eight Nations*. Tokyo: Japan Center for International Exchange 1980, 17-31

– 'Report on the Pacific Basin Cooperation Concept.' In John Crawford and Greg Seow, eds., *Pacific Economic Co-operation: Suggestions for Action*. Selangor: Heinemann Educational 1981, 183-204

The Pacific Community Concept: Views from Eight Nations. Tokyo: Japan Center for International Exchange 1980

Pacific Economic Cooperation Conference (PECC). *Issues for Pacific Economic Cooperation: A Report of the Third Pacific Economic Cooperation Conference, Bali, November 1983*. Jakarta: Centre for Strategic and International Studies 1984

– *Pacific Economic Cooperation – Issues and Opportunities: Report of the Fourth Pacific Economic Cooperation Conference, Seoul, April 29-May 1, 1985*. Seoul: Korea Development Institute 1985

– *Pacific Economic Cooperation Conference IV: Announcement Seoul, Korea, April 29-May 1, 1985*. Seoul: Korea Development Institute 1985

– *Pacific Trade Policy Cooperation: Goals and Initiatives*. Seoul: Korea Development Institute 1986

– *PECC Work Programme, 1991-1992*. Singapore: PECC Secretariat 1991

– *Report of the Fifth Pacific Economic Cooperation Conference, Vancouver, November 16-19, 1986*. Ottawa: Canadian Chamber of Commerce 1987

– *Report of the Sixth Pacific Economic Cooperation Conference, Osaka, May 17-20, 1988*. Tokyo: Japan National Committee for Pacific Economic Cooperation 1988

– *Report of the Seventh Pacific Economic Cooperation Conference, Auckland, November 12-15, 1989*. Wellington: New Zealand Committee for Pacific Economic Cooperation 1990

Pacific Economic Cooperation Council (PECC). *Pacific Economic Outlook, 1992-1993*. San Francisco: U.S. National Committee for Pacific Economic Cooperation 1992

A Pacific Perspective: New Horizons in the Japan-Australia Relationship: An address by His Excellency Mr. Yasuhiro Nakasone, Prime Minister of Japan, to the National Press Club, Canberra, 16 January 1985. Canberra: Australia-Japan Research Centre, Research School of Pacific Studies, Australian National University 1985

'Pacific Rim.' *Japan Quarterly* 15 (April/June 1980):147-51

Pacific Trade and Development Conference (PAFTAD). *The Pacific Trade and Development Conference: The First Twenty Years*. Canberra: PAFTAD International Secretariat, April 1989

– International Steering Committee. 'The Pacific Trade and Development Conference Series.' In John Crawford and Greg Seow, eds., *Pacific Economic Co-operation: Suggestions for Action*. Selangor: Heinemann Educational 1981, 26

– Secretariat. 'Pacific Trade and Development Conference Series: List of Participants (1968-84).' Australia-Japan Research Centre, Research School of Pacific Studies, Australian National University, Canberra 1985

Padover, Saul K., ed. *On America and the Civil War: The Karl Marx Library, Volume III*. New York: McGraw-Hill 1972

Palmer, Norman D. *The New Regionalism in Asia and the Pacific.* Lexington: Lexington 1991

Parsons, Talcott. 'Order and Community in the International Social System.' In James N. Rosenau, ed., *International Politics and Foreign Policy: A Reader in Research and Theory.* New York: Free Press 1961, 126-9

Patrick, Hugh T. 'Summary.' In Kiyoshi Kojima, ed., *Structural Adjustments in Asian-Pacific Trade.* Tokyo: Japan Economic Research Centre 1973, 461-76

Payne, Anthony J. *The Politics of the Caribbean Community 1961-79: Regional Integration Amongst New States.* Manchester: Manchester University Press 1980

Pentland, Charles. *International Theory and European Integration.* London: Faber and Faber 1973

Perry, John Curtis. 'Private Philanthropy and Foreign Affairs: The Case of John D. Rockefeller and Japan.' *Asian Perspective* 8 (Fall/Winter 1984):268-84

Perry, Stewart E. 'Notes on the Role of the National: A Social-Psychological Concept for the Study of International Relations.' In James N. Rosenau, ed., *International Politics and Foreign Policy: A Reader in Research and Theory.* New York: Free Press 1961, 87-97

Petrov, D. 'Imperialism Forms New Blocs in the Asian Pacific Region.' *Far Eastern Affairs* (Moscow), no. 1 (1987):70-80

Pickard, Bertram. *The Greater United Nations: An Essay Concerning the Place and Significance of International Non-Governmental Organizations.* New York: Carnegie Endowment for International Peace 1956

Plischke, Elmer. 'The Optimum Scope of Instruction in Diplomacy.' In Smith Simpson, ed., *Instruction in Diplomacy: The Liberal Arts Approach.* Philadelphia: American Academy of Political and Social Science 1972, 1-25

Porter, Gareth and Janet Welsh Brown. *Global Environmental Politics.* Boulder, CO: Westview 1991

Prem Tinsulanonda, 'Pacific Economic Interdependence.' In Hadi Soesastro and Han Sung-Joo, eds., *Pacific Economic Cooperation: The Next Phase.* Jakarta: Centre for Strategic and International Studies 1983, 202-3

Presthus, Robert. *Elite Accommodation in Canadian Politics.* New York: Cambridge University Press 1973

– *Elites in the Policy Process.* New York: Cambridge University Press 1974

Puchala, Donald J. 'The Integration Theorists and the Study of International Relations.' In Charles W. Kegley, Jr. and Eugene R. Wittkopf, ed., *The Global Agenda: Issues and Perspectives*, 2nd edition. New York: Random House 1988, 198-215

Puchala, Donald J. and Raymond F. Hopkins. 'International Regimes: Lessons from Inductive Analysis.' *International Organization* 36 (Spring 1982):245-75

Quo, F. Quei, ed. *Politics of the Pacific Rim: Perspectives on the 1980s.* Burnaby, BC: SFU Publications 1982

Randolph, R. Sean. 'Pacific Overtures.' *Foreign Policy*, no. 57 (Winter 1984-5):128-42

– 'Scenarios and Pathways Towards Greater Pan-Pacific Co-operation.' In Hiroshi Matsumoto and Noordin Sopiee, eds., *Into the Pacific Era: Southeast Asia and Its Place in the Pacific.* Kuala Lumpur/Tokyo: Institute of Strategic and International Studies/Association of Promotion of International Cooperation 1986, 43-9

– 'Towards Pan-Pacific Cooperation: An American View.' *Euro-Asia Business Review* 4 (February 1985):33-6

Regional Dimensions of Indonesia-Australia Relations. Jakarta: Centre for Strategic and International Studies 1984

Reifman, Alfred. 'An Asian-Pacific Regional Economic Organisation: A Skeptical View.' In John Crawford and Greg Seow, eds., *Pacific Economic Co-operation: Suggestions for Action.* Selangor: Heinemann Educational 1981, 205-6

Renouf, Alan. *Malcolm Fraser and Australian Foreign Policy.* Sydney: Australian Professional Publications 1986

Renwick, Neil. 'International Relations and Political Economy.' Working Paper No. 4, Department of International Relations, Research School of Pacific Studies, Australian National University, n.d.

Resnick, Philip. 'BC Capitalism and the Empire of the Pacific.' *BC Studies*, no. 67 (Autumn 1985):29-46

Reuber, Grant L. 'Problems of Development Assistance and Economic Cooperation Among Large and Small States in the Pacific Region.' In Leslie V. Castle and Frank Holmes, eds., *Cooperation and Development in the Asia/Pacific Region.* Tokyo: Japan Economic Research Center 1976, 9-37

Reynolds, P.A. *An Introduction to International Relations.* London: Longman 1971

– 'Non-state Actors and International Outcomes.' *British Journal of International Studies* 5 (July 1979):91-111

Reynolds, Philip A. and Robert D. McKinlay. 'The Concept of Interdependence: Its Uses and Misuses.' In Kjell Goldmann and Gunnar Sjstedt, eds., *Power, Capabilities, Interdependence: Problems in the Study of International Influence.* London: Sage 1979, 141-66

Rix, Alan. *Coming to Terms: The Politics of Australia's Trade with Japan, 1945-57.* Sydney: Allen and Unwin 1986

Rizvi, Hasan-Askari. 'Problems and Prospects of South Asian Regional Cooperation.' *Regional Studies* 2 (Spring 1984):13-24

Robertson, R.T. 'From Community to Cooperation to Self-Reliance: Death of the Pacific Basin Concept.' *Journal of International Relations* (Japan), no. 17 (July 1986):66-80

Robison, Richard. *Indonesia: The Rise of Capital.* North Sydney: Allen and Unwin 1986

Rogowski, Ronald. 'Rationalist Theories of Politics: A Midterm Report.' *World Politics* 30 (January 1978):296-323

Rosenau, James N. *Turbulence in World Politics: A Theory of Change and Continuity.* Princeton: Princeton University Press 1990

Rosenau, James N., ed. *International Politics and Foreign Policy: A Reader in Research and Theory.* New York: Free Press 1961

Rosenau, James N. and Ernst-Otto Czempiel, eds. *Governance Without Government: Order and Change in World Politics.* Cambridge: Cambridge University Press 1992

Ross, Robert S. 'China's Strategic Role in Asia.' In James W. Morley, ed., *The Pacific Basin: New Challenges for the United States.* New York: Academy of Political Science 1986, 116-28

Roth, William V., Jr. 'New Perspective on the Pacific Basin.' In John Crawford and Greg Seow, eds., *Pacific Economic Co-operation: Suggestions for Action.* Selangor: Heinemann Educational 1981, 46-9

Rothstein, Robert L. 'The Rise and Fall of the North-South Dialogue.' *Pacific Focus* 1 (Spring 1986):75-95

Royal Institute of International Affairs. *The Pattern of Pacific Security: A Report by a Chatham House Study Group.* London 1946

Ruggie, John Gerard. 'International Regimes, Transactions and Change: Embedded Liberalism in the Postwar Economic Order.' *International Organization* 36 (Spring 1982):379-415

Russett, Bruce M. and John D. Sullivan. 'Collective Goods and International Organization.' *International Organization* 25 (Autumn 1971):845-65

Sadli, Mohammad. 'Foreign Investment in Developing Countries: Indonesia.' In Peter Drysdale, ed., *Direct Foreign Investment in Asia and the Pacific.* Canberra: Australian National University Press 1972, 201-26

Saito Shiro. *Japan at the Summit: Japan's Role in the Western Alliance and Asian Pacific Co-operation.* London: Routledge 1990

Samoteikin, Evgeni. 'The Goals of Vladivostok.' In Ramesh Thakur and Carlyle A. Thayer, eds., *The Soviet Union as an Asian Pacific Power: Implications of Gorbachev's 1986 Vladivostok Initiative.* Boulder, CO: Westview 1987, 11-18

Sato Eisaku. 'Pacific Asia.' *Pacific Community* 1 (October 1969):1-3

Sato Seizaburo. 'Transcending Diversity.' *Look Japan* 34 (June 1988):12-13

Satow, Ernest. *A Guide to Diplomatic Practice.* Ed. Neville Blank. 4th edition. London: Longmans, Green 1957

Schattschneider, Elmer Eric. *The Semisovereign People: A Realist's View of Democracy in America.* New York: Holt, Reinhart and Winston 1960

Scheinman, Lawrence. 'Security and a Transnational System: The Case of Nuclear Energy.' In Robert O. Keohane and Joseph S. Nye, Jr., eds., *Transnational Relations and World Politics.* Cambridge, MA: Harvard University Press 1973, 276-99

Schmitter, Philippe C. 'The Organizational Development of International Organizations.' *International Organization* 25 (Autumn 1971):917-37

Scott, Andrew M. 'The Logic of International Interaction.' *International Studies Quarterly* 21 (September 1977):429-60

– *The Revolution in Statecraft: Informal Penetration.* New York: Random House 1968

Scott, Brian. 'Pacific Role in Promoting Trade Liberalization and Economic Recovery.' *Asia Pacific Community*, no. 26 (Fall 1984):16-30

Seo Keijiro. 'Asahan Project: A Shining Example of Economic Cooperation.' *Journal of Japanese Trade and Industry*, no. 2 (March/April 1985):20-3

Shibusawa, Masahide, Zakaria Haji Ahmad, and Brian Bridges. *Pacific Asia in the 1990s.* London: Routledge 1992.

Shinohara Miyohei. 'The Future of Chinese Economic Growth and the Role of Hong Kong.' In Toshio Shishido and Ryuzo Sato, eds., *Economic Policy and Development: New Perspectives (Essays in Honor of Dr. Saburo Okita).* Dover, MA: Auburn House 1985, 127-46

Shishido Toshio and Ryuzo Sato, eds. *Economic Policy and Development: New*

Perspectives (Essays in Honor of Dr. Saburo Okita). Dover, MA: Auburn House 1985

Shultz, George. 'The United States and East Asia: A Partnership for the Future.' In Hadi Soesastro and Han Sung-Joo, eds., *Pacific Economic Cooperation: The Next Phase.* Jakarta: Centre for Strategic and International Studies 1983, 290-300

Sicat, Gerardo P. 'ASEAN and the Pacific Region.' In John Crawford and Greg Seow, eds., *Pacific Economic Co-operation: Suggestions for Action.* Selangor: Heinemann Educational 1981, 216-24

– 'National Economic Management and Technocracy in Developing Countries.' In Toshio Shishido and Ryuzo Sato, eds., *Economic Policy and Development: New Perspectives (Essays in Honor of Dr. Saburo Okita).* Dover, MA: Auburn House 1985, 81-94

Simandjuntak, Djisman S. 'The Global Economy in the 1990s.' *Indonesian Quarterly* 15 (April 1987):226-38

Simpson, Smith, ed. *Instruction in Diplomacy: The Liberal Arts Approach.* Philadelphia: American Academy of Political and Social Science 1972

Singh, Bilveer. 'Gorbachev and a Pacific Community.' *Pacific Review* 1 (1989):227-35

Sinha, Radha. 'Japan and ASEAN: A Special Relationship.' *World Today* 38 (December 1982):483-92

Skidmore, David and Valerie M. Hudson, eds. *The Limits of State Autonomy: Societal Groups and Foreign Policy Formulation.* Boulder, CO: Westview 1992

Skjelsbaek, Kjell. 'The Growth of International Nongovernmental Organizations in the Twentieth Century.' In Robert O. Keohane and Joseph S. Nye, Jr., eds., *Transnational Relations and World Politics.* Cambridge, MA: Harvard University Press 1973, 70-92

Smith, Charles. 'Economic Cooperation in the Pacific Basin.' *Pacific Community* 2 (July 1971):721-31

Smith, Michael. 'The Pacific Basin's Stake in the New Trade Round.' In PECC, *Pacific Trade Policy Cooperation: Goals and Initiatives.* Seoul: Korea Development Institute 1986, 45-52

– *Western Europe and the United States: The Uncertain Alliance.* London: Allen and Unwin 1984

Smith, Steve, ed. *International Relations: British and American Perspectives.* Oxford: Basil Blackwell/British International Studies Association 1985

Sneider, Richard L. 'The Evolving Pacific Community: Reality or Rhetoric.' In John Crawford and Greg Seow, eds., *Pacific Economic Co-operation: Suggestions for Action.* Selangor: Heinemann Educational 1981, 225-7

Sneider, Richard L. and Mark Borthwick. 'Institutions for Pacific Regional Cooperation.' *Asian Survey* 23 (December 1983):1,245-54

Snyder, Richard C., H.W. Bruck, and Burton Sapin. 'The Decision-Making Approach to the Study of International Politics.' In James N. Rosenau, ed., *International Politics and Foreign Policy: A Reader in Research and Theory.* New York: Free Press 1961, 186-92

Soesastro, Hadi. 'ASEAN and the Political Economy of Pacific Cooperation.' *Asian Survey* 23 (December 1983):1255-70

– 'Institutional Aspects of Pacific Economic Cooperation.' In Hadi Soesastro and

Han Sung-Joo, eds., *Pacific Economic Cooperation: The Next Phase*. Jakarta: Centre for Strategic and International Studies 1983, 3-52
- 'The Western Pacific in the Year 2000: Economic Trends and Their Implications.' *Indonesian Quarterly* 12 (October 1984):410-15
Soesastro, Hadi and Han Sung-Joo, eds. *Pacific Economic Cooperation: The Next Phase*. Jakarta: Centre for Strategic and International Studies 1983
Soesastro, Hadi and Mari Pangestu, eds. *Technological Challenge in the Pacific*. Sydney: Allen and Unwin 1990
Soesastro, M. Hadi, Han Gwang Choo, and Robert A. Armstrong. *Pacific Economic Development Report 1992-1993*. Singapore: PECC Secretariat 1992
Solidum, Estrella D. 'The Pacific Community in Search of a Form.' *Asian Perspective* 9 (Fall/Winter 1985):184-219
Soo Young Auh. 'Pacific Community Concept: A Korean Perspective.' *Asia Pacific Community*, no. 20 (Spring 1983):66-79
Sopiee, Noordin. 'ASEAN and the Pacific Basin Concept: Questions and Imperatives.' In Hadi Soesastro and Han Sung-Joo, eds., *Pacific Economic Cooperation: The Next Phase*. Jakarta: Centre for Strategic and International Studies 1983, 198-201
Soroos, Marvin S. *Beyond Sovereignty: The Challenge of Global Policy*. Columbia: University of South Carolina Press 1986
Sours, Marvin H. 'Transpacific Interdependencies.' In Gavin Boyd, ed., *Region Building in the Pacific*. New York: Pergamon 1982, 103-42
Spero, Joan Edelman. *The Politics of International Economic Relations*. 2nd edition. New York: St. Martin's 1981
Spinelli, Altiero. 'The Growth of the European Movement Since World War II.' In C. Grove Haines, ed., *European Integration*. Baltimore: Johns Hopkins Press 1957, 37-63
Stamp, Elizabeth. 'Oxfam and Development.' In Peter Willetts, eds., *Pressure Groups in the Global System: The Transnational Relations of Issue-Orientated Non-Governmental Organizations*. London: Frances Pinter 1982, 84-104
Starke, J.G. *An Introduction to International Law*. 8th edition. London: Butterworth's 1977
Stein, Arthur A. 'Coordination and Collaboration: Regimes in an Anarchic World.' *International Organization* 36 (Spring 1982):299-324
Strang, Lord. *The Foreign Office*. London: Allen and Unwin 1955
Strange, Susan. 'Cave! hic dragones: A Critique of Regime Analysis.' *International Organization* 36 (Spring 1982):479-96
- 'States, Firms and Diplomacy.' *International Affairs* 68 (January 1992):1-15
Subroto. 'Aid, Trade, and Economic Development: Experience of Indonesia.' In Kiyoshi Kojima, ed., *Pacific Trade and Development, II*. Tokyo: Japan Economic Research Center 1969, 351-66
- 'Prospects for Pacific Economic Cooperation: An Indonesian View.' In PECC, *Report of the Fifth Pacific Economic Cooperation Conference, Vancouver, November 16-19, 1986*. Ottawa: Canadian Chamber of Commerce 1987, 59-62
Suhartono, R.B. 'Industrial Cooperation in ASEAN.' In Hiromichi Mutoh et al., eds., *Industrial Policies for Pacific Economic Growth*. Sydney: Allen and Unwin 1986, 255-68

Sycip, David. 'Is Regional Economic Cooperation PECC's Goal?' *Euro-Asia Business Review* 5 (January 1986):37-8
- 'The Pacific Community Concept.' *Asia Pacific Community*, no. 11 (Winter 1981):39-41
- 'Why Not a Pacific Economic Community Initiative?' *Asian Pacific Community*, no. 17 (Summer 1982):71-3
Tan Chwee Huat. 'Trade and Comparative Economic Development in ASEAN Countries.' *Journal of Asian-Pacific and World Perspectives* 7 (1984):21-30
Tan, Augustine H.H. and Basant Kapur, eds. *Pacific Growth and Financial Interdependence*. Sydney: Allen and Unwin 1986
Taylor, Phillip. *Nonstate Actors in International Politics: From Transregional to Substate Organizations*. Boulder, CO: Westview 1984
Taylor, Robert. *The Sino-Japanese Axis: A New Force in Asia?* London: Athlone 1985
Thakur, Ramesh and Carlyle A. Thayer, eds. *The Soviet Union as an Asian Pacific Power: Implications of Gorbachev's 1986 Vladivostok Initiative*. Boulder, CO: Westview 1987
Thanat Khoman. 'The Pacific Basin Cooperation Concept.' In John Crawford and Greg Seow, eds., *Pacific Economic Co-operation: Suggestions for Action*. Selangor: Heinemann Educational 1981, 21-4
- 'Pacific Interdependence: Development of Pacific Economic Cooperation Concept.' In Hadi Soesastro and Han Sung-Joo, eds., *Pacific Economic Cooperation: The Next Phase*. Jakarta: Centre for Strategic and International Studies 1983, 208-13
- 'Reconstruction of Asia.' *Pacific Community* 1 (October 1969):20-30
Thomas, John N. *The Institute of Pacific Relations: Asian Scholars and American Politics*. Seattle: University of Washington Press 1974
Thomson, Graeme A. 'Trade Issues for the Pacific Basin: Resource-Endowed Exporter Perspectives.' In PECC, *Pacific Trade Policy Cooperation: Goals and Initiatives*. Seoul: Korea Development Institute 1986, 100-12
Thorne, Christopher. *Allies of a Kind: The United States, Britain, and the War Against Japan, 1941-1945*. New York: Oxford University Press 1978
- 'Chatham House, Whitehall and Far Eastern Issues: 1941-45.' *International Affairs* 54 (January 1978):1-29
- *The Issue of War: States, Societies, and the Far Eastern Conflict of 1941-1945*. London: Hamish Hamilton 1985
- *The Limits of Foreign Policy: The West, the League and the Far Eastern Crisis of 1931-33*. New York: Capricorn 1973
Thornton, Robert L. 'Governments and Airlines.' In Robert O. Keohane and Joseph S. Nye, Jr., eds., *Transnational Relations and World Politics*. Cambridge, MA: Harvard University Press 1973, 191-203
Tinker, Catherine. 'Making UNCED Work: Building the Legal and Institutional Framework for Sustainable Development at the Earth Summit and Beyond.' *UNA-USA Occasional Papers*, no. 4 (March 1992)
Toledano, Ralph de. *Spies, Dupes and Diplomats*. New York: Duell, Sloan and Pearce 1952
Toynbee, Arnold. *The World and the West*. London: Oxford University Press 1954
Trezise, Philip H. *The Atlantic Connection: Prospects, Problems, and Policies*. Washington: Brookings Institution 1975

Trible, Paul. 'Report on the Congressional Study Group.' In Robert L. Downen and Bruce J. Dickson, eds., *The Emerging Pacific Community: A Regional Perspective*. Boulder, CO: Westview 1984, 13-17

Trigg, Eric A. 'PECC's Progress: An Insider's View.' *Asia Pacific Business* 2 (Fall 1986):38

Trotter, Ann. 'New Zealand and the Pacific Community Concept.' *World Today* 39 (July/August 1983):312-18

Tsokhas, Kosmas. *A Class Apart?: Businessmen and Australian Politics 1960-1980*. Melbourne: Oxford University Press 1984

Tung, Rosalie L. 'Handshakes Across the Sea: Cross-Cultural Negotiating for Business Success.' *Organizational Dynamics* 19 (Winter 1991):30-40

Tupouniua, Sione, Ron Crocombe, and Claire Slatter. *The Pacific Way: Social Issues In National Development*. Suva: South Pacific Social Sciences Association 1975

Uhalley, Stephen, Jr. 'China and the Pacific Basin: Questions and Apprehensions.' *Contemporary Southeast Asia* 8 (March 1987):298-307

United States National Committee for Pacific Economic Cooperation. *Japan-U.S. Relations and the Pacific Basin*. San Francisco: United States National Committee for Pacific Economic Cooperation 1987

Vallier, Ivan. 'The Roman Catholic Church: A Transnational Actor.' In Robert O. Keohane and Joseph S. Nye, Jr., eds., *Transnational Relations and World Politics*. Cambridge, MA: Harvard University Press 1973, 129-52

Vance, Cyrus. 'The United States and the Pacific Nations.' In John Crawford and Greg Seow, eds., *Pacific Economic Co-operation: Suggestions for Action*. Selangor: Heinemann Educational 1981, 228-9

Vernon, Raymond. 'Multinational Business and National Goals.' In Robert O. Keohane and Joseph S. Nye, Jr., eds., *Transnational Relations and World Politics*. Cambridge, MA: Harvard University Press 1973, 343-55

Vernon, James. 'The Pacific Basin Economic Council.' In John Crawford and Greg Seow, eds., *Pacific Economic Co-operation: Suggestions for Action*. Selangor: Heinemann Educational 1981, 25

Vicuna, Francisco Orrego. 'The Pacific Islands in a Latin American Perspective: Towards a Special Relationship?' In Paul F. Hooper, eds., *Building a Pacific Community*. Honolulu: East-West Center 1982, 94-118

Walters, Robert S. 'International Organizations and Political Communication: The Use of UNCTAD by Less Developed Countries.' *International Organization* 25 (Autumn 1971):818-35

Waltz, Kenneth N. *Theory of International Politics*. Don Mills, ON: Addison-Wesley 1979

Wanandi, Jusuf. 'ASEAN and Pacific Basin Economic Cooperation.' *Indonesian Quarterly* 13 (January 1985):74-82

– 'ASEAN and Pacific Basin Economic Co-operation.' In Hiroshi Matsumoto and Noordin Sopiee, eds., *Into the Pacific Era: Southeast Asia and Its Place in the Pacific*. Kuala Lumpur/Tokyo: Institute of Strategic and International Studies/Association of Promotion of International Cooperation 1986, 25-32

– 'Pacific Economic Cooperation: An Indonesian View.' *Asian Survey* 23 (December 1983):1,271-80

– 'The Role of PECC in the 1990's and Pacific Institutions.' In PECC, *Report of the Seventh Pacific Economic Cooperation Conference, Auckland, November 12-15, 1989.* Wellington: New Zealand Committee for Pacific Economic Cooperation 1990, 21-8

– *Security Dimensions of the Asia Pacific Region in the 1980's.* Jakarta: Centre for Strategic and International Studies 1979

Warwick, Donald P. 'Transnational Participation and International Peace.' In Robert O. Keohane and Joseph S. Nye, Jr., eds., *Transnational Relations and World Politics.* Cambridge, MA: Harvard University Press 1973, 305-24

Watanabe Akio. 'Foreign Policy Making, Japanese Style.' *International Affairs* 54 (January 1978):75-88

Watanabe Takeshi. 'Pan-Pacific Solidarity Without Domination.' In *The Pacific Community Concept: Views from Eight Nations.* Tokyo: Japan Center for International Exchange 1980, 99-102

Watson, Adam. *Diplomacy: The Dialogue Between States.* London: Methuen 1982

– 'From a European to a Global International System.' *Jerusalem Journal of International Relations* 11 (1989):17-26

Weatherbee, Donald E. 'Indonesia in 1985: Chills and Thaws.' *Asian Survey* 26 ((February 1986):141-9

Wells, Louis T., Jr. 'The Multinational Business Enterprise: What Kind of International Organization?' In Robert O. Keohane and Joseph S. Nye, Jr., eds., *Transnational Relations and World Politics.* Cambridge, MA: Harvard University Press 1973, 97-114

Weltman, John J. *Systems Theory in International Relations: A Study in Metaphoric Hypertrophy.* Lexington, MA: D.C. Heath 1973

Western Co-operation: A Reference Handbook. London: Central Office of Information 1953

White, Lyman Cromwell. *International Non-Governmental Organizations: Their Purposes, Methods, and Accomplishments.* New Brunswick, N.J.: Rutgers University Press 1951

– *The Structure of Private International Organizations.* Philadelphia: George S. Ferguson 1933

Whitlam, E. Gough. *A Pacific Community.* Cambridge, MA: Harvard University Press 1981

Wight, Martin. *Power Politics.* Edited by Hedley Bull and Carsten Holbraad. 2nd edition. Harmondsworth: Penguin/Royal Institute of International Affairs 1986

– 'Western Values in International Relations.' In Herbert Butterfield and Martin Wight, eds., *Diplomatic Investigations: Essays in the Theory of International Politics.* London: George Allen and Unwin 1966, 89-131

– 'Why Is There No International Theory?' In Herbert Butterfield and Martin Wight, eds., *Diplomatic Investigations: Essays in the Theory of International Politics.* London: Allen and Unwin 1966, 17-34

Wijarso.'Energy Opportunities and Challenges: Impact on the Pacific in the 1980s.' In John Crawford and Greg Seow, eds., *Pacific Economic Co-operation: Suggestions for Action.* Selangor: Heinemann Educational 1981, 57-8

Wilkinson, Bruce W. 'Canadian Trade, The Kennedy Round and a Pacific Free

Trade Area.' In Kiyoshi Kojima, ed., *Pacific Trade and Development, I*. Tokyo: Japan Economic Research Center 1968, 30-71

– 'A Re-Estimation of the Effects of the Formation of a Pacific Free Trade Agreement.' In Kiyoshi Kojima, ed., *Pacific Trade and Development, II*. Tokyo: Japan Economic Research Center 1969, 53-95

Willetts, Peter. 'The Impact of Promotional Pressure Groups on Global Politics.' In Peter Willetts, ed., *Pressure Groups in the Global System: The Transnational Relations of Issue-Orientated Non-Governmental Organizations*. London: Frances Pinter 1982, 179-200

– 'Pressure Groups as Transnational Actors.' In Peter Willetts, ed., *Pressure Groups in the Global System: The Transnational Relations of Issue-Orientated Non-Governmental Organizations*. London: Frances Pinter 1982, 1-27

Willetts, Peter, ed. *Pressure Groups in the Global System: The Transnational Relations of Issue-Orientated Non-Governmental Organizations*. London: Frances Pinter 1982

Williams, Charlotte. 'The Pacific Community: A Modest Proposal.' Research Paper No. 55, Australia-Japan Economic Relations Research Project, Australia-Japan Research Centre, Research School of Pacific Studies, Australian National University, March 1979

Wilson, Clifton E. *Diplomatic Privileges and Immunities*. Tucson, Arizona: University of Arizona Press 1967

Wilson, Dick. 'The Pacific Basin is Coming Together.' *Asia Pacific Community*, no. 30 (Fall 1985):1-12

Wionczek, Miguel S. 'Future of Japanese-Latin American Relations in the Pacific Basin Community.' *Asia Pacific Community*, no. 16 (Spring 1982):59-72

– 'Pacific Trade and Development Cooperation with Latin America.' *Asia Pacific Community*, no. 9 (Summer 1980):21-41

Wolfers, Arnold. *Discord and Collaboration: Essays on International Politics*. Baltimore: Johns Hopkins Press 1971

Wong, John. 'The Integration of China into the Western Pacific Basin Economy: Implications for ASEAN.' In Teruyuki Iwasaki, ed., *Economic Interdependence in the Western Pacific Basin in Perspective*. Tokyo: Institute for Developing Economics 1984, 208-32

Woodard, Garry. 'The Pacific Community: Start, Stop. Start?' *Asia Pacific Community*, no. 25 (Summer 1984):116-24

Woods, Lawrence T. 'The Business of Canada's Pacific Relations.' *Canadian Journal of Administrative Sciences* 4 (December 1987):410-25

– 'Delicate Diplomatic Debuts: Chinese and Soviet Participation in the Pacific Economic Cooperation Conference.' *Pacific Affairs* 63 (Summer 1990):210-27

– 'Diplomacy and Culture: Lessons from the Asian-Pacific Region.' *Asian Culture Quarterly* 19 (Autumn 1991):1-12

– 'A House Divided: The Pacific Basin Economic Council and Regional Diplomacy,' *Australian Journal of International Affairs* 45 (1991):264-79

– 'Japanese and Australian Approaches to Regional Economic Diplomacy.' *Asian Pacific Review*, no. 8 (Winter 1988):1-11

– 'Meeting Mikhail: Attitudes towards Soviet Involvement in Pacific Cooperation.' *Pacific Review* 3 (1990):214-21

– 'Nongovernmental Organizations and Pacific Cooperation: Back to the Future?' *Pacific Review* 4 (1991):312-21.
– 'Regional Diplomacy and the Institute of Pacific Relations,' *Journal of Developing Societies* 8 (1992):212-22
Woodsworth, Charles J. *Canada and the Orient: A Study in International Relations.* Toronto: Macmillan/Canadian Institute of International Affairs 1941
Wright, Quincy. 'Diplomatic Machinery in the Pacific Area.' Prepared for the Sixth Conference of the Institute of Pacific Relations, Yosemite Park, California, 15-29 August 1936. *Secretariat Papers,* no. 2A, Secretariat, Institute of Pacific Relations, New York 1936
Yahuda, Michael B. 'The Pacific Community: Not Yet.' *Pacific Review* 1 (1988):119-27
Yakubovsky, V. 'Emergence of the Pacific Economic Complex and Some Aspects of the Economic Relations Between the Soviet Union and the Pacific Countries.' In Kiyoshi Kojima and Miguel S. Wionczek, eds., *Technology Transfer in Pacific Economic Development.* Tokyo: Japan Economic Research Center 1975, 18-29
– 'Foreign Trade of the USSR with the Countries of the Asian-Pacific Region.' In Hedley Bull, ed., *Asia and the Western Pacific: Towards a New International Order.* Sydney: Thomas Nelson and Sons/The Australian Institute of International Affairs 1975, 341-54
Yamane Hiroko. 'Japan as an Asian/Pacific Power.' *Asian Survey* 27 (December 1987):1,302-8
Yamazawa Ippei. 'An Estimate of the Effects of PAFTA Preferences Through an Advance Cut.' In Kiyoshi Kojima, ed., *Pacific Trade and Development, II.* Tokyo: Japan Economic Research Center 1969, 129-35
Yasuba, Yasukichi. 'Economists and Society in Postwar Japan.' Research Paper No. 29, Australia-Japan Economic Relations Research Project, Australia-Japan Research Centre, Research School of Pacific Studies, Australian National University, Canberra, July 1975
Yee, Herbert S. 'China and the Pacific Community Concept.' *World Today* 39 (February 1983):68-74
Yoffie, David B. *Power and Protectionism: Strategies of the Newly Industrializing Countries.* New York: Columbia University Press 1983
Yoffie, David B. and Robert O. Keohane. 'Responding to the New Protectionism: Strategies for the Advanced Developing Countries in the Pacific Basin.' In Wontack Hong and Lawrence B. Krause, eds., *Trade and Growth of the Advanced Developing Countries in the Pacific Basin.* Seoul: Korea Development Institute 1981, 560-89
Yondorf, Walter. 'Monnet and the Action Committee: The Formative Period of the European Communities.' *International Organization* 19 (Autumn 1965):885-912
Young, Oran R. 'Regime Dynamics: The Rise and Fall of International Regimes.' *International Organization* 36 (Spring 1982):277-97
Young, Stephen M. 'Gorbachev's Asian Policy: Balancing the New and the Old.' *Asian Survey* 28 (March 1988):317-39
Zagoria, Donald S. 'Soviet-American Rivalry in Asia.' In James W. Morley, ed.,

The Pacific Basin: New Challenges for the United States. New York: Academy of Political Science 1986, 103-15

– 'The Soviet Union's Military-Political Strategy in the Far East.' *Korea and World Affairs* 10 (Summer 1986):346-69

Government Documents

Australia. Department of External Affairs. 'Pacific Basin Economic Co-operation Committee.' *Current Notes on International Affairs* 39 (May 1968):202-6

– Department of Foreign Affairs. 'Address by Mr. J.S. Dawkins, Australian Minister for Trade at the Pacific Basin Economic Council Eighteenth Annual General Meeting, Auckland, New Zealand, 16 May 1985.' *Backgrounder* 479 (22 May 1985):A5-A13

– Department of Foreign Affairs. *Annual Report 1984-85*. Canberra: Australian Government Publishing Service 1985

– Department of Foreign Affairs. 'Ministerial Meeting of Fair Traders in Agriculture.' *Backgrounder* 540 (4 September 1986):7-8

– Department of Foreign Affairs. 'National Pacific Co-operation Committee.' News Release. No. M125, 29 August 1984

– Department of Foreign Affairs. 'Pacific Basin Economic Council.' *Australian Foreign Affairs Record* 55 (March 1984):192-7

– Department of Foreign Affairs. 'Pacific Basin Economic Council Meeting: Australian Statement.' *Australian Foreign Affairs Record* 56 (May 1985): 413-16

– Department of Foreign Affairs. 'Pacific Community Seminar: ANU Seminar.' *Backgrounder* 3 September 1980, 1-2

– Department of Foreign Affairs. 'Pacific Economic Co-operation: Australia and Japan.' *Australian Foreign Affairs Record* 56 (March 1985):173-7

– Department of Foreign Affairs. 'Pacific Economic Co-operation Conference.' *Australian Foreign Affairs Review* 56 (May 1985):411-13

– Department of Foreign Affairs. 'Pacific Economic Co-operation Conference: Australian Statement.' *Australian Foreign Affairs Record* 56 (April 1985):307-8

– Department of Foreign Affairs. 'Pacific Economic Co-operation Conference Meeting, Seoul, 1985.' *Backgrounder* 477 (8 May 1985):A42-45

– Department of Foreign Affairs. 'Speech by the Prime Minister, Mr. Bob Hawke, M.P., to the Australian-Thai Chamber of Commerce, Bangkok, 22 November 1983.' *Australian Foreign Affairs Record* 54 (November 1983):688-94

– Department of Foreign Affairs and Trade. 'APEC Comes of Age.' *Backgrounder* 2 (8 December 1991):1-7

– Department of Foreign Affairs and Trade, 'APEC Ministers Meet in Bangkok,' *Insight* 1 (21 September 1992):3

– Department of the Prime Minister and Cabinet. 'Regional Co-operation: Challenges for Korea and Australia.' Speech by the Prime Minister to Luncheon of Korean Business Associations, Seoul, Korea, 31 January 1989

– Senate Standing Committee on Foreign Affairs and Defence. 'Australia and Pacific Trade and Development.' In John Crawford and Greg Seow, eds., *Pacific Economic Co-operation: Suggestions for Action*. Selangor: Heinemann Educational 1981, 214-15

Canada. Department of External Affairs. *Briefing Book for the Canadian Committee of PBEC, 17th Annual PBEC Meeting, 21-24 May 1984, Vancouver, Canada*

– Department of External Affairs. 'Changes in World Trade and Investment (Speech by Mrs. Sylvia Ostry, Ambassador for Multilateral Trade Negotiations, to the 25th Anniversary Conference of the Atlantic Institute of International Affairs, Brussels, Belgium, 20 November 1986).' *Statements and Speeches* (Canadian Foreign Policy Series)

– Department of External Affairs. 'Notes for an address by the Right Honourable Joe Clark, Secretary of State for External Affairs, to the Fifth Pacific Economic Cooperation Conference, Vancouver, 16 November 1986.' *Statements and Speeches* (Canadian Foreign Policy Series)

– Department of External Affairs. *Pacific Basin Economic Council: Briefing Book for the Canadian Committee, 21st Annual Meeting, May 23-25, 1988, Sydney, Australia*

– Department of External Affairs. 'Secretary of State for External Affairs Addresses the First Meeting of the National Committee on Pacific Cooperation.' *Communiqué*, no. 144 (4 October 1985)

– Department of External Affairs. 'Text of a Speech Delivered by the Honourable Mitchell Sharp, Secretary of State for External Affairs, to the Foreign Correspondents' Club, Tokyo (Entitled: Canada and the Pacific).' Press Release, 15 April 1969

– Secretary of State for External Affairs. 'Notes for a speech by the Honourable Allan J. MacEachen, Deputy Prime Minister and Secretary of State for External Affairs to the Seventeenth International General Meeting of the Pacific Basin Economic Council.' Statement, 22 May 1984

Indonesia. Department of Information. *Indonesia 1986: An Official Handbook.* Jakarta: Directorate of Foreign Information Services 1986

New Zealand. Ministry of Foreign Affairs. 'Agreement on Uruguay Round.' *New Zealand Foreign Affairs Review* 36 (July/September 1986):4-5

– Ministry of Foreign Affairs. 'Cairns Declaration.' *New Zealand Foreign Affairs Review* 36 (July/September 1986):5-6

– Ministry of Foreign Affairs. 'Pacific Basin Economic Council.' *New Zealand Foreign Affairs Review* 35 (April/June 1985):81-2

– Ministry of Foreign Affairs. 'Pacific Economic Cooperation.' *New Zealand Foreign Affairs Review* 35 (April/June 1985):82

United States. Congressional Research Service, Library of Congress. 'An Asian-Pacific Regional Economic Organization: An Exploratory Concept Paper.' Prepared for the Committee on Foreign Relations, United States Senate. U.S. Government Printing Office, Washington, July 1979

– *Institute of Pacific Relations: Hearings Before the Subcommittee to Investigate the Administration of the Internal Security Act and Other Internal Security Laws of the Committee on the Judiciary, United States Senate, Eighty-Second Congress.* Washington: U.S. Government Printing Office 1951-3, Parts 1-15

– Joint Economic Committee, Congress of the United States, ed. *Pacific Region Interdependencies: A Compendium of Papers.* Washington: U.S. Government Printing Office 1981

Index

Set in Stone by Brenda and Neil West, Typographics West

Printed and bound in Canada by D.W. Friesen & Sons Ltd.

Copy-editor: Joanne Richardson

Indexer: Perry Millar